Clear Grammar 4

Activities for Spoken and Written Communication

Keith S. Folse
Deborah Mitchell
Barbara Smith-Palinkas
Donna M. Tortorella

The University of Michigan Press
Ann Arbor

We would like to thank the numerous professionals who gave their expert advice in the design of the grammar presentations and some of the activities used in this textbook. We would also like to thank the students who tried out these exercises and gave us valuable feedback.

Special thanks go to the staff of the University of Michigan Press who have worked so diligently toward the success of this project, particularly Kelly Sippell, Mary Erwin, Giles Brown, and Chris Milton.

Copyright © by the University of Michigan 2003
All rights reserved
ISBN 0-472-08886-6
Published in the United States of America by
The University of Michigan Press
Manufactured in the United States of America

2012   2011   2010   2009   5   4   3   2

Illustrations by Barbara Goodsit
Photograph of an Akita from the American Kennel Club. Copyright © Kent and Donna Dannen.
Photographs of Susan B. Anthony (LC-USZ62-85580) and Muhammad Ali (LC-USZ62-115435) from Library of Congress

ISBN 978-0-472-08886-7

Contents

To the Teacher

Clear Grammar 4 is the newest addition to the *Clear Grammar* series. *Clear Grammar 4* covers grammar points for high-intermediate to advanced learners of English, including past perfect tense, word forms, conditionals, adverb clauses, noun clauses, reduction of adjective and adverb clauses, past modals, subject-verb agreement, prepositions, and a review of verb tenses.

Clear Grammar 1 contains presentations and exercises on basic grammar points such as the verb *to be,* regular verbs, simple question and negative forms, and prepositions. *Clear Grammar 2* continues this series with articles, *be + going to,* irregular past tense, *how* questions, adverbs of frequency, object pronouns, *one* and *other,* possessive, comparison and superlative, modals, and problem words. *Clear Grammar 3* covers phrasal verbs, past progressive tense, present perfect tense, adverbs of manner, prepositions after verbs and adjectives, passive voice, relative clauses, infinitives and gerunds, connectors, and direct and indirect objects.

Clear Grammar 4 contains exercises that provide relevant practice in the basic grammar points for high-intermediate to advanced students of English as a second language (ESL). This book assumes that the student has a good reading and writing ability in English, and it is designed to be used by adult learners, that is, high school age and up. It is suitable for either intensive or nonintensive programs found at community colleges, universities, adult education programs, conversation programs, and secondary school settings.

An important feature of this book is the number and variety of types of exercises included. Teachers and learners need a large number of practice opportunities. An advantage of this book is that it contains approximately 175 exercises and activities. Furthermore, whenever possible, two smaller exercises have been included instead of one long exercise so that one may be done in classes with the teacher's guidance and the other can be sent home for independent learning. A second advantage of this book is the variety of types of practice exercises and learning activities. For example, approximately 20 percent of the exercises are speaking or some other type of interactive activities. Some grammar points can be practiced at the single-sentence level while other points may be learned better if seen within a larger context.

A strong attempt has been made to provide engaging activities in addition to the traditional single sentences with one blank. To this end, the written exercises are divided between sentence-level exercises and multisentence- and dialogue-level activities. Therefore, the resultant structure of this book is approximately 20 percent speaking/ interactive exercises, 40 percent single-sentence practices, and 40 percent multisentence or minidialogue activities.

These last figures clearly illustrate an extremely important difference between the *Clear Grammar* series and other grammar books. While some ESL grammar books have included some speaking activities and others have included a few multisentence exercises, the four books in this series make use of contextualized exercises where possible. These features represent current views toward the learning of grammar in a second language, namely, that speaking practice is as important as written practice and that some grammar points are more apparent to students when these points are seen within a real and somewhat longer context.

Because learners learn in different ways based on their individual learning differences, the presentation of grammar in this series, and especially in this volume, has been varied to include both traditional deductive and inductive presentations. In the deductive presentations (see units 2, 3, 5, 7, 8, 10, 11), the grammar rules are stated explicitly, and then learners work exercises that help solidify the stated patterns in their minds. In the inductive presentations (see units 4, 6, 9), on the other hand, learners are given correct examples and incorrect examples of the grammar and are to figure out the grammatical patterns and exceptions. This presentation is also followed by a series of written exercises and speaking activities that gradually become more difficult.

Clear Grammar 4 has six main goals:

1. to teach the basic grammar points necessary for high-intermediate to advanced ESL students;
2. to provide ample written practice in these structures at the single-sentence level as well as at the multisentence and dialogue levels;
3. to provide a wide array of practices at varying cognitive levels (i.e., not just knowledge and comprehension but also synthesis and evaluation);
4. to provide oral communication work practicing these structures through a variety of activities and games;
5. to provide ample opportunities for students to check their progress while studying these structures; and
6. to serve as a grammar reference that is written with language and terms that a high-intermediate-level ESL student can understand without a great deal of teacher assistance.

Clear Grammar 4 consists of twelve units. Unit 1 is a review of the grammatical structures covered in *Clear Grammar 3*. Unit 12 is a review of the new material covered in *Clear Grammar 4*. Each of the other ten units covers a single grammar area, but sometimes a particular area may have several subdivisions. An example is unit 6, "Noun Clauses," in which six usages of noun clauses are examined. Another example is unit 5, "Adverb Clauses," which teaches nine classes of adverb clauses.

The units may be taught in any order. However, it is recommended that the general sequencing of the units be followed whenever possible. An attempt has been made to recycle material from one unit into the following units where appropriate. For example, once reduced clauses have been covered, sentences in subsequent units may contain this grammatical structure for further reinforcement.

Though a great deal of variety of materials exists in the book, there is a general pattern within each unit. The units begin with some kind of grammar presentation. Sometimes this presentation is inductive; other times it is deductive. This presentation is then followed by a list of the most likely mistakes (i.e., potential problems) for each structure. This is followed by a series of written exercises arranged from least to most cognitively demanding. After the written work are one or more speaking activities. This is followed by a multiple choice quiz. At the end of each unit there are a review test and suggestions for possible writing practice. The exact guidelines for each class (e.g., amount of writing expected of students and the exact form in which they should prepare writing exercises—handwritten or typed, single or double spaced, etc.) are left completely up to the individual instructor, as no one knows the specific teaching situation better than that teacher.

A unique feature of all four volumes of the *Clear Grammar* series is the inclusion of Challenge Boxes. Each Challenge Box presents a single question that requires a higher level of knowledge and understanding of the particular grammar point. Sometimes the Challenge Box requires learners to analyze the most difficult item in the previous exercise. Other times the Challenge Box presents a new item that is more difficult than the items in the previous exercise. In both cases, the purpose of this activity is twofold: (1) to raise students' understanding of the grammar point by dealing with a very difficult question about the grammatical point, and (2) to motivate the better students who might not have been challenged sufficiently by the previous exercise.

General Lesson Format

1. Grammar Presentation

    These presentations vary in method. In some units, they are deductive; in others, inductive; and in others, consciousness raising. Second language learners have a wide range of learning styles and employ an even greater range of learner strategies. It is believed that having a variety of presentation types for the grammatical structures is therefore advantageous. (Where the presentations are inductive, the answers are provided at the end of the unit.)

2. List of Potential Errors with Corrections

    In this section of the unit, there is a list of several of the most commonly made errors. Following each error is the corrected form so that students can see not only what they should avoid but also how it should be corrected. Our students represent a wide range of linguistic groups, and every effort has been made to take this into account in selecting which kinds of errors to include here.

3. Written Exercises

    Teachers and students want a large number of written exercises to allow for ample practice of the newly learned structure. The exercises have been sequenced so that the early exercises require only passive knowledge of the grammar point. For example, students circle one of two answers or put a check mark by the correct word. These exercises are followed by others that are more cognitively demanding and require active production of the language structure. In this way, students can comfortably move from passive knowledge to active production of a structure.

    The written exercises in this book are short enough to be done in a small amount of time, yet they are thorough enough to provide sufficient practice for the structure in question. These exercises may be done in class or as homework. Furthermore, they may be checked quickly either by individual students or by the class.

4. Speaking Activities

   Each unit has at least one (and often several) speaking activities. The design of these speaking activities is based on second-language acquisition research by C. Doughty, M. Long, T. Pica, and P. Porter showing that certain types of activities encourage L2 learners to produce a greater amount and a higher quality of language.

   The instructions for these activities are clearly written at the top of the exercise. Students are almost always directed to work with a partner. In this case, it is important for the teacher to make sure that students do not see their partner's material ahead of time as this will not facilitate speaking. (However, not all speaking activities are set up in this manner. See the directions for the individual exercises for further clarification.)

5. Multiple Choice Exercise

   Because students often have such a hard time with this particular format and because it is similar to the format found on many standardized language tests, each unit includes an eight-question multiple choice exercise. It is important to discuss not only why the correct answers are correct but also why the distractors are not correct.

6. Review Test

   Equally as important as the teaching of a given grammar point is the measurement of the learning that has taken place. To this end, the last exercise in every unit is a review test. This review test has several *very* different kinds of questions on it. For example, one kind of question may require a simple completion while another may require error identification. This variety allows all students an opportunity to demonstrate their knowledge without interference caused by the type of question.

7. Extended Writing Activity

   At the end of each unit is a suggestion for a writing activity. The nature of the exact assignment is left up to the individual teacher. It should be noted that the main purpose of this writing activity is to incorporate yet another of the four skills in the learning of grammar.

Answer Key

In the back of the book, there is a section that contains the answers for all exercises in this text. These answers are provided so that students may check to see if their answers are correct. It is supposed that students will use the answer key after they have actually done the exercises. It is further hoped that students will use the answer key to detect their mistakes and then return to the exercises to discover the source of their error. The answer key also makes it possible for students engaged in independent study to use this textbook. (Where unit presentations are inductive, the answers are provided at the end of the unit.)

Grammar Terminology

In this book, grammar is not viewed as a theoretical science that requires complex terminology. Surely the main purpose of studying grammar in a foreign language is to be able to function better in that language, that is, to produce *accurate* communication (not just communication). To that end, the main focus of the presentations in this book is on being able to use English accurately and not on learning labels that are of little use.

However, this does not mean that terminology is or should be avoided. Terms such as *reduced adverb clauses* and *present perfect progressive tense* are introduced and explained. However, grammar terminology is introduced only when it is necessary. Furthermore, when it is introduced, explanations have been adjusted to reflect the level of the learner's English ability. Complex grammar terminology serves no justifiable purpose and is to be avoided at all costs in good ESL classes and materials.

Using This Book in Your Curriculum

The number of hours needed to complete this book depends to a large extent on the students in your class. Some groups may need up to 60 or 70 hours to finish all the material, while a more advanced group might be able to omit certain units and/or do more work as homework, therefore using less class time. In this case, the students could finish the material in approximately 35 to 40 hours. The results of the diagnostic test (at the end of the book) can help you decide which units, if any, can be omitted or should be assigned as homework to certain students only in order to use group class time the most effectively.

Another factor that will greatly influence the number of class hours needed to complete this material successfully is whether or not the oral activities are done in class. It is recommended that teachers make every effort to do these speaking fluency activities in order to build up students' speaking ability and their confidence in their ability to use spoken English. An instructor in a course in which time is an important factor may want to consider ways of correcting student homework (e.g., posting homework answer sheets on the wall) that are less time consuming rather than omitting the speaking fluency activities.

A diagnostic test is included at the back of the book. More information about this test is given in the next section. In order to make the best use of (limited) class time, the results of this test can guide you in choosing which units to cover and which units to omit if necessary.

About the Diagnostic Test

The diagnostic test is printed on perforated pages. Have the students remove this test and take it at the first class meeting. The test consists of twenty-two questions, two for each of the eleven units. (The twelfth unit of the book is a review of the entire book, and thus no question matches it solely.) The test is set up in two parts, each part consisting of eleven questions. You may set your own time limit, but a recommended time limit is twenty minutes for all twenty-two questions. (Answers are not provided.)

The scoring for the test is fairly straightforward. On the test sheet, note in which units the student has missed both questions, in which the student has missed only one of the two questions, and in which the student has not missed either of the questions. You will need to make a composite picture of the results for your whole group. The units for which the most students have missed both questions are the units that your class should focus on first.

Online Placement Testing

Correct placement of a learner at the start of any language course is important. Students may take a placement test at www.press.umich.edu/esl/compsite/cleargrammar/ to find out if they should start their studies with *Clear Grammar* 1, 2, 3, or 4. Students take the test completely online. At the end of the examination, an appropriate *Clear Grammar* book level will be suggested based on the student's test results.

Testing

Evaluation is extremely important in any language classroom, and it has a definite role in the grammar classroom. Frequent testing, not just major exams but small quizzes or checks, is vital to allow the learners to see what they have mastered and what still needs further work and to facilitate the teacher in gauging whether individual students have understood and retained the contents of the class.

Testing can come in many forms. Some teachers prefer cloze activities; others prefer multiple choice. Some teachers prefer discrete grammar items; others insist on context. Some include listening and/or speaking; others deal only with printed language. The most important things to keep in mind when testing are (1) students should know what kind of questions to expect, that is, they should know what they will have to do, because this affects how they should study, and (2) the test should test what was taught and nothing else. This second point is the mark of a good test and is essential to the fair treatment of the students.

About the Final Test

In addition to the diagnostic test, there is a final test on page 249. This is meant to be done toward the end of the course when most, if not all, of the book has been covered. This test is also printed on perforated pages and should be removed early in the course to prevent students from looking ahead. For this reason, some teachers will have students remove this test at the first class meeting and then collect these tests. It is not recommended that the results of this particular test be used as the sole deciding factor in whether a student moves from one level or course to the next. This is especially true if you have not had your students answer this type of question during the course. In general, this type of test is more difficult than regular multiple choice or cloze, and any student who scores at least 70 percent is probably ready to move on to a higher level of grammar study.

This test has two parts, each of which has the same directions. Students are to find the grammatical error in each sentence and correct it. Each of the two parts has eleven sentences, one sentence for each of the units in the book (except the final review unit, of course). The questions are in numerical order matching the corresponding units in the book. Thus, question number 7 in each part deals with material found in unit 7. It is possible to give the first part of this quiz as a progress check midway through the course and then to give the other half at the end to compare results. Again, it is not recommended that any decision regarding promotion to the next level of study be based solely on the results of this single exam.

References

Doughty, C., and T. Pica. 1986. "Information gap" tasks: Do they facilitate second language acquisition? *TESOL Quarterly* 20:305–25.

Long, M. 1989. Task, group, and task-group interactions. Paper delivered at RELC Regional Seminar, Singapore.

Long, M., and P. Porter. 1985. Group work, interlanguage talk, and second language acquisition. *TESOL Quarterly* 19:207–28.

Pica, T., and C. Doughty. 1985. Input and interaction in the communicative language classroom: A comparison of teacher fronted and group activities. In Susan M. Gass and Carolyn G. Madden, eds., *Input in Second Language Acquisition* (Rowley, MA: Newbury House).

Pica, T., and C. Doughty. 1985. The role of group work in classroom second language acquisition. *Studies in Second Language Acquisition* 7:233–48.

Unit 1

Review of Book 3

1. phrasal verbs
2. past progressive tense
3. past participle forms
4. adverbs of manner and related terms
5. prepositions after verbs and adjectives
6. passive voice
7. relative clauses
8. infinitives and gerunds
9. connectors
10. VERB + direct or indirect object

Will the real Dolly COME ON down!

Exercise 1.   Phrasal Verbs. Write the correct preposition (and sometimes pronoun) after the verb.

Situation 1.   In this conversation, a child is asking his mother for help with his homework.

Child: Mom, I need to write a paper about cloning. Do you know anything about it?

Mother: Not much. Did you try looking ❶ _____ _____ on the Internet?

Child: I tried to do a search, but the answer came ❷ _____ *unavailable.*

Mother: Try leaving ❸ _____ all the unnecessary words and type in only the word *cloning.*

Child: I still can't get it!

Mother: Check the spelling. Did you type ❹ _____ _____ correctly?

Child: Oh, I spelled it wrong. Now I've got it. Thanks for your help.

Mother: You're welcome.

Situation 2. In this conversation, the same child is asking a librarian for help with his research.

Child: Excuse me. Could you please help me find ❺ _____ something about cloning?

Librarian: Did you try an Internet search?

Child: Yes, but the information I found was difficult to understand, and I wasn't able to get ❻ _____ all the technical terms. Can you help me find some magazines with pictures?

Librarian: I came ❼ _____ an article in *National Geographic* yesterday. It had a picture of Dolly, the clone. The magazine should still be on the rack, but you can't always count ❽ _____ _____ .

Later

Child: I found the article and went ❾ _____ _____ quickly. I think I'd like to borrow it.

Librarian: You can check ❿ _____ _____ at the counter.

Child: Thanks.

Librarian: Any time.

Exercise 2.   Phrasal Verbs. Match the beginning of the sentence with the correct ending to find the meanings of the **phrasal verbs**.

___ 1. When someone yells, "<u>Come on</u>,"

___ 2. When someone asks you to <u>eat out</u>,

___ 3. When a person's date doesn't <u>show up</u>,

___ 4. When an airplane is late <u>taking off</u>,

___ 5. When someone riding in your car asks you to <u>slow down</u>,

___ 6. When someone on the phone tells you to <u>hold on</u>,

___ 7. When your boyfriend or girlfriend tells you they want to <u>break up</u>,

___ 8. When someone says the car alarm <u>went off</u>,

___ 9. When you hear that someone didn't <u>wake up</u> in time for class,

___ 10. When someone tells you to <u>grow up</u>,

A. it means that the peson thinks you are acting immature.

B. it means that the person doesn't want to have a relationship with you.

C. it means that the person overslept.

D. it means that the person doesn't want you to drive that fast.

E. it means that it made a loud noise.

F. it means that the person wants you to go to a restaurant.

G. it means that the person is left waiting alone.

H. it means that it doesn't leave on time.

I. it means that the person wants you to hurry up.

J. it means that the person wants you to wait.

Speaking Activity

Exercise 3.   Past Progressive Tense. You are going to do some research to find out how much interest people have in cloning. Use the following questions to survey between ten and fifteen people. Write down their answers.

1. Do you know why Dolly, the sheep, is famous?

_____

2. When she was born in 1996, her birth was kept secret by the doctors at the institute. Why do you think they did that?

_____

3. Were you watching TV when you first heard the news?

_____

4. When the news broke, was it a headline in your local newspaper?

_____

5. While you were thinking about cloning, were any ethical issues coming to mind?

_____

6. Did your family discuss the topic of cloning while they were eating?

_____

7. While you and your friends were talking, did you discuss the implications of cloning?

_____

8. Were teachers and students talking about it in school?

_____

9. When Dolly was born, she was considered unique because her DNA was taken from an adult sheep, not an embryo. Why do you think this was so important?

_____

10. When a Massachusetts biotech company revealed the news that it had successfully cloned a human embryo on November 27, 2001, the news stirred up a lot of controversy. Why do you think this happened?

_____

Exercise 4. Past Progressive Tense. Disagree with the following sentences. Use the verbs from the word bank in your explanations. Use each verb only once. One verb will not be used.

lead	try	research	eat	think	get	ask	~~sleep~~

1. The doctors at the Roslin Institute were waiting anxiously for Dolly's birth.

No, *they weren't. They were sleeping* when she was born.

2. The people in the town were rejoicing at her birth.

No, _____ . They thought that Dolly _____

_____ too much attention.

3. Dolly was living on a farm when she became famous.

   No, _____ . _____ a quiet life at

   the Roslin Institute.

4. Dolly was grazing in the meadows with the other sheep.

   No, _____ . _____ pellets of

   sheep food.

5. People all over the world were ignoring Dr. Wilmut's discovery.

   No, _____ . _____ Dr. Wilmut to

   clone dead family members and pets.

6. Dr. Wilmut was trying to become famous.

   No, _____ . _____ animal

   embryology.

Exercise 5.   Past Participle Forms. Write in the missing forms.

Present	Past	Past Participle
1. become	became	_____
2. forget	_____	forgotten
3. _____	brought	brought
4. read	_____	read
5. _____	wore	worn
6. run	_____	run
7. grow	grew	_____
8. _____	said	said
9. sleep	slept	_____
10. draw	drew	_____

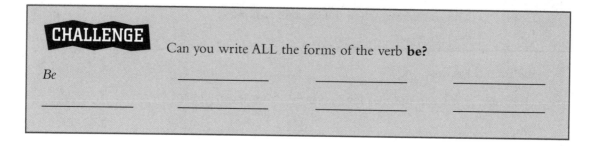

CHALLENGE Can you write ALL the forms of the verb **be**?

Be

_____ _____ _____

_____ _____ _____ _____

Exercise 6. Adverbs of Manner and Related Terms. Underline the correct adjective or adverb forms.

One ❶ (warm, warmly) summer day in July, a very ❷ (famous, famously) athlete decided to practice diving at the nearby community swimming pool. While he was busy impressing the spectators with his smooth moves, some jealous guys ❸ (humorous, humorously) hid his clothes. The athlete ❹ (hard, hardly) noticed what they were up to. The only thought on his mind was how ❺ (good, well) he was executing his dives. The spectators ❻ (quick, quickly) began to tire of his showing off. Looking around before his next dive, the athlete ❼ (sudden, suddenly) realized that no one was watching him. Therefore, he decided to "wow" them with one more death-defying feat. The dive, considered ❽ (scientific, scientifically) impossible, defied the laws of gravity. When the athlete emerged from the water, he got a round of applause from the audience and a few snickers from the jokesters.

Exercise 7.   Prepositions after Verbs and Adjectives. Find the ten mistakes and correct them.

Situation: Returning to the library setting first mentioned in this unit, the same child asks the same librarian for help again.

Student: Hello again!

Librarian: Well, hello. How can I help you today?

Student: I have to look to some more sources. I don't have enough.

Librarian: Did your teacher approve on the sources you have?

Student: Yes. I have sources from the Internet and magazines. Now I need to think off another kind.

Librarian: Did you speak for any experts and ask them to advice?

Student: Our class wrote questions with *how* that we asked the doctors at the Roslin Institute during our long-distance learning class. We even took a survey and talked from people in town about their opinions of cloning.

Librarian: I know a source you haven't mentioned yet.

     What does a library mostly consist from?

Student: Oh, I forgot to books!

Librarian: When you look in the library catalog, concentrate in *cloning*.

Student: Thanks of your help.

Librarian: You're welcome.

Exercise 8.   Prepositions after Verbs and Adjectives. Fill in the blanks with one of the following:

used to + VERB

OR

be used to + GERUND (VERB + *-ing*)

The student *used to ask* his mother for help with his homework. Whenever
(ask)

she was very busy, she ❶ _____ him to look it up on the Internet.
(tell)

Consequently, the student would go to the library when he needed help. It is obvious

that he ❷ _____ with the librarian who was so ❸ _____ him
(talk)   (see)

around. In the past, he ❹ _____ magazine and newspaper articles for
                                    (read)

information. Now he goes straight to the librarian's desk. She ❺ _____ him
                                                                      (see)

there so often that she sometimes puts books aside for him. She ❻ _____ until
                                                                        (wait)

he got there, but now she is prepared. He ❼ _____ a lot of time, but now
                                                  (waste)

he gets right to work. He ❽ _____ the library at closing time with his
                                  (leave)

work unfinished, but now he ❾ _____ home in time for dinner.
                                     (be)

Exercise 9.   Prepositions after Verbs and Adjectives. Fill in the blank before the
                    preposition with the correct adjective from the word bank. Each
                    paragraph should make sense. Use each word only once.
                    (Sometimes different combinations of answers are possible.)

1. *Note:* Remember, *about* implies relation to.

sorry	curious	confused	crazy	excited	worried	happy

Dr. Wilmut, an inquisitive embryologist, *was* _____ *about* cloning

adult genetic material. He and his team tried to clone 277 udder cells. They *were*

_____ *about* the 29 embryos that developed. After growing the embryos

in the lab for a week, the doctors *were* _____ *about* transferring them to

surrogate mothers. Blackface sheep were chosen as surrogates so that the doctors

wouldn't *be* _____ *about* the sheep's looks.

2. *Note:* Remember, *of* implies origin, component parts, cause, relation, or about.

jealous	scared	guilty	aware	proud	afraid	sick

Doctors at the Roslin Institute *were* _____ *of* how the public would

react to Dolly, so they kept her birth a secret. They *were* _____ *of* the

positive and negative implications of cloning. However, they *were* _____ *of*

more negative than positive feedback. After about a year, they decided to reveal their

experiment to the public because they *were* really very _____ *of* their

discovery.

3. *Note:* Remember, *to* implies motion toward.

similar	harmful	polite	accustomed	related	married	relevant

Since Dolly was not born out of a union of a sperm and an egg, she *was*

_____ *to* her biological mother's cells only. Her looks *were* _____

to her biological mother's. Her surrogate mother's looks *were* not _____ *to*

Dolly's appearance. Scientists *are* _____ *to* using constants and variables in

their experiments. For this reason, they used a surrogate with different physical

characteristics. Using sheep that looked similar would have *been* _____ *to*

the experiment.

4. *Note:* Remember, *with* implies association.

finished	disappointed	satisfied	bored	fed up	impressed	familiar

At first, Dolly *was* _____ *with* her life; she behaved like a perfectly

ordinary sheep. As time went on, she was becoming more and more famous, which

made her aware that she was different. She *was* _____ *with* her own

notoriety. Not like other sheep, she *was* too _____ *with* people who wanted

to feed and pet her. She *was* _____ *with* living in a pen with other sheep.

Consequently, she would assert herself by turning over her trough as soon as she *was*

_____ *with* her food. She *was* _____ *with* life as an ordinary sheep

and would bleat loudly whenever there were visitors.

Exercise 10.   Passive Voice. Rewrite the following sentences in passive voice.

1. Scientists research cloning at the Roslin Institute in Scotland.

   _____

2. Doctors are developing drugs for human use.

   _____

3. For many years, scientists have used animals in research.

   _____

4. Dr. Wilmut cloned Dolly from the udder cells of a ewe.

_____

5. Dr. Wilmut was experimenting with adult cells rather than embryonic cells.

_____

6. Dr. Wilmut and his team had achieved a scientific milestone when Dolly was born.

_____

7. Cloning is going to open a new frontier for the science of medicine.

_____

8. Because of these experiments, people might expect cures for widespread diseases.

_____

9. Scientists could find a remedy for the common cold.

_____

10. Scientists should consider questions about ethics.

_____

11. Scientists have to prolong human life.

_____

Speaking Activity

Exercise 11.   Passive Voice: Role Play

Situation: You and your partner are scientists who are working on the same experiment. You are discussing a problem that occurred. After you are finished talking, work together to write down the steps that were taken and what happened to your experiment. Use **passive voice** wherever possible.

Scientist A: While you were home sleeping, something went wrong with the experiment. You notice it when you arrive the next morning, and you are very angry!

Scientist B: You set up the experiment and checked it twice. You had to wait for hours for it to run its course. Therefore, you decided to take a nap. When you wake up, your partner has already arrived, and he is very angry. You explain what you did and what you know. All the while, you are trying to calm your partner down.

example: The experiment was checked twice.

Exercise 12.   Passive Voice. Write the correct adjective (participial *-ing, -ed*) forms on the lines.

In the 1970s, cloning was the "hot topic" of many science fiction writers. They

were ❶ _____ in exploring the subject as deeply as they could. However,
        (interest)

the information that they received was so ❷ _____ that they began to
                                              (confuse)

make up many of their "facts." The stories they wrote were ❸ _____.
                                                                (shock)

Readers were ❹ _____ at what they were reading. The ❺ _____
                  (amaze)   (astonish)

tales were both ❻ _____ and ❼ _____. Readers couldn't get
                    (fascinate)   (frighten)

enough; as a result, books went flying off the shelves. Writers wrote

more and more so that readers could read more and more. The high

demand was ❽ _____ to authors while the avid readers
                (satisfy)

were ❾ _____ with the volumes of material being made
        (satisfy)

available.

Exercise 13.   Relative Clauses. Find the mistakes and correct them.
                    Some sentences may not have any mistakes.

1. Whose the doctor that cloned Dolly?

2. The Roslin Institute is the establishment noted for its work in embryology.

3. Ian Wilmut is the doctor who's collaborator was Keith Campbell.

4. Dr. Wilmut and Dr. Campbell got 29 embryos out of 277 udder cells that they tried to clone.

5. The cells that were used for Dolly taken from the frozen cells of a ewe.

6. A blackface sheep was distinctively different from Dolly, was chosen as a surrogate mother. (Note: Dolly was a white-faced sheep.)

7. The people who were present at Dolly's birth not aware of the impact it would have.

8. Dolly is the sheep who's birth was kept a secret.

9. Who's the person which kept it a secret?

10. Dolly's birth, which kept a secret for a year, sparked a debate about cloning.

Exercise 14.   Infinitives and Gerunds. The following are three bibliographic entries that the student researching cloning could have written. In the conversation between the student and his teacher, fill in the blanks with either the infinitive (*to* + VERB) or the gerund (VERB + *-ing*) form of the verbs given.

Bibliography

Campbell, Keith, and Ian Wilmut. <u>The Cloning of Dolly.</u> Scotland: Edinburgh University Press, 2000.

Peterson, Jerry L. "Cloning Becomes Reality." <u>National Geographic.</u> June 1998: 16–20.

Wilmut, Ian. Videoconference interview. 10 December 2001.

Teacher: These are really good sources. What made you decide **❶** _____ the
(cite)

interview in your bibliography?

Student: I considered **❷** _____ it out, but then I had already planned
(leave)

❸ _____ some of Dr. Wilmut's ideas in my paper, so I had to give
(use)

him credit.

Teacher: Did you know how **❹** _____ up the citation, or did you get help?
(write)

Student: I thought about **❺** _____ the librarian, but I looked it up instead.
(ask)

I learned how **❻** _____ it from the *MLA Handbook*.
(cite)

Teacher: I'd like **❼** _____ where you found the book.
(know)

Student: I found it in the library. Actually, I know the librarian really well, and she

offered **❽** _____ for material whenever anything new arrived.
(look)

Teacher: Did she suggest **❾** _____ the magazine?
(read)

Student: Yes. She said she had seen a cover with Dolly on it, so she told me to keep on

❿ _____ until I found it, and I did.
(search)

Teacher: You must enjoy **⓫** _____ to the library.
(go)

Student: Yup. I go there a lot. The librarian is used to **⓬** _____ me there.
(see)

Exercise 15.   Infinitives and Gerunds. Find the mistakes and correct them. *Every* sentence has at least one mistake.

1. The student's mother told him search the Internet for information.

2. His mother said, "To look on the Internet for information about cloning."

3. Did the librarian invite him browsing through magazines?

4. She wanted him to found the copy with Dolly on the cover.

5. Did the student expect to don't use any sources?

6. The teacher urged that he used a variety of sources.

7. The teacher allowed he writes three different sources.

8. The student should have said her he also used a survey.

9. Did she teach her class how to writes citations correctly?

10. The student taught himself to looking in the *MLA Handbook* for the right way to citing sources.

Speaking Activity

Exercise 16.   Infinitives and Gerunds. Role play. Work with a partner. One of you is student A and the other is student B. Student A questions in situation 1A while student B responds from situation 1B. Then student A questions in situation 2A while student B responds from situation 2B. As often as possible, use the main verbs: *make, help, let, have.*

Student A

Situation 1A: You have just arrived in Scotland, and your partner meets you at the airport. You need to get to the Roslin Institute tomorrow for an important interview. You need a good map of the city, but you don't have time to go to a store to buy one. Ask your friend for help.

Example: Can you help me get to the Roslin Institute?

Situation 2A: Suddenly you feel sick and won't be able to go to the institute for your interview. Get your friend to telephone them and tell them.

Student B

Situation 1B: You are very busy and can't talk to your friend. Ask him or her to wait.

Situation 2B: You are talking on your cell phone to a business associate who is telling you that you are late for a meeting. You need to be at this meeting, which should take about an hour. You can't talk to your friend until afterward.

Exercise 17.   Connectors. Write three possible answers for the following questions. Use *to* + VERB, *in order to* + VERB, and *for* + NOUN.

1. Why did the student go to the library?

_____

_____

_____

2. Why did he talk to the librarian?

   _____

   _____

   _____

3. Why did he interview Dr. Wilmut?

   _____

   _____

   _____

4. Why did Dr. Wilmut clone Dolly?

   _____

   _____

   _____

5. Why did Dr. Wilmut keep Dolly's birth a secret for a year?

   _____

   _____

   _____

Exercise 18.   Connectors. Rewrite these sentences using the following at least
                     once: *and . . . too, and so . . . , and . . . either, and neither . . .*

1. Dolly Parton is famous. Dolly, the sheep, is famous.
   Dolly Parton is famous, and so is Dolly, the sheep.

2. Dolly Parton does not live in England. Dolly, the sheep, does not live in England.

   _____

3. The Roslin Institute has become well known because of its cloning experiment. The
   Massachusetts biotech firm has become well known because of its cloning experiment.

   _____

4. Dr. Wilmut was not present at Dolly's birth. Dr. Campbell was not present at Dolly's
   birth.

   _____

5. When she was young, Dolly had a fear of humans. The other sheep in the pen had a
   fear of humans.

   _____

Exercise 19.   Connectors. Look carefully at the connector, add punctuation and capitalization if needed, and then complete the sentence.

1. The Roslin Institute is famous for using adult cells to clone a sheep however _____

    _____

2. The Massachusetts biotech firm cloned human embryo cells therefore _____

    _____

3. (result) Cloning has opened a new frontier for medicine so now _____

    _____

4. (reason) Dr. Wilmut kept Dolly's birth a secret so the public would not _____

    _____

5. When Dolly was young, she was kept in a pen with other sheep but _____

    _____

Exercise 20.   VERB + Direct or Indirect Object. Fill in the blanks with the verbs from the word bank, as well as the missing prepositions. For the correct tense, look for time marker clues.

announce   describe   explain   introduce   mention   repeat   report   say   speak   suggest

❶ When Dolly was born, none of the doctors at the institute _____ a word

_____ anyone. ❷ They couldn't even _____ it _____

their wives. ❸ A year later, Dr. Wilmut _____ Dolly's birth _____

the world. ❹ He _____ his experiment in detail _____ the

scientific community first. ❺ Once the media heard the news, they _____

their questions over and over _____ every doctor at the institute.

answer	cash	change	close	do	open	prescribe	pronounce

Dolly was getting spoiled. ❻ People would _____ anything

_____ her. ❼ They would _____ the gate _____ her so

that she could go out to pasture. ❽ They would _____ the gate _____

her when she was finished. ❾ They would give her treats even though the doctors

_____ a special diet _____ her. ❿ Ultimately, Dr. Wilmut

_____ pens _____ Dolly so that she could have privacy.

Exercise 21.   VERB + Direct or Indirect Object. Put the sentences in correct word order.

1. good luck / wished / the student / the librarian

_____

2. a lot of / himself / he / time / saved

_____

3. asked / he / a question / his mother

_____

4. him / for an overdue book / the librarian / money / charged

_____

5. more money / him / cost / it / than expected

_____

Exercise 22.   VERB + Direct or Indirect Object. Write these sentences in the *other* pattern.

subject + VERB + direct object + PREPOSITION + indirect object
OR
subject + VERB + indirect object + direct object

1. Dr. Wilmut gave Dolly a different pen.

_____

2. Dr. Wilmut did Dolly a favor.

_____

3. He wrote a dedication in his book to Dolly.

_____

4. Visitors bought Dolly treats.

_____

5. They would pass the treats through the fence to Dolly.

_____

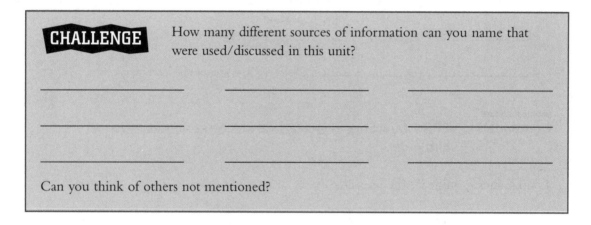

CHALLENGE How many different sources of information can you name that were used/discussed in this unit?

_____   _____   _____

_____   _____   _____

_____   _____   _____

Can you think of others not mentioned?

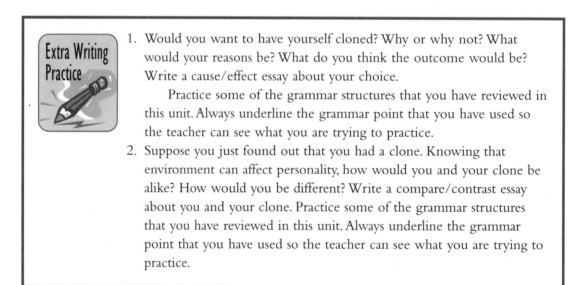

Extra Writing Practice

1. Would you want to have yourself cloned? Why or why not? What would your reasons be? What do you think the outcome would be? Write a cause/effect essay about your choice.

   Practice some of the grammar structures that you have reviewed in this unit. Always underline the grammar point that you have used so the teacher can see what you are trying to practice.

2. Suppose you just found out that you had a clone. Knowing that environment can affect personality, how would you and your clone be alike? How would you be different? Write a compare/contrast essay about you and your clone. Practice some of the grammar structures that you have reviewed in this unit. Always underline the grammar point that you have used so the teacher can see what you are trying to practice.

Unit 2

Past Perfect Tense

1. form: *had* + PAST PARTICIPLE
2. question form
3. past perfect progressive tense
4. negative form

When to Use Past Perfect

Use **past perfect** for past actions that occurred before another past event, action, or time.

Example		*Key Word*
Reporter:	Here's the photo I took of that 42-pound kingfish that John **had caught** only moments before the contest ended. (1)	before
Editor:	Wow! How long **had** he **been fishing** when he caught it? (2)	when . . .

19

Reporter: Not long. He **had** already **returned** to the docks by the time I arrived there. (3)

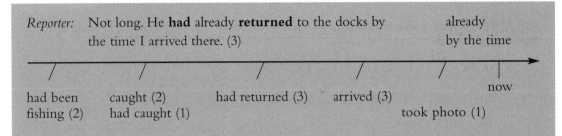

Note: The past perfect tense needs to refer to a simple past verb in order to point to its earlier time. Although the simple past tense verb is usually in the same sentence as the past perfect verb, the two actions may be in separate sentences.

Past Perfect Tense of Verbs

Past perfect tense consists of two parts: **had + PAST PARTICIPLE.** It is also possible to use a contraction for **had**: I'd, you'd, he'd, she'd, we'd, they'd.

	walk	**speak**	**be**
I	I had walked	I'd spoken	I had been
you	You had walked	You'd spoken	You had been
he	He had walked	He'd spoken	He'd been
she	She had walked	She'd spoken	She had been
it	It had walked	It had spoken	It had been
we	We had walked	We'd spoken	We had been
they	They had walked	They had spoken	They had been

Question Form

Making a question with present perfect tense is very easy. You put **had** before the subject.

statement: He **had completed** his homework before he went out.
question: **Had** <u>he</u> **completed** his homework before he went out?

statement: They **had been** home for 20 minutes by the time the rain started.
question: How long **had** <u>they</u> **been** home by the time the rain started?

NOTE TO ADVANCED STUDENTS

Past perfect is also used in **if** clauses and clauses after **wish.** In these cases, it refers to an action that did not happen in the past. Past perfect with **if** clauses and with **wish** is discussed in unit 4.

If I **had studied** last night, I would have passed the test today.
(= I did not study.) (= I did not pass the test.)

I wish you **had told** me this news yesterday.
(= You did not tell me the news yesterday.)

CHALLENGE   1. Where had Mike studied before attending the University of Copenhagen?
2. What had Mike studied before he changed schools?
3. What had caused Mike to change his major?
4. Who had been his adviser?

All of these sentences are correct. Why don't sentences 3 and 4 use **had** before the subject?

Exercise 1.   In the blank spaces, write the correct past perfect form of each verb.

	go		*fall*		*close*
I	*had gone*	you	_____	she	_____
you	*had gone*	it	_____	they	_____
they	*had gone*	Joe	_____	I	_____
he	*had gone*	we	_____	Jane	_____

Exercise 2.   Change the following sentences into questions using the past perfect. Make the question about the underlined words. Follow the example.

1. Linda had already made her Christmas candy <u>in November.</u>

   Question: *When had Linda made her Christmas candy?*

2. Kumiko had seen the movie <u>twice</u> before she read the book.

   Question: _____

3. Miki had lived <u>in Idaho</u> before she moved to Tampa.

   Question: _____

4. Serhat had spent <u>14 hours</u> working on his class project before it was completed.

   Question: _____

5. Caroline had studied <u>medicine</u> before she got her MBA.

   Question: _____

6. <u>Lisana</u> had eaten all of the cake before Amna came home.

   Question: _____

7. Mindo had read <u>*The Lord of the Rings*</u> by the end of the semester.

   Question: _____

Past Perfect Progressive Tense

Past perfect progressive has three parts: **had + been + VERB + -ing.**
The past perfect progressive tense is used to emphasize the duration of an event or action that was in progress before another event, action, or time.

> *example:* John <u>had been fishing</u> for one hour when he caught a kingfish.

> *example:* Rod <u>had been playing</u> the piano when the phone rang.

Without the progressive, *Rod <u>had played</u> the piano when the phone rang* means that Rod had finished playing the piano before the phone rang.

Exercise 3.   In the blank spaces, write the correct past perfect progressive form of each verb. You may need to review the spelling rules for adding *-ing.*

sleep *had been sleeping*   listen _____

sit *had been sitting*   plan _____

live _____   write _____

cry _____   eat _____

CAREFUL! Do not make these common mistakes.

1. Do *not* use the progressive form of past perfect with *nonaction* verbs.
   wrong: Betty hadn't been seeing her brother for several years.
   correct: Betty hadn't seen her brother for several years.

2. Do *not* use the progressive form of the past perfect with actions that are *repeated* a given number of times.
   wrong: Ariadne had been playing tennis twice before last night.
   correct: Ariadne had played tennis twice before last night.

3. Do not write the contraction **it'd** for **it had.** When Americans speak quickly, **"it had"** often sounds like **"it'd,"** but this form is *incorrect* in written English.

Negative Form

Making a negative with past perfect tense is easy. Add the word **not** after **had: had not.**
It is also possible to use a contraction: **hadn't.**

affirmative: I **had** finished writing my report when Sally called.

negative: I **hadn't** finished writing my report when Sally called.

affirmative: They**'d** been at the park for more than four hours when the wind
started to blow.

negative: They **had not** been at the park for very long when the wind
started to blow.

Exercise 4.   Write these statements or questions in the *negative* form of the
past perfect or past perfect progressive verb. Follow the example.

1. When Mom came in the door, she knew that the kids (napping).
   When Mom came in the door, she knew that the kids hadn't been napping.

2. I went skiing yesterday, but I (be) on skis since 1994.

   _____

3. Dave and Linda (dating) very long when they got married.

   _____

4. Brenda told the veterinarian that her cat (eat) for several days.

   _____

5. On his way to work, Ray suddenly remembered that he (turn off) the coffeemaker.

   _____

6. Where Marshall (travel) before he got married? He is a world traveler.

   _____

Exercise 5.   Read each sentence. If the event in A began first, circle A. If the
event in B began first, circle B. If the two events began or happened
at the same time, then circle C.

1. Gail had been fishing for three hours when it began raining.

   (A) raining   (B) fishing   (C) They happened at the same time.

2. By lunchtime, Pat had already picked all the strawberries that her basket could hold.

   (A) eating lunch   (B) picking strawberries (C) They happend at the same time.

3. When Kelly got to the hospital, the baby was born.

   (A) Kelly arrived.   (B) The baby was born.   (C) They happened at the same time.

4. When Kelly got to the hospital, the baby had been born.

   (A) Kelly arrived.   (B) The baby was born.   (C) They happened at the same time.

5. Steve began working as a geologist after they moved to Colorado.

   (A) He worked.   (B) They moved.   (C) They happened at the same time.

6. Steve had worked as a geologist when they moved to Colorado.

   (A) He worked.   (B) They moved.   (C) They happened at the same time.

Exercise 6.   Combine the following sentences with the word in parentheses.
Change one of the verbs to past perfect or past perfect progressive
in order to make the sentence correct. Follow the example.

1. Gary photographed the whale (1). (before) It dove under the water (2).

   Gary had photographed the whale before it dove under the water.

2. The children already ate (1). (when) Their father came home (2).

   _____

3. The girls were tired (2). (because) They were dancing all morning (1).

   _____

4. The baby was sick for two days (1). (so) Kerri and John decided to stay home (2).

   _____

5. Sally never used the Internet (1). (until) John taught her how (2).

   _____

6. I read the entire trilogy (1). (by the time) My vacation ended (2).

   _____

7. John Grisham didn't even write the final chapter (1). (when) The publisher began to advertise the book (2).

   _____

8. The printing press was used in China (1). (before) Gutenberg invented movable type (2).

   _____

9. Susan B. Anthony taught school (1). (before) She joined the struggle for women's rights in 1848 (2).

   _____

   _____

   _____

10. Susan B. Anthony died (1). (by the time) Women received the right to vote in 1920 (2).

    _____

    _____

    _____

Exercise 7. Practice with Forms. Fill in the spaces with the correct affirmative and negative forms of the verbs. Follow the example.

Present Affirmative	Present Negative	Past Affirmative	Past Negative	Past Perfect Affirmative	Past Perfect Negative
1. I eat	I don't eat	I ate	I didn't eat	I had eaten	I hadn't eaten
2. he works					
3. we go					
4. they are					
5. they live					
6. you have					
7. it takes					
8. she has					
9. I see					
10. you do					

Speaking Activity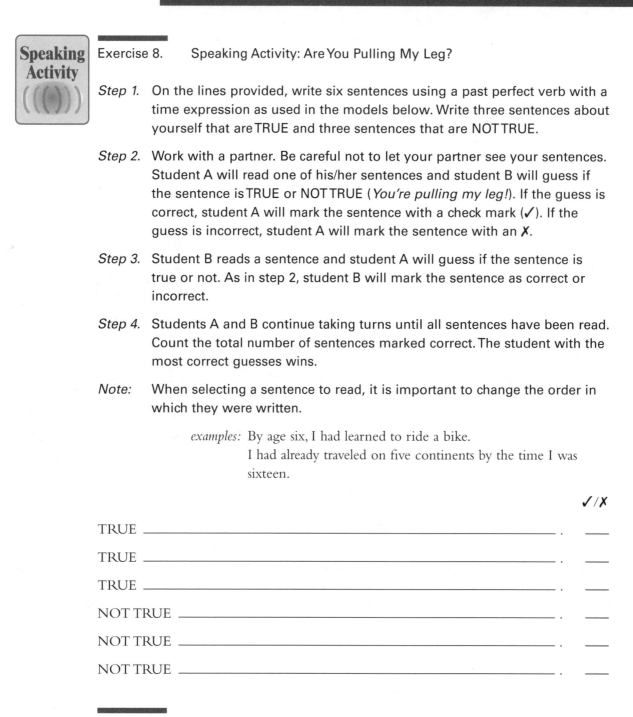

Exercise 8.   Speaking Activity: Are You Pulling My Leg?

Step 1.   On the lines provided, write six sentences using a past perfect verb with a time expression as used in the models below. Write three sentences about yourself that are TRUE and three sentences that are NOT TRUE.

Step 2.   Work with a partner. Be careful not to let your partner see your sentences. Student A will read one of his/her sentences and student B will guess if the sentence is TRUE or NOT TRUE (*You're pulling my leg!*). If the guess is correct, student A will mark the sentence with a check mark (✓). If the guess is incorrect, student A will mark the sentence with an ✗.

Step 3.   Student B reads a sentence and student A will guess if the sentence is true or not. As in step 2, student B will mark the sentence as correct or incorrect.

Step 4.   Students A and B continue taking turns until all sentences have been read. Count the total number of sentences marked correct. The student with the most correct guesses wins.

Note: When selecting a sentence to read, it is important to change the order in which they were written.

> *examples:* By age six, I had learned to ride a bike.
> I had already traveled on five continents by the time I was sixteen.

                                                                      ✓/✗

TRUE _____ . ____

TRUE _____ . ____

TRUE _____ . ____

NOT TRUE _____ . ____

NOT TRUE _____ . ____

NOT TRUE _____ . ____

Exercise 9.   Complete the following sentences with the correct form of the verb in parentheses. Use either past perfect or simple past.

Urashima: A Japanese Folktale

Once upon a time, a young fisherman named Urashima rescued a turtle from some boys who were teasing and hitting her with sticks. Then one day while he was fishing, a turtle swam up to his boat and said, "Urashima, you saved my life; now I have a reward for you. Please, get on my back." Urashima was surprised, but he

(get) ❶ _____ on the turtle's back as she (request) ❷ _____ .

The turtle dove under the water and took Urashima to a dazzling palace where

he met an elegant princess. She prepared a delicious banquet for him and together

they were entertained by a host of colorful fish dancing to beautiful music. Soon he

(begin) ❸ _____ to wonder how long he (be) ❹ _____ away

from home.

"I need to go home now," he told the princess. She didn't want him to leave,

but she complied with his wish. The turtle took Urashima back to the beach

where he lived. However, things seemed different to Urashima. His house (stand)

❺ _____ near the hill, but now nothing (be) ❻ _____ there.

He saw an old woman and asked her if she (know) ❼ _____ what

(happen) ❽ _____ to Urashima's house. She answered, "A young man

named Urashima (live) ❾ _____ in this town 100 years ago. One day he

went fishing and (never come back) ❿ _____ ."

Urashima was very distressed. Then he remembered that he had a pearl-covered

box that the princess (give) ⓫ _____ him before he (leave)

⓬ _____ the palace. She (tell) ⓭ _____ him not to open it

unless he (need) ⓮ _____ help. Urashima sat down and opened the box.

A mysterious white cloud came out of the box and suddenly Urashima turned into a

white crane. As he (fly) ⓯ _____ away, he looked down and saw the turtle

looking up.

 **CHALLENGE**   A1. They had eaten before they arrived.
                    A2. They ate before they arrived.

                    B1. She fell asleep after the movie had ended.
                    B2. She fell asleep after the movie ended.

Sentences 1 and 2 in each set have the same meaning even though the B sentences do not use past perfect tense. Can you explain why?

Exercise 10.   Dialogues. Underline the correct verb tense in the parentheses. The first one has been done for you.

A. *Roger:*   Who do you think is the best boxer in the world?

   Marshall: Evander Holyfield. He is the only three-time heavyweight-boxing champion in the world.

   Roger: Not so. Twenty years earlier, Muhammed Ali ❶ (hold, <u>held</u>) that same title.

   Marshall: Yes, but before Holyfield held the heavyweight title, he ❷ (has been, had been) a world champion in the cruiserweight class.

   Roger: But Ali ❸ (had won, had winned) a gold medal in the 1960 Olympics before he ❹ (turned, had turned) professional.

   Marshall: Yes, but don't forget that when Ali held his titles, all three boxing organizations were unified. However, by the time Holyfield ❺ (begun, began) his career, the organizations ❻ (had split up, have split up) and he had to be recognized separately by all three.

   Roger: All right, Marshall. You win. I'm throwing in the towel.

B. *Linda:*   ❼ (Had Julia Roberts ever received, Had ever Julia Roberts received)

an Academy Award before she ❽ (had been starring, starred) in *Erin*

Brockovich?

Valerie: No. That was her first Academy Award even though she ❾ (had had, has

had) several hit movies prior to her role as Erin Brockovich.

C. *Steve:*   ❿ (Have you enjoyed, Did you enjoy) the symphony orchestra last night?

Freida: Oh, yes. I ⓫ (had never heard, didn't hear) Mozart's *Requiem* before.

Steve: Did you know that he ⓬ (had working, had been working) on that piece

for months before he died?

Freida: That's fascinating. What else do you know about Mozart?

Steve: Well, he ⓭ (began, begun) composing music when he was just

five years old, and by the time of his death at age 35, he ⓮ (wrote, had

written) over 600 pieces.

Freida: Wow. Maybe ⓯ (he had worked, had he worked) himself to death.

NOTE TO ADVANCED STUDENTS

Although the use of the words *before* and *after* may eliminate the need for the use of the
past perfect in a single sentence, the need for past perfect becomes obvious in longer texts
and also in reported speech. More about reported speech is discussed in unit 6.

Exercise 11.   Multiple Choice. Circle the letter of the answer that best completes
each sentence.

1. Unfortunately, by the time the plane started to land, the movie _____ , so the

passengers were not able to see how the movie ended.

(A) did not finish   (C) not finishing

(B) had not finished   (D) was not finishing

2. Millions of years ago, huge animals called dinosaurs _____ in certain areas of the

world.

(A) had been living   (C) had lived

(B) did not finish   (D) lived

3. The teacher asked Jay to be quiet. Jay kept on talking. When the teacher asked Jay for

   the third time to be quiet, she _____ enough. She asked him to leave the room. Jay

   was quite embarrassed, but he gathered his books, stood up, and left the room.

   (A) had had   (C) was having

   (B) had   (D) had been having

4. In 2002, Sarah went to Germany and Belgium. She _____ to either of these

   countries before, so she didn't know what to expect.

   (A) did not go   (C) had not gone

   (B) was not going   (D) had not been going

5. In 1500, sailors _____ Holland, Spain, and Portugal in order to search for spices.

   (A) had left   (C) had been leaving

   (B) leave   (D) left

6. When Steve Fossett first attempted his solo balloon flight around the world, he

   _____ that he would encounter 10 days of thunderstorms over Argentina.

   Consequently, his balloon was damaged and he was forced to end his trip.

   (A) was anticipating   (C) had anticipated not

   (B) hadn't anticipate   (D) had not anticipated

7. Joanne had seen some bad storms in the past, but she _____ through a hurricane

   until Hurricane Michelle hit this area last summer.

   (A) had never   (C) has never been

   (B) had never been   (D) was never

8. Alexander Graham Bell _____ on a multiple telegraph system for several years when

   he coincidentally discovered that the sound of a human voice could be transmitted as

   an electrical impulse through wires.

   (A) had been working   (C) worked

   (B) has been working   (D) had worked

. Exercise 12.   Review Test

Part 1.   Fill in the blanks with the correct form of the verb in parentheses.

Last night I cooked a special meal for some of my friends. Four of my good

friends (come) ❶ ———————————————— to my house to eat chicken and

rice, which (be) ❷ ———————————————— one of my favorite things to

cook. Earlier yeasterday morning I (go) ❸ ———————————————— to

the store to buy the chicken, rice, vegetables, and other ingredients. Because I wanted

this to be a really great meal, I (buy) ❹ ———————————————— the best

ingredients that I could afford. For example, instead of getting regular rice, I (get)

❺ ———————————————— extra long grain rice from Thailand. I

(never/buy) ❻ ———————————————— that kind of rice before, but I

(choose) ❼ ———————————————— that kind of rice because I thought it

would be great for the dish that I (make) ❽ ———————————————— . I

(start) ❾ ———————————————— to cook the food around four o'clock.

I (cook) ❿ ———————————————— the chicken and rice for about thirty

minutes when my friend Zack (call) ⓫ ———————————————— to say

that he could not make it, so instead of six people, there (be)

⓬ ———————————————— only five people at dinner last night. I (be)

⓭ ———————————————— really surprised when Zack called to say that he

couldn't come to dinner. I (know) ⓮ ———————————————— Zack all

my life and (invite) ⓯ ———————————————— Zack to my house for dinner on

many occasions. Before last night, he (not cancel) ⓰ ———————————————— a

dinner invitation even one time. In any case, Zack (not attend) ⓱ ————————————

the dinner party last night. In the end, the dish (turn) ⓲ ————————————————

out fine, and I think that everyone (have) ⓳ ———————————————— a great

time. If I (know) ⓴ ———————————————— that Thai rice was so good and

was going to make this chicken and rice dish so delicious, I would have started to use

it a long time ago.

Part 2. Error Correction. Read each sentence carefully. Look at the underlined parts. If the underlined parts are correct, circle the word *correct.* If an underlined part is wrong, circle the word *wrong* and write the correct form above the words that are wrong.

correct   wrong   1. <u>How long have</u> you <u>been waiting</u> by the time the plumber <u>arrived</u>?

correct   wrong   2. The Civil Rights Act <u>brought</u> equality to African-Americans who <u>had been struggled</u> with the problems of segregation and discrimination <u>for over one hundred years</u>.

correct   wrong   3. How far <u>the cheetah had chased</u> the antelope <u>before</u> it <u>got</u> away?

correct   wrong   4. June <u>hadn't</u> <u>studied</u> for the test, yet she <u>passed</u> it.

correct   wrong   5. Christopher Columbus <u>had originally thought</u> that he <u>could sail</u> west to reach Asia; instead, he <u>had landed in</u> the Americas.

correct   wrong   6. I <u>had never saw</u> a live octopus until I <u>learned</u> to snorkel. Since then, I <u>have seen</u> several.

correct   wrong   7. How long <u>they had been traveling</u> in Costa Rica when they <u>decided</u> to leave the country and <u>cross</u> into Panama?

correct   wrong   8. Mel Gibson <u>had wanted</u> to be a journalist when he <u>was</u> in high school, but he later <u>had changed</u> his career to acting.

Extra Writing Practice

Situation: You have just won an Olympic medal and a magazine has asked you to write an article that tells your story. (Choose any sport.) When did you first become interested in the sport? How had you become interested in it? How many years had you engaged in the sport before you decided to compete? How long had you practiced for the Olympics? Where? How often? With whom? When? Add any other details that you need in order to make this story interesting.

Be sure to practice simple past, past perfect, and past perfect progressive verbs. For example, you might write, "I <u>had been dreaming</u> about the Olympics for years when I finally met my skating coach, Dorothy Hamill." Always underline the grammar point that you have used so the teacher can see what you are trying to practice. Remember that past perfect tense does not occur as often as simple past tense, so you will have to write a lot to have enough sentences that have past perfect in them.

Unit 3

Word Forms

1. verb endings
2. adjective endings
3. adverb ending
4. noun endings

Ahh... we are FINALLY going to have our mountain vacation.

I hope so... I forgot to FINALIZE the hotel reservations!

Certain word endings, called suffixes, can be used to create new words. These new words usually have a meaning similar to the original word, but the function, or part of speech, will change.

example: The <u>adjective</u> **final** becomes a <u>verb</u> by adding **-ize: finalize.**

By the *final* week of school, we were ready for a vacation.
adjective

Have you called Global Travel to *finalize* our vacation plans?
verb

The functions of content words within a sentence are **verb, adjective, adverb,** and **noun.**

verb	**adjective**	**adverb**	**noun**
finalize	*final*	*finally*	*finalization*

VERBS★	are actions or existence words that describe what nouns do.	
Ending†	**Meaning**	**Example**
–ate	to cause, to become, to supply with	motivate, oxygenate
–en	to make something have a certain quality	darken, lighten
–ify	to cause or make into something	identify, solidify, unify
–ize	to become	generalize, finalize

★Verbs are placed after subjects.
†Verbs can be made from nouns or adjectives plus these word endings.

It is important to check for spelling changes when adding word endings.

vowel dropped: clear + **-ify**   =   clarify
vowel added: different + **-ate** =   differentiate

Exercise 1. Create verbs from these nouns or adjectives by adding the
appropriate ending. You may use a dictionary to check the spelling.
The first one is done for you.

1. class   _classify_

2. diverse   _____

3. final   _____

4. alien   _____

5. light   _____

6. clear   _____

7. ideal   _____

8. different _____

ADJECTIVES★	describe nouns or pronouns.	
Ending†	**Meaning**	**Example**
–able, –ible	having a particular quality	comfortable, reversible
–al	of or relating to something	musical, occasional
–ant, –ent	someone who does something	persistent
–an, –ian, –ean	relating to someone or something from a place; relating to someone who has a certain knowledge or belief	American, technician, vegetarian
–ary	belonging to	planetary
–ate	having, containing, or having to do with something	compassionate
–ful	full of	beautiful
–ic	of or relating to a particular thing	periodic
–ish	having qualities of, or tending to be	bluish, childish
–ive	having a particular quality	expensive
–less	without something	useless
–ous, –ious	having qualities of	dangerous
–y	having the character of	curly, funny

★Adjectives are placed before nouns or after linking verbs (*be, become, seem, appear, taste, look*).
†Adjectives can be made from nouns or verbs with these word endings.

Order of Adjectives

Usually no more than two or three adjectives appear in any one phrase, yet whenever you use multiple adjectives you should follow this sequence:

1. opinion, 2. size, 3. shape, 4. condition, 5. age, 6. color, 7. origin

> *example 1:* a magnificent, small, oval, shiny, antique, silver, French spoon

> *example 2:* OR WITH ONLY THREE: a small, shiny, silver spoon

---

Exercise 2. Create adjectives from these nouns or verbs by adding the appropriate ending. The first one is done for you.

1. sense   *sensible*

2. peril   _____

3. classic   _____

4. accuracy   _____

5. violence   _____

6. monotony   _____

7. style   _____

8. help   _____

CHALLENGE A past participle verb (**-ed/-en**) or a present participle verb (**-ing**) can function as an adjective in addition to the list presented.

What is the difference in meaning between **comfortable, comforting, comforted?**

ADVERBS★	describe verbs, adjectives, or adverbs.	
Ending†	**Meaning**	**Example**
–ly	in a particular way or at times	easily, occasionally

★Adverbs can be placed at the beginning of a sentence, end of a sentence, or between the subject and verb. Adverbs can also be placed in front of adjectives or other adverbs.
†Adverbs can be made from adjectives with this word ending.

Not all words that end in **-ly** are adverbs. Here are a few.

early   Adjective: Gary is in his **early** twenties.
       Adverb: Carlos has to wake up **early.**

daily   Adjective: Our library subscribes to four **daily** newspapers.
       Adverb: Kumiko exercises **daily.**

oily   Adjective: Irma doesn't like **oily** foods.

lonely   Adjective: Ronald was a very **lonely** child.

Also, not all adverbs end in **-ly.** *examples:* fast, well, soon, always, here

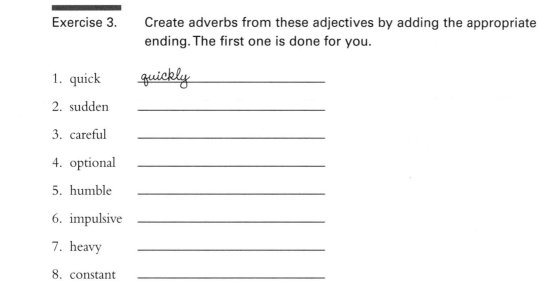

Exercise 3.   Create adverbs from these adjectives by adding the appropriate
                ending. The first one is done for you.

1. quick   *quickly* _____

2. sudden   _____

3. careful   _____

4. optional   _____

5. humble   _____

6. impulsive   _____

7. heavy   _____

8. constant   _____

NOUNS★	are people, places, things, or ideas.	
Ending†	**Meaning**	**Example**
-al	the act of doing something	rehearsal, denial
-ence, -ance, -cy	action or process; quality	performance, confidence
-ent, -ant	someone or something that does something	president, resident
-er, -or, -ar, -r	someone or something that does something	teacher, elevator, printer
-ity, -ty,	having a quality	equality, specialty
-tion, -ion	act or result of doing something	attention, impression
-ism	a belief or set of ideas	capitalism
-ist	a person who performs a specific action; a person with certain beliefs	typist, capitalist
-ment	a result of doing something; a place of action	development, department
-ness	state or condition	happiness
-ure	an act or process	failure, pressure
-ship	a state or quality; an art or skill	friendship, sportsmanship

★Nouns can be subjects, subject complements, objects, or objects of a preposition.
†Nouns can be created from verbs and adjectives with these word endings.

Exercise 4. Create nouns from these verbs or adjectives by adding the appropriate ending. Follow the example.

1. invest   *investor* _____

2. conform   _____

3. impress   _____

4. confide   _____

5. personal   _____

6. improve   _____

7. integrate   _____

8. compose   _____

Some nouns have the same spelling and a similar meaning as the verb.

	Verb	**Noun**
copy	Please **copy** this information.	I have a **copy** of it.
promise	I **promise** to pay you.	I made a **promise.**
struggle	He **struggles** with homonyms.	This is a **struggle.**

Exercise 5. In each blank, write the part of speech that is underlined: *noun, verb, adj* (adjective), or *adv* (adverb).

1. Are you going to the <u>play</u> tonight?   _____

2. Eliza and Donny <u>regret</u> not selling their stock last year.   _____

3. Kaan received a letter of <u>refusal</u> from admissions.   _____

4. The teacher gave Tom some <u>additional</u> homework.   _____

5. Mark and Cathy really had a lot of <u>fun</u> in New Orleans.   _____

6. Roberto's jokes are always very <u>funny</u>.   _____

7. Atsuko had <u>thoroughly</u> researched her essay topic.   _____

8. Good language learners make willing and <u>accurate</u> guesses.   _____

9. Most homeowner insurance policies are renewed <u>annually</u>.   _____

Exercise 6.   Underline the correct word form. Follow the example.

1. No one is ever sure of the schedule, so it is important to have (<u>flexibility</u>, flexible).

2. This shirt is (reversible, reversion). It has two sides.

3. Daniel is in (deny, denial) about his grades. He doesn't want to believe it.

4. The Strattons have elegant (Victorian, Victority) furniture in their house.

5. If you put oil on the wooden table, you will (darkly, darken) its color.

6. Did the teacher (clarify, clarity) the instructions?

7. Mindo comes to class with (regularity, regularly).

8. Read (slowly, slow) so that you won't make any careless mistakes.

9. You will always have her support because (faithfulness, faithfully) has been called her best quality.

10. Hospitals carefully (sanitize, sanitary) everything to prevent the spread of disease.

Speaking Activity

Exercise 7.   Speaking Activity: Word Branches

Step 1. Work with a partner or in a small group. Determine a length of time to play, such as 15–20 minutes. Select one person to be the scorekeeper and one person to begin the activity.

Step 2. Student A calls out a verb, adjective, adverb, or noun with any of the suffixes used in this unit. (No proper nouns or animals are allowed.) Student B has two choices: either change the form of the word, or use the same suffix and change the word. For example, if student A calls out *automatic,* then student B could call out either *automatically* or *automation* as a way of changing the form. However, student B would also have the option of using the suffix (*-ic* in the case of *automatic*) to make a new word, such as *periodic.* If student B calls out *automatically,* for instance, then student C now has the choice to use *automation* or a new word that ends in *-ly.* The game continues in this way.

Step 3. Keeping score. For each correct change in form, the player receives one point. For each correct new word with the same suffix, the player receives two points. Using the above example, *automatically* would receive one point, but *periodic* would have received two.

Step 4. Challenge your opponent. If the opponent thinks that the player has used a word that does not exist, then the dispute can be settled by referring to a dictionary or asking the teacher. If the student who challenges is correct, the student gets three points and the other player loses a turn.

Step 5. At the end of the set time, add the total points for each player. The player with the highest number of points wins the game.

Exercise 8.   Read each sentence carefully. Look at the underlined parts. If one of the underlined parts is wrong, circle it and write the correct form above it. Circle the word *wrong* as well. If the underlined parts are correct, circle the word *correct*.

correct   wrong   1. Siberia has a <u>substantial</u> number of <u>natural</u> resources.

correct   wrong   2. Olympic clocks must be very <u>accuracy</u> to be <u>useful</u>.

correct   wrong   3. Members of the book club <u>automatically</u> receive <u>preferentially</u> prices.

correct   wrong   4. Pavarotti gave an <u>impressive</u> <u>performance</u> at Carnegie Hall last night.

correct   wrong   5. Judge Hernandez told the <u>prosecute</u> to present her <u>evidence</u> to the court.

correct   wrong   6. <u>Politics</u> debates are part of the <u>democratic</u> process.

correct   wrong   7. Graciela's black, <u>wavy</u> hair seems very <u>attraction</u>.

Speaking Activity

Exercise 9a.   Speaking Activity: Crossword Puzzle, Student A

Two students, A and B, work to complete this puzzle. Student A works on the first crossword puzzle (on p. 41) while student B works on the second crossword puzzle (on p. 42). Do NOT look at your partner's puzzle at any time. First use the clues beneath the puzzle to fill in as many of the words as possible. Then take turns asking each other questions about the information that is missing from your puzzle. When giving an answer to your partner, be sure to use a complete sentence with the noun clause as provided in the clue.

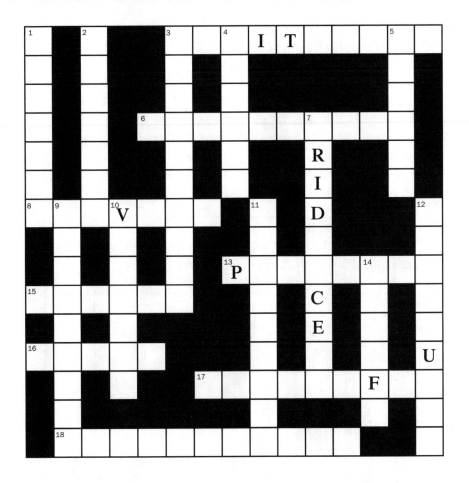

Clues for Student A

Across

3. adjective form of *add*
6. adjective form of *convenience*
8. After she broke her ankle, Sabine had to _____ her leg at night.
15. We took a water *purifier* when we went camping so that we could _____ our water.
16. having a lot of *hills*
18. adjective form of *sympathy*

Down

2. The pyramids of Giza are made from _____ stone blocks that weigh several tons each.
3. completely and totally
4. a person who drives a car, bus, or taxi
7. Some tropical fish appear _____ when the sun shines on them. They are shiny and the colors seem to change.
10. able to be seen (adjective)
11. Rob is very _____ to have won the lottery.
12. done with detail and caution (adverb)

Speaking Activity

Exercise 9b.   Speaking Activity: Crossword Puzzle, Student B

Two students, A and B, work to complete this puzzle. Student A works on the first crossword puzzle (on p. 41) while student B works on the second crossword puzzle (on this page). Do NOT look at your partner's puzzle at any time. First use the clues beneath the puzzle to fill in as many of the words as possible. Then take turns asking each other questions about the information that is missing from your puzzle. When giving an answer to your partner, be sure to use a complete sentence with the noun clause as provided in the clue.

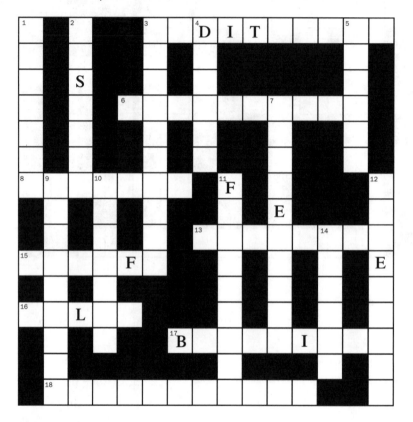

Clues for Student B

Across

8. *elevator* is the noun form of this verb
13. a captive
15. to remove the dirty parts
17. A very attractive woman is _____.
18. A person who tries to understand another person's problems is very _____ .

Down

1. adjective form of *abuse*
3. in an *absolute* manner
5. noun form of *apathetic*
9. expensive, beautiful, comfortable
10. Due to the thick fog, the Golden Gate Bridge was not _____ from the city.
11. lucky
12. Before taking the test, please read the directions _____ .
14. to give *notice*

Exercise 10.   Fill in each blank with the correct word form in order to make each sentence grammatically correct. Follow the example.

1. Some doctors say that exercise can help relieve (depress) _depression_ .

2. Those who (regular) _____ exercise will achieve long-term health benefits.

3. Exercising can even help you to feel better and have more (confident)

   _____ .

4. Each New Year many people (haste) _____
   begin a new program of exercise, which they often
   abandon after a few weeks or months.

5. One reason they quit is because they were
   overenthusiastic and didn't set (real) _____ goals.

6. The best plan is to start a program (slow) _____
   and build up from there.

7. Additionally, the program should be (enjoy) _____ .

8. One way to enjoy your exercise program is to add (vary) _____ .

9. Be sure to (diverse) _____ your activities between group sports and
   individual routines.

10. Finally, a fitness trainer can help to (individual) _____ your program.

Exercise 11.   Word Groups. Circle the word that does not belong in each group because it is a different part of speech from the other two words.

1. repetitious, persistent, regression

2. accommodate, compassionate, dictate

3. virtually, frivolous, inhibited

4. available, responsible, submission

5. frequent, resident, efficient

6. creative, final, appear

7. happily, quickly, lovely

8. floppy, stylish, attribute

9. originate, friendship, violation

10. eternity, extend, environment

Exercise 12.   Multiple Choice. Circle the letter of the correct answer.

1. If you treat strangers _____ , they will usually be nice to you.

    (A) civilize   (C) civilization

    (B) civilly   (D) civilian

2. When you oppose someone, you often _____ with him/her.

    (A) conflict   (C) confliction

    (B) conflictingly   (D) conflictive

3. Typically, rabbits _____ surroundings that provide them with a protective cover.

    (A) desire   (C) desirously

    (B) desirous   (D) desirousness

4. If you have enough _____ , you can accomplish most any goal.

    (A) determine   (C) determinable

    (B) determinedly   (D) determination

5. Jorge put in all the effort that was _____ possible to pass his classes. He couldn't
    have done any more.

    (A) humanize   (C) human

    (B) humanly   (D) humanism

6. We hope that the senators will soon pass _____ creating public health care.

    (A) legislate   (C) legislative

    (B) legislature   (D) legislation

7. My personal tailor, Angel, has satisfactorily done my clothing _____ for years.

    (A) alter   (C) alterable

    (B) alterably   (D) alterations

8. Meteorologists usually have no problem with the _____ of hurricanes because of
    satellite and aircraft sensors.

    (A) predict   (C) predictability

    (B) predictable   (D) predictive

9. During the final round, the Buccaneers were respected as _____ football players.

(A) competitive

(C) competition

(B) competitively

(D) compete

10. Tampa was unable to host the Olympic games due to the negative _____ that had

been created by traffic congestion on the highways.

(A) impress

(C) impressively

(B) impressive

(D) impression

Exercise 13.   Review Test

Part 1.   Identifying the Correct Part of Speech. Circle the letter of the part of speech that correctly identifies each of the following word forms.

1. components

(A) noun

(C) adjective

(B) verb

(D) adverb

2. cynicism

(A) noun

(C) adjective

(B) verb

(D) adverb

3. moralize

(A) noun

(C) adjective

(B) verb

(D) adverb

4. individuality

(A) noun

(C) adjective

(B) verb

(D) adverb

5. accommodation

(A) noun

(C) adjective

(B) verb

(D) adverb

6. revolutionary

(A) noun

(C) adjective

(B) verb

(D) adverb

7. selfish

    (A) noun   (C) adjective

    (B) verb   (D) adverb

8. lighten

    (A) noun   (C) adjective

    (B) verb   (D) adverb

9. cloudy

    (A) noun   (C) adjective

    (B) verb   (D) adverb

10. instrumental

    (A) noun   (C) adjective

    (B) verb   (D) adverb

Part 2.   Error Identification. If the underlined portion of the sentence is correct, write correct on the line. If it has an error, circle the error and write the correction on the line.

Reading in a Second Language

Good second-language readers need to be able to ❶ <u>recognizition</u> a large number of words ❷ <u>automatically</u>. Since second-language readers will always be at a disadvantage because of their ❸ <u>limit</u> vocabulary knowledge, they must make use of context clues to ❹ <u>inference</u> the meaning of the numerous unknown words they will encounter. Unfortunately, it is the second-language readers' very limited vocabulary knowledge that hinders their being ❺ <u>ability</u> to make ❻ <u>fully</u> use of context clues as well. In other words, ❼ <u>compared</u> to first-language readers, second-language readers' lack of vocabulary ❽ <u>know</u> forces them to guess word meanings more often; however, this very lack of vocabulary knowledge also ❾ <u>severe</u> limits second-language readers' ability to make use of context clues for guessing. One solution, then, would be to teach second language readers a ❿ <u>sufficiently</u> number of lexical items.

1. _____

2. _____

3. _____

4. _____

5. _____

6. _____

7. _____

8. _____

9. _____

10. _____

Extra Writing Practice

Situation: You are working for Universal Studios in Hollywood, one of the biggest theme parks in the United States, as a new creative director. Karen Walkenstein has found several actors and actresses who will work for free if they can play the following roles. She has asked you to fully develop the characters for **three or four** of these actors/actresses. You will need to create a setting and describe these characters in as much detail as you can. Use various forms of nouns, adjectives, adverbs, and verbs that you have been learning. For each verb, find an adverb. For each noun, find at least one adjective. Underline each new word for your teacher.

- housepainter
- musician
- bus driver
- farmer
- artist

- store manager
- farmer
- florist
- teacher

example:

It's a <u>gorgeous</u> summer day in this area of California, and <u>countless</u> people are <u>busily</u> shopping at an <u>enjoyable</u> outdoor market. Three of the more <u>progressive</u> stands are <u>operated</u> by a <u>farmer</u>, a <u>florist</u>, and a <u>musician</u>. The <u>cheerful</u> farmer has <u>delicious</u>, <u>colorful</u> vegetables. The <u>musician</u> is <u>suspicious</u> of everyone. The <u>talkative</u> <u>florist</u> refuses to sell <u>yellowish</u> flowers.

Unit 4

Conditionals: *If* Clauses and *Wish*

1. the grammar of conditionals
2. real conditions in the present and future
3. unreal conditions in the present and future
4. unreal conditions in the past
5. progressive forms and mixed conditionals
6. sentences with *wish*

Discover Grammar

1. Look at the sentences below. Some of them state situations that are real or that are possible. Others state situations that are not real or that will probably never happen. Read the sentences and decide whether the underlined situation is real or is possible. Then circle *yes* or *no* in front of each sentence.

2. After you have finished, discuss your answers with a partner.

   yes   no   1. <u>If tornadoes touch down</u>, they can cause damage to buildings.

   yes   no   2. <u>If it snowed 6 inches in Miami</u>, it would be front page news.

   yes   no   3. Your garden will grow faster <u>if you water it</u>.

   yes   no   4. <u>If people had feathers</u>, they could fly like birds.

   yes   no   5. <u>If money grew on trees</u>, we would all be rich.

   yes   no   6. <u>If I had invented the computer</u>, I would have become famous.

   yes   no   7. She goes swimming <u>if she wants to relax</u>.

   yes   no   8. He wishes <u>he could live forever</u>.

This unit deals with conditional sentences and sentences with *wish*. The underlined clauses in numbers 1, 3, and 7 are real conditions, i.e., it is possible for the situations to happen or occur. The remaining clauses describe unreal conditions (those that cannot happen or that probably never will).

Look at the two verb forms in each sentence. Write them on the lines below. Sentence 1 has been done for you.

<u>Real</u>

touch, can cause

_____

_____

_____

_____

<u>Unreal</u>

_____

_____

_____

_____

_____

What is similar about the verbs in the first group? What is similar about those in the second group? Write your answers below and then share them with a partner or the rest of the class.

First group: _____

Second group: _____

[Check page 66 for the answers.]

The Grammar of Conditionals

1. Conditional sentences usually have two clauses. The **if** clause states the condition, and the main clause states the result.

   If tornadoes touch down,   they can cause damage to buildings.
   if clause ⟶ condition   main clause ⟶ result

2. It is possible to reverse the order of the clauses of a conditional sentence without changing its meaning.

   Tornadoes can cause damage to buildings   if they touch down.
   main clause ⟶ result   **if** clause ⟶ condition

3. Notice that the punctuation changes depending on the order of the clauses.
   if clause,   result   vs.   result   **if** clause

4. The verb forms in the clauses change depending on two things:

   (1) whether the condition is real or unreal, and (2) whether the condition is in the present, past, or future. Look at the examples below.

   Real Condition in the Present and Future
   > If the weather **changes** suddenly, I **get** a headache. (real, present)
   > If it **snows** a lot tonight, they **will call off** school tomorrow. (real, future)
   > If you **have** time, you **should visit** the local museum. (real, future)

If Clause	Result Clause
simple present	simple present
simple present	**will/be going to + base form of VERB**
simple present	**should/can/may/might + base form of VERB**

   Unreal Conditions in the Present and Future and Past
   > If I **were** rich, I **would travel** around the world. (unreal, present)
   > If you **took** flying lessons, you **could become** a pilot. (unreal, future)
   > If she **had come** earlier, she **would have met** him. (unreal, past)

If Clause	Result Clause
simple past	**would★/could + base form of VERB**
past perfect	**would★ have/could have/might have + base form of VERB**

   Wishes in the Present and Future and Past
   > I wish I **were** home right now. (unreal, present)
   > He wishes she **would call** him. (unreal, future)
   > They wish they **had studied** harder for the exam. (unreal, past)

   ★*Note:* **'d** can be substituted for <u>would</u> or for <u>had</u>.

5. The **if** clause and/or the result clause in a conditional can be affirmative or negative.

> If I **get** a raise, I **will celebrate.**
> If I **get** a raise, I **won't spend** it foolishly.
> If I **don't get** a raise, I **will be** upset.
> If I **don't get** a raise, I **won't stay** there much longer.

However, only the result clause is used to form a conditional question.

> **Will** you **celebrate** if you **get** a raise? OR If you **get** a raise, **will** you **celebrate?**
> **Will** you **be** upset if you **don't get** a raise? OR If you **don't get** a raise, **will** you **be upset?**

6. It is possible to make unreal conditional statements about the present, future, or past without using *if*. These conditional statements, used only with the verbs **to be, to have,** or **should** are called inverted conditionals because the subject and verb are inverted. Notice that *if* is omitted in these inverted conditionals. (See exercise 10 for practice with this special form.)

> **Were** he here, he **would lead** the discussion skillfully.
> **Had** they **known** about the fundraiser, they **would have made** a donation.
> **Should** you **find** an electronic dictionary, please let me know. I've lost mine.

Real Conditions in the Present and Future

Real conditions express situations that can happen in the present or future. They are often used when stating facts or general knowledge or when describing people's habits. Conditions in the present use the simple present tense form of the verb in both the **if** clause and the result.

> If it **rains** a lot, some streets in my neighborhood **flood.**
> You **can't go** to the concert if you **don't buy** a ticket.
> They **volunteer** at the animal shelter on the weekends if they **have** time.

Conditions in the future use the simple present tense form of the verb in the **if** clause and **will, going to, can, may, should,** or **might** and the base form of the verb in the result clause.

> You **are not going to do** well if you **don't study.**
> I **will call** you later if it **is not** too late.
> If you **play** the lottery, you **may win.**

Exercise 1.   Circle the correct verb forms. Follow the example.

1. Every weekend, if the weather is nice, I (spend, spent) time outside with my children.

2. If you (are, will be) too busy to talk now, I can call you later.

3. If it (rained, rains) on the weekend, she stays inside and reads.

4. He (rakes, raked) leaves after work if he has time.

5. If I (got, get) some time off in December, I may take a vacation.

6. You (will enjoy, are enjoying) your trip to Ireland more if you plan ahead.

7. If she (doesn't put in, didn't put in) extra hours today, she can't take tomorrow off.

8. They're going to go fishing if it (doesn't rain, won't rain) tomorrow.

9. I'm free tonight if anyone (asked, should ask).

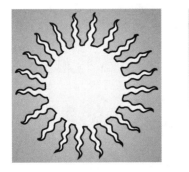  

Exercise 2.   Use the information below to form real conditions in the present or future. Follow the example.

1. If / today / be / Monday—tomorrow / be / Tuesday

   If today is Monday, tomorrow is Tuesday.

2. If/there/be/24 hours/day—there/be/168 hours/week

   _____

3. If/it/be/summer/north of the equator—it/be/winter/south of the equator

   _____

4. If/I/have/free time/evening—I/visit/you/tomorrow

   _____

5. If/they/vacation/Florida in February—they/eat/fresh strawberries

   _____

6. You/be/sorry—if/you/pass up/opportunity/this time

   _____

7. He/get/ticket—if/parking meter/expire

   _____

8. They/not/come—if/they/get/not/personal invitation

   _____

9. He/star/movie—if/price/be/right

   _____

Unreal Conditions in the Present and Future

Unreal conditions in the present or future express situations that are untrue in the present and that probably will not happen in the future. Although it is possible that the situation could change and become true in the future, it probably will not. Unreal conditions in the present or future use the simple past form in the **if** clause and **would** or **could** plus the base form of the verb in the result clause.

> If he **had** time, he **would take up** rock climbing.
> She **would not be** so lonely if she **knew** more people.
> If you **were** I,* what **would** you **do?**
> We **could skip** the next exercise if we all **understood** it.

*_Note:_ It is very common to hear the pronoun **me** used instead of **I** in this type of clause.

CAREFUL! Do not make these common mistakes.

1. Use **were** instead of **was** for all persons, singular and plural, in unreal conditions in the present or future. **Was** is used only in very informal situations.

   wrong: If I **was** you, I **would memorize** this rule about unreal conditions.
   correct: If I **were** you, I **would memorize** this rule about unreal conditions.

2. Remember that although the condition contains the past tense form of a verb, the condition is about the present or future, not the past.

   If she **were** the manager of the department now, she **would set** everyone's work schedule. = She is <u>not</u> the manager of the department, so she <u>does not</u> set everyone's work schedule.

Exercise 3.   Underline the condition that is untrue or probably won't happen.

1. If I were you, I would accept the job in San Antonio.

2. I think she would marry him if she truly loved him.

3. We'd all be relieved if she postponed the exam on conditionals.

4. If they hurried up, they could still catch the last bus downtown.

5. If he had the time, I'm sure he'd help you move into your new place.

6. Could you explain these idioms to me if I asked you?

7. I'll bet you would like the movie if it didn't star what's-her-name!

8. If my VCR worked, I'd invite you over to watch a movie tonight.

Exercise 4.   Terry and Ken are discussing whether Terry should accept a job promotion she was offered by her employer. Accepting the promotion means moving out of state. Fill in the blanks with the correct form of the verb to make unreal conditions. Follow the example.

Terry: I have to let the company know this week whether or not I'm going to accept the position of regional manager they offered me.

Ken: If there ❶ _weren't_ (be, not) so many factors to consider, this ❷ _would be_ (be) easy!

Terry: I know. If we ❸ _____ (like, not) living here in Denver so much, I

     ❹ _____ (jump) at the chance to move to San Francisco.

Ken: Yes, and if your salary ❺ _____ (stay) the same, it ❻ _____

     (be) easier to turn this job down, but they've offered you a big increase.

Terry: I've been talking to some people at work about it. One of them said, "Terry, if I

     ❼ _____ (be) you, I ❽ _____ (accept) that promotion in a

     heartbeat!"

Ken: I was thinking that if San Francisco ❾ _____ (be) closer, you

     ❿ _____ (commute) to work, but it's just too far for that.

Terry: Hmmm . . . How ⓫ _____ you _____ (feel) if I just

     ⓬ _____ (come) home on the weekends?

Ken: I ⓭ _____ (like, not) it if I only ⓮ _____ (see) you two days

     a week.

Terry: Well, if I ⓯ _____ (take) the promotion, you ⓰ _____

     (have) to quit your job. How ⓱ _____ you _____ (feel)

     about that?

Ken: I ⓲ _____ (be) okay with quitting if it ⓳ _____ (mean) that

     we ⓴ _____ (be) together.

Terry: Then I guess we've decided! It's the right decision, isn't it?

Ken: If it ㉑_____ (be, not), you ㉒ _____ (have, not) that big

     smile on your face!

Speaking Activity

Exercise 5.   Speaking Activity

Form a small group with two or three of your classmates. Make a chain of conditionals: the first person offers a sentence using an unreal conditional in the present or future. The second person changes the result clause in the original sentence to an *if* clause and adds a new result clause. The third person changes the new result clause to an *if* clause and adds a new result clause. See how long you can keep the chain going. See the example below if you need help getting started.

     example: Person 1—If I had more time, I'd go to school full-time.

                   Person 2—If I went to school full-time, I would study

                           architecture.

                   Person 3—If I studied architecture, I could design my own

                           house.

                   Person 1—If I designed my own house, I would . . .

Exercise 6. Complete the following sentences to form real and unreal conditionals in the present or future. Follow the example.

1. If I don't finish this tonight, *I won't be able to hand it in tomorrow* .

2. They wouldn't discover the secret if _____ .

3. I'm three years older than Maiko is, so if I'm 29, _____ .

4. If I weren't so afraid of heights, _____ .

5. If Mark cuts his hair any shorter, _____ .

6. You can't work in a deli if _____ .

7. It would look better if _____ .

8. If Laura wants to succeed in her career, _____ .

9. If we ran instead of walked, _____ .

10. He'd return the gift she gave him if _____ .

11. We need to leave right now if _____ .

12. If you have time tomorrow, _____ ?

13. If you surprised her with flowers, _____ .

14. Could those students pass the exam if _____ ?

Unreal Conditions in the Past

Unreal conditions in the past express situations that did not happen. Consequently, it is impossible for the results of the situations to happen. Unreal conditions in the past are often used to express a regret about the situation. Unreal conditions in the past use the past perfect form in the **if** clause and **would have, could have,** or **might have** plus the past participle of the verb in the result clause.

> I **could have gotten** the job if I **had sent** in my résumé on time. = I didn't get the job because I didn't send my résumé in on time.
>
> If they **hadn't read** the book, the ending of the movie **would have been** a surprise. = They read the book, so the ending of the movie was not a surprise.
>
> He **might have won** the tournament if he **had trained** harder and more often. = He didn't win the tournament because he didn't train hard or often.

CAREFUL! Do not make these common mistakes.

1. Do not get confused by the contracted forms used with conditionals.
   If he **had** more time, he**'d take up** a new sport.
   he**'d take up** = he **would take up**
   If he**'d had** more time, he**'d have taken up** a new sport.
   he**'d had** = he **had had**;   he**'d have taken up** = he **would have taken up**

2. The spoken contracted form of **would have (would've)** sounds like **"would of."** Do not substitute *of* for *have* in writing.

3. Do not use **would have** in the **if** clause for unreal past conditionals where **had +**
   PAST PARTICIPLE is needed.
   wrong: If I would have won the scholarship, I would have felt proud.
   correct: If I had won the scholarship, I would have felt proud.

Exercise 7.   Fill in the blanks with the correct form of the verb to make unreal conditions in the past. Follow the example.

1. If I _had seen_ (see) the paper, I _would have known_ (know) about the sale at Macy's.

2. She _____ (be) on time if she _____ (miss, not) the train.

3. _____ you _____ (go) to Daniel's party if you _____ (have, not) to work overtime?

4. I _____ (help) you if you _____ (ask) me. It wouldn't have been a problem.

5. She _____ (run, not) the Boston Marathon if she _____ (train, not) so rigorously for it.

6. If Orville and Wilbur Wright _____ (invent, not) the airplane, someone else _____ (do) it, don't you think?

7. If they _____ (follow) their parents' advice, Ray and Lisa _____ (be, not) in such a fix.

8. _____ they _____ (avoid) the fee if

they _____ (pay) the bill by credit card instead of by check?

9. I _____ (recognize, not) you if I _____

(hear, not) your voice. You look totally different!

Exercise 8

Part 1.   Look at the sentences above and write what really happened.
Follow the example.

1. *I didn't see the paper, so I didn't know about the sale at Macy's.*

2. _____

3. _____

4. _____

5. _____

6. _____

7. _____

8. _____

9. _____

Part 2.   The sentences below express actual situations. Write the unreal condition
for each situation. Follow the example.

1. I wasn't hungry, so I didn't eat. → *If I had been hungry, I would have eaten.*

2. He didn't feel well, so he stayed home.

3. He retired from his job early, so he was able to travel to exotic places.

4. She wasn't at home, so she didn't get the package UPS tried to deliver.

5. They skipped the concert because tickets were outrageously expensive.

Part 3.   Write actual situations of your own. Give your sentences to a classmate
and have your classmate write the unreal condition for each sentence.

1. _____

2. _____

3. _____

4. _____

5. _____

Speaking Activity

Exercise 9.   Speaking Activity

Choose a partner. With your partner, discuss one thing you could change or would like to do over in your life. Tell your partner how you would change things. Use the real and unreal conditional forms you have learned so far in this unit. Your partner will ask you questions. When you have finished, it's your partner's turn to tell you changes he or she would make and your turn to ask questions. If you can't think of anything you would change, practice with one of the examples from below.

> *examples:* I wish I had studied English earlier in my life. If I had studied English in elementary school, I would have learned it much faster.
>
> I wish I had not bought the car I own. If I hadn't bought it, I would have saved money on gas and repairs and insurance.
>
> I wish I spoke English more fluently. If I knew more vocabulary, I would have more confidence in speaking.

Exercise 10.   Read the sentences below. Where possible, omit the word *if* and invert the subject and verb to form an inverted conditional sentence. Review the rule on page 51 if you need help. Follow the example.

1. They would have bought the car if they had been able to afford it.

   Had they been able to afford it, they would have bought the car.

2. If you come late, you'll miss the beginning of the movie.

   _____

3. If Elaine were a true friend, she'd stand by you no matter what.

   _____

4. Please let me know if any new job openings should become available.

   _____

5. You'd be too tired to go out dancing tonight if you stayed up late last night.

   _____

6. If you liked sports, I'd invite you to see the Lakers play.

   _____

7. If IBM had offered Kari a job anywhere but Chicago, she'd have taken it.

   _____

8. They would know what a hula hoop is if they

   had grown up in the 1950s.

   _____

   _____

   _____

9. Dharma would send Smriti roses if she weren't

   allergic to them.

   _____

   _____

   _____

Progressive Forms and Mixed Conditionals

It is possible for conditional sentences to use the progressive forms of the verb.

   If I **weren't studying** for tomorrow's exam right now, I **could go** to the mall
   with you.
   If we **were driving** a convertible in this rainstorm, we**'d be getting** soaked!
   If they **hadn't been standing** on the corner, the bus **would never have stopped.**
   If you **had been waiting** where we agreed to meet, we **could be enjoying** a
   relaxing dinner right now.

It is also possible for conditional sentences to have different tenses in each clause.

   past/present: If she **had studied** a couple of hours last night, she **would feel** more
                     confident about the test.
                     If I **hadn't missed** the bus, I**'d be sitting** in class right now.

   present/past: If he **were** a citizen, he **would have voted** in the last election.
                     If she **were** a true friend, she **would have remembered** my birthday.

Exercise 11.   Fill in the blanks with the correct verbs to form progressive and
                     mixed conditional sentences. Follow the example.

1. If you ___*weren't studying*___ (studying, not), I ___*would turn on*___

   (turn on) the TV. (present/present)

2. If it _____ (snowing) now, we _____

   (build) a snowman. (present/present)

3. If you _____ (paying) attention, you _____ (answer) the question. (past/present)

4. If they _____ (ask) me yesterday, they _____ (be, not) in trouble today. (past/present)

5. You _____ (sign, not) up for this class if you _____ (be) an English teacher. (past/present)

6. If we _____ (talking, not) so loudly, we _____ (understood) what he said. (past/past)

7. If she _____ (be) a real artist, she _____ (stop, not) painting. (present/past)

8. The picture _____ (be) better if they _____ (smiling). (past/past)

9. If you _____ (eat, not) those peanuts, you _____ (be) so thirsty now. (past/present)

Sentences with *Wish*

Sentences with *wish* are similar in meaning to unreal conditions in the present, future, or past. The situation is not true, does not exist, or did not happen. Using *wish* expresses the fact that you want the opposite of the real situation to be true. Look at the examples below.

> I wish I **were** at home. = I am not at home.
> I wish I **could go** to the party with you. = I can't go to the party with you.
> I wish she **would call** me. = She won't call me, but I want her to call me.
> He wishes they **could go/were going** to Canada on vacation. = They aren't going to Canada on vacation.

present/future: **wish + subject + past tense form of VERB**
wish + subject + could/would + base form of VERB
wish + subject + be + base form of VERB + -ing

> I wish he **had picked** me up on time. = He didn't pick me up on time.
> They wish they **could have stayed** in Orlando longer. = They didn't stay in Orlando for as long as they wanted to stay there.

past: **wish + subject + had + PAST PARTICIPLE**
wish + subject + could/would + have + PAST PARTICIPLE

Exercise 12.   Underline the correct form of the verb to make sentences with
                    wish. Follow the example.

1. I have to work this coming summer. I wish I (can, <u>could</u>) go to Europe instead.

2. We need a break from work once in a while. There are days when we all wish we
   (could call, could have called) in sick.

3. I'm sorry you won't be coming with us. I wish you (were, are) going to come.

4. Carl just won't give in. Rhonda really wishes he (will, would) change his mind and
   take dancing lessons.

5. My sister Bev doesn't know how to sew very well. She wishes she (knows, knew) how
   so she could make her own kitchen curtains.

6. Many children watch too much television. Most parents wish their kids (watched, were
   watching) less TV.

7. I didn't know it was Anna's birthday today. I wish I (knew, had known) it was. I would
   have given her a card.

8. They missed the start of class by coming in late. Their instructor wishes they (came,
   had come) on time and (did not interrupt, had not interrupted) her lecture.

9. We forgot to put out the recycling bin this morning. I wish we (had remembered,
   remembered) to put it out.

Exercise 13.   Fill in the blanks with the correct forms of the verbs in parentheses.
                    Follow the example.

Lee is celebrating his 80th birthday today. His children and grandchildren are with
him, asking him if he has any regrets in life. Here's what he has to say.

Here I am, celebrating my 80th birthday. Some

days I wish I ❶ _____*were*_____ (be) still young

enough to start over. I wish I ❷ _____

(go) back to school, but I can't. I'm too old. For over

40 years I worked as an accountant. I enjoyed my

career, but I wish I ❸ _____

(study) art. My family encouraged me to attend the Art

Institute in Chicago when I was a young man, but I didn't take their advice. I wish I

4 _____ (listen) to them and **5** _____

(enroll) in the Institute.

To you, my grandchildren, I say, "Listen to your parents." I know you don't fully

understand my advice today. I wish you **6** _____ (do). I

wish you **7** _____ (know) how important it is to think

carefully before making decisions that can affect your entire life.

No one is going to hold your hand as you go through life. I wish I **8** _____

_____ (be) there for you as you grow up. Your parents will certainly

be there for you. So, today, even though it's my birthday we're celebrating, I have a

wish for you! I wish you **9** _____ (give) some serious

thought today to your future plans. I know that if you don't, someday you'll wish

you **10** _____ (listen) to me today!

Exercise 14.   Multiple Choice. Circle the letter of the correct answer.

1. If you park in a restricted area, you _____ a ticket on your windshield.

    (A) would find   (C) will find

    (B) found   (D) could found

2. I get nervous if I _____ in front of a group.

    (A) had to speak   (C) spoke

    (B) have to speak   (D) will speak

3. If today _____ Friday, we could sleep in tomorrow morning.

    (A) is   (C) were

    (B) will be   (D) was

4. If you _____ more sleep, you _____ be so tired all of the time.

    (A) get/would   (C) got/won't

    (B) got/wouldn't   (D) don't get/aren't going to

5. He _____ $20 in finance charges if he _____ his bill by the due date.

   (A) had saved/pays   (C) could save/will pay

   (B) could have saved/will pay   (D) could have saved/had paid

6. They _____ such a big van _____ the price of gas would skyrocket.

   (A) would have bought/if they   (C) wouldn't have bought/if had
       knew   they known

   (B) wouldn't have bought/had   (D) wouldn't have bought/had
       they known   they knew

7. If I _____ so much in this class, I _____ here.

   (A) wasn't learning/would be   (C) am not learning/won't be

   (B) weren't learning/wouldn't be (D) wasn't learning/wouldn't be

8. I wish I _____ myself better in English, but I _____ .

   (A) will express/won't   (C) could express/can't

   (B) would express/won't   (D) can express/can't

Exercise 15.   Review Test

Part 1.   Read these sentences. Fill in the blanks with the correct verb forms.

1. My grandmother always used to say, "If it rains, it _____ (pour)."

2. Do you believe that if you _____ (walk) under a ladder, you'll have bad luck?

3. Imagine—if money _____ (grow) on trees, we'd all be rich!

4. I don't understand the meaning of the proverb, "If wishes _____ (be) horses, beggars would ride."

5. If John Pemberton _____ (invent, not) Coca-Cola in 1886, we _____ (drink, not) it today.

6. If you _____ (living) in the U.S. in 1824, you _____ (be) one of the first Americans to taste pretzels.

7. Do you ever wish you _____ (be) someone famous?

8. _____ we _____ (study, not) inverted conditionals earlier in this

unit, we _____ (know) the answer to this!

Part 2. Read each sentence and look at the underlined verbs. If the verbs are correct, circle the word *correct.* If they are wrong, circle the word *wrong* and write the correct forms above the verbs.

correct wrong   1. If I get home before 10:00 P.M., I usually <u>watch</u> the local news.

correct wrong   2. She'll sell me her old car if the bank <u>approves</u> her loan for a new

                   one.

correct wrong   3. I <u>had volunteered</u> to work at the library a few hours a week if they

                   needed help.

correct wrong   4. Were he to ask, he <u>could receive</u> extra tutoring help after class.

correct wrong   5. If we <u>would have bought</u> them online, we could have gotten our

                   opera tickets for half price.

correct wrong   6. <u>Hadn't you been</u> so late, you wouldn't have missed the kick-off.

correct wrong   7. If I <u>wasn't taking</u> this review quiz, I'd be sitting in some little café

                   drinking coffee.

correct wrong   8. I'm confused. I wish I <u>have understood</u> the rules for making

                   sentences with *wish.*

correct wrong   9. They would have come to the

                   concert if they <u>hadn't been</u>

                   <u>studying</u> for their American

                   Studies exam.

correct wrong   10. If I <u>had studied</u> this chapter more

                   thoroughly, I wouldn't be so

                   confused by this sentence.

Extra Writing Practice

Situation: Employees at the company where you work are not very motivated. You have some ideas on how to change that, and your supervisor has asked you to put them in writing. Write a short report listing and explaining some of your ideas. Be sure to use conditional sentences in your report. For example, you could write, "If people had a more flexible schedule, they could come in later and leave later. If the company took this action, this would reduce tardiness." Underline the grammar point that you have used so that the teacher can see what you are trying to practice. (In this case, underline the word *if* and the subject and verb of that clause as well as the subject and verb of the main clause.)

Answers to DISCOVER GRAMMAR on page 49:

Real: touch, can cause; will grow, water; goes, wants to relax
Unreal: snowed, would be; had, could fly; grew, would be; had invented, would have become; could live
First group: The verbs and modals are in the present or future tense.
Second group: The verbs and modals are in the past or past perfect tense.

Unit 5

Adverb Clauses

The Grammar of Adverb Clauses

1. An adverb clause consists of a subordinating connector (i.e., an adverb) followed by a subject and a verb. Note that the adverb clause is never the main clause of a sentence.

ADVERB CLAUSE,   MAIN CLAUSE

When   the students   finished   the exam, the teacher collected the papers.

connector + subject + VERB   **subject + VERB**

2. It is possible to reverse the order of most adverb clauses without changing the meaning of the sentence.

MAIN CLAUSE   ADVERB CLAUSE

The teacher collected the papers   when   the students   finished   the exam.

subject + VERB   **connector + subject + VERB**

3. Notice that the punctuation changes depending on the order of the clauses:

Adverb clause, main clause.   vs.   Main clause adverb clause.

4. This unit will introduce nine different kinds of adverb clauses according to the function of the clause. In general, the kind of adverb clause depends on the question that the adverb clause answers. Adverb clauses generally answer one of these questions: When? Where? Why? How? Adverb clauses function the same way that adverbs function.

CAREFUL! Do not make these common mistakes.

1. Do not forget to use a comma when the adverb clause comes first in a sentence.
   wrong: As soon as I arrive in London I will call you.
   correct: As soon as I arrive in London, I will call you.

2. Do not forget to use a (subordinating) connector to introduce an adverb clause.
   wrong: The singer finished her song, the audience stood up and applauded wildly.
   correct: When the singer finished her song, the audience stood up and applauded wildly.
   wrong: The war ended, half a million people had died.
   correct: By the time that the war ended, half a million people had died.

Exercise 1.   Each of these sentences contains an adverb clause, which has been underlined. Add a comma if it is necessary. Follow the example.

❶ _Whenever I have the munchies,_ I like to make popcorn. ❷ Popcorn is my first choice for a snack <u>because it is easy to make</u>. ❸ <u>Because it is so easy to make</u> even those who don't know how to cook can pop popcorn. ❹ Popcorn is also a good snack food <u>because it can be a healthy food to eat</u>. ❺ <u>As long as you don't drench your popcorn in butter</u> popcorn is low in calories. ❻ However, many people prefer to pour melted butter all over their popcorn <u>until it turns bright yellow</u>. ❼ Of course, people do this <u>so that it will taste better</u>. ❽ Unfortunately, <u>since butter contains so much fat</u> popcorn loses its value as a healthy snack. ❾ <u>Now that several companies have come out with popcorn in convenient microwavable pouches</u> more and more people are munching on

popcorn even at their offices. ❿ <u>Even if you are not a good cook</u> you can certainly make popcorn, one of the easiest, healthiest, and most popular snacks!

Adverb Clauses of Time

Common adverbs that introduce adverb clauses of time are

after	Most of the students were happy <u>after they heard the exam results</u>.
before	<u>Before the rain started</u>, Brenda and I played two sets of tennis.
when	Lyndon Johnson became president <u>when Kennedy died in 1963</u>.
while	<u>While they were watching TV</u>, I was cleaning the kitchen.
as	The audience stood up <u>as the actors returned to the stage</u>.
whenever	<u>Whenever it gets too cold</u>, we have to cover the plants with sheets.
since	The company has grown by leaps and bounds <u>since it started here</u>.
until	<u>Until I checked my email</u>, I didn't know that Jack had a new job.
till	We stayed in the hotel room <u>till the maid knocked on the door</u>.
as soon as	<u>As soon as you arrive home</u>, please call me to tell me you're OK.
as long as	She has been my best friend <u>as long as I can remember</u>.
once	<u>Once I took the medicine</u>, I felt much better.
by the time that	They had eaten all of the cookies <u>by the time that I arrived</u>.

CAREFUL! Do not make these common mistakes.

1. When you want to express a future action of a sentence that has an adverb clause, do not use future tense with adverb clauses of time (but use future tense in the main clause).

   wrong: As soon as I will arrive in Sydney, I will call you.

   correct: As soon as I arrive in Sydney, I will call you.

2. With **by the time that,** the verb in the main clause should be in past perfect for a past action and in future perfect for a future action.

   wrong: By the time that the war ended, half a million people died.

   correct: By the time that the war ended, half a million people had died.

3. With **by the time that,** the verb in the main clause should be in future perfect for a future action.

   wrong: By the time the war ends, half a million people will die.

   correct: By the time the war ends, half a million people will have died.

Note: Future perfect tense consists of **will have + PAST PARTICIPLE.** It is used to show that one future action will be completed before a second future action.

Exercise 2.   Underline the correct connector. The first one has been done
               for you.

I have been teaching English to nonnative speakers ❶ (when, <u>since</u>) I graduated in
1990. ❷ (Whenever, While) I was a student, I often wondered if I would ever be
able to find a good teaching job. ❸ (As soon as, Until) I graduated, I landed a really
good job teaching English in an intensive
program for adults. I was very interested
in teaching English overseas, but I knew
that I needed some classroom experience
❹ (before, as) I could teach in another
country. I taught in the U.S. ❺ (once,
till) I felt that I had enough experience
to venture on to another country.

❻ (After, Whenever) I had taught in the U.S. for five years, I decided that it was
time to go overseas. I applied for a job in Saudi Arabia, and ❼ (once, by the time) I
got the job, I had started taking Arabic lessons to help me prepare for my new life.
❽ (As soon as, By the time) I landed in Saudi Arabia, I had learned the alphabet as
well as some simple grammar and vocabulary. I learned a great deal about teaching
English outside an English-speaking country and about Saudi Arabia ❾ (while,
before) I was living there. My teaching time in Saudi Arabia was a very long time ago,
but I can still remember so much of my life there ❿ (whenever, till) I think of it.

Adverb Clauses of Reason

Common adverbs that introduce adverb clauses of reason are

since	<u>Since Joe got sick</u>, we decided not to attend the party.
because	The price of car insurance has gone up <u>because car theft is on the rise</u>.
as	<u>As the term paper is due tomorrow</u>, we need to stay home tonight to do it.
so that	We enrolled in a Spanish course <u>so that we could improve our Spanish</u>.
inasmuch as	<u>Inasmuch as the patient felt better</u>, she was able to leave the hospital.
given that	She had to take the course again <u>given that she did not pass the final</u>.
now that	<u>Now that the stores are having their annual clearance sales</u>, today is the perfect day to go shopping.

Be careful with the two meanings of **since.** When **since** means **because,** various verb tenses are possible. When **since** means **from the starting time of,** the most common verb tense is present perfect.

careful: Since I arrived in Brazil, I have seen many of my good friends. (= TIME)
careful: Since I arrived late, I didn't see many of my good friends. (= BECAUSE)

Exercise 3.   Complete these sentences so that your information matches the situation. The first one has been done for you. Remember that there are many different possible responses.

Situation: Mr. and Mrs. Vickers are in a pet store with their twin seven-year-old daughters, Mandy and Misty, who want to get a pet. Mr. Vickers is not crazy about the idea because his daughters may not take good care of the animal. Mrs. Vickers is allergic to cats. Mandy likes dogs, but Misty would like to have a cat. Three of them do not want a bird, and nobody wants a snake.

1. The twins want a pet because *they want something cute and cuddly to play with* .

2. Given that Mrs. Vickers is allergic to cats, _____
_____ .

3. They probably do not want a bird since _____
_____ .

4. Mr. and Mrs. Vickers want their girls to have a pet so that _____

_____ .

5. In the end, they decided to get a dog since _____

_____ .

Adverb Clauses of Opposition

Common adverbs that introduce adverb clauses of opposition are

although	<u>Although they worked very hard</u>, they didn't finish on time.
even though	The cars cost more <u>even though they are smaller than those vans</u>.
though	<u>Though I called him up several times</u>, no one answered.
despite the fact that	She decided to travel to Cuba <u>despite the fact that this was prohibited by the State Department</u>.
in spite of the fact that	<u>In spite of the fact that this dictionary has more words in it</u>, the other dictionary seems to have more information about each word.

CAREFUL! Do not make these common mistakes.

1. Do not use the conjunction **but** when you use an adverb clause of opposition.
   wrong: Although we planned the trip carefully, but we encountered many problems.
   correct: Although we planned the trip carefully, we encountered many problems.

2. Do not forget to use the preposition **of** with **in spite.** Do not use an additional preposition with **despite.**
   wrong: Despite of the fact that it was cold, we drove to the ocean.
   correct: Despite the fact that it was cold, we drove to the ocean.
   wrong: In spite the fact that it was cold, we drove to the ocean.
   correct: In spite of the fact that it was cold, we drove to the ocean.

3. Be careful with **though, even though,** and **although.** These three connectors have basically the same meaning and usage. They should be followed by a subject and a verb.
   confusion: (Although? Even though? Though?) she studied the night before, she failed the exam.
   correct: Although she studied the night before, she failed the exam.
   correct: Even though she studied the night before, she failed the exam.
   correct: Though she studied the night before, she failed the exam.

Exercise 4. Editing. In each sentence, there is one error. Circle the error, write the correction above it, and then on the line below each sentence write your reason for making this change. (*Hint:* There are different kinds of errors in these sentences, not just errors with adverb clauses.) Follow the example.

1. I'm going to write about my neighbor because ⟨she the⟩ *is* most interesting person that I know.

   The clause needs to have a verb.

2. She has ninety-seven years old.

   _____

3. In spite the fact that she is ninety-seven years old, she lives alone.

   _____

4. Even she is quite old, she still does a great many things by herself. For example, she is frequently outside watering or even weeding her lawn.

   _____

5. Her companion is a fourteen-year-old cat named Cocoa. Despite the fact that Cocoa is not brown. Her name is Cocoa.

   _____

6. Although she will turn one hundred in a few years, but my neighbor is full of energy.

   _____

Adverb Clauses of Direct Contrast

Common adverbs that introduce adverb clauses of direct contrast are

while　　<u>While Chile has a long coast</u>, its neighbor Bolivia does not.

whereas　The Aztecs lived in the central part of Mexico, <u>whereas the Incas lived in the southern part of the country</u>.

Punctuation Note: With adverbs of direct contrast, it is good to use a comma even if the adverb clause comes second.

> *example:* The wind did a great deal of damage, whereas the heavy rain did not.

CAREFUL! Do not make these common mistakes.

1. Do not forget that **while** has two meanings. When it means **during the time that,** the verb tense is often present progressive or past progressive. When it means **contrast,** various verb tenses are possible.
   correct: While I was cleaning the kitchen, she was washing the car. (= TIME)
   correct: While this TV has a great picture, the price is too high for me. (= CONTRAST)

2. **Whereas** is not common in conversation. Do not try to use this in your daily speech.
   strange: Jack: "I ate eggs for breakfast whereas my wife had only toast."
   natural: Jack: "I ate eggs for breakfast while my wife had only toast."

Exercise 5.　　Write complete sentences to contrast the food items.

1. Whereas pizza is high in calories, _____ .

2. While pizza and tacos _____ .

3. While Joe likes pizza, _____ .

What to eat? Pizza? Salad? Tacos?

4. Whereas some of the ingredients in pizza contain a lot of oil, _____

_____ .

5. Salads have dressing on top, whereas _____ .

6. For meat lovers, pizzas and tacos can be a dream come true, while _____

_____ .

Adverb Clauses of Condition

Common adverbs that introduce adverb clauses of condition are

if	If the weather is nice tomorrow, I think we will go to the beach.
only if	We will go to the beach only if the weather is nice tomorrow.
even if	Even if the weather is nice tomorrow, we will not go to the beach.
whether or not	We will go to the beach tomorrow whether or not the weather is nice.
unless	Unless the weather is nice, we will not go to the beach tomorrow.
provided that	We will go to the beach tomorrow provided that the weather is nice.
in case	In case the weather is not nice tomorrow, we will not go to the beach.
in the event that	The school trip will be canceled in the event that the weather is bad tomorrow.

Exercise 6.   Editing. In each sentence, there is one error. Circle the error, write the correction above it, and then on the line below each sentence write your reason for making this change.

1. If is lightning, what should you do?

_____

2. Whether or no you have taken lightning seriously in the past, it is important to take several precautions during a lightning storm.

_____

3. Whether you are outdoors, do not seek shelter under a tree as lightning might strike the tree.

_____

4. Even it is raining really hard, do not be tempted to wait out the lightning storm under the tree.

_____

5. If you outdoors, you should avoid water, high ground, and open spaces.

_____

6. Provided that you can maintain a minimum of fifteen feet between you and anyone else, it is safe to wait out the storm with someone else. Thus, it is best not to wait out the storm in a small group.

_____

_____

7. In an event that the storm is really severe, crouch down and cover your ears with your hands to reduce any ear damage from the thunder.

_____

_____

Lightning

8. You will be safe in a vehicle if only it is a fully enclosed metal vehicle and all the windows are shut. Thus, a convertible is not a safe option.

_____

9. If are you indoors, avoid water and do not go near windows or doors.

_____

10. Unless it is not an emergency, do not use the telephone.

_____

11. Finally, you should unplug all appliances in your house in a severe storm even you are not using them.

_____

12. You can survive a thunderstorm that provided you follow these important precautions.

_____

Adverb Clauses of Place

Common adverbs that introduce adverb clauses of place are

where   The town of Preston was built <u>where two rivers meet</u>.
wherever   <u>Wherever I have lived</u>, I have made new friends quite easily.
anywhere   It is important to drive more carefully <u>anywhere it has just rained</u>.
everywhere   <u>Everywhere I shop</u>, people tell me "Have a good day!"

Exercise 7.   Underline the correct connector words.

Jan: Wow, I'm so excited to finally be boarding the plane! This is going to be a great

          trip.

Luke: I agree. I can't wait to get to Rome.

Jan: But first we have to find our seats. This is my first time on such a big plane. Wow.

          This is bigger than I had imagined it would be. Hey, let's sit here.

Luke: Don't be silly. We can't sit ❶ (everywhere, wherever) we want. We have to sit in

          our assigned seats. What numbers are on our boarding passes?"

Jan: 42A and 42B.

Luke: OK, I see row 42. It's back there. Keep walking. It's just past the galley.

Jan: Let's sit here. These are good seats.

Luke: No, you can't sit ❷ (where, that) you want. You have an assigned seat.

Jan: OK, here we are. I'll take the aisle, and you can have the window, OK?

Luke: Sure, it doesn't matter to me. Look, I'm so tired that I'll sit ❸ (everywhere, wherever) you tell me to sit. I just want to sit down a.s.a.p.

Jan: Hey, what about my backpack? Where does it go?

Luke: You can put it under the seat in front of you or in the overhead bin. If you use the overhead bin, it's better to put it in a place ❹ (where, wherever) you can reach it easily if you need to get something like your passport out of it.

Flight Attendant: May I help you?

Jan: Yes, I'm looking for a place to put my bag.

Flight Attendant: Well, it's probably too big to fit under the seat in front of you, and we're running out of overhead bin space, so why don't you look in the compartments around here and put it ❺ (anywhere, everywhere) you can find a spot.

Jan: OK, thanks.

Adverb Clauses of Result

Common adverbs that introduce adverb clauses of result are

so (adjective) that	It was so hot that you could fry an egg on the sidewalk!
such (ADJECTIVE + NOUN) that	They were such delicious chocolates that no one could eat just one.

CAREFUL! Do not make these common mistakes.

1. In conversation or informal writing, the word **that** is often omitted with these two subordinating adverbs.
   informal: It was such a good book I recommended it to all my friends.
   formal: It was such a good book that I recommended it to all my friends.

2. Do not use a comma with adverb clauses of result.
   wrong: The exam was so hard, no one passed it.
   informal: The exam was so hard no one passed it.
   formal: The exam was so hard that no one passed it.

3. Do not use **such** with only an adjective or **so** with only a noun.
   wrong: The exam was such hard that no one passed it.
   correct: The exam was so hard that no one passed it.
   correct: The exam was such a hard test that no one passed it.

Exercise 8.   Write *so, such, such a,* or *such an* on the lines.

In today's cooking program, we're going to learn how to make meatballs.

Making meatballs is not ❶ _____ hard thing to do in itself, but there

are several steps to go through. As with everything that we cook on this show, it's

❷ _____ important to have fresh ingredients. Look at these onions. These

onions look ❸ _____ fresh that you can almost see the dirt on them as if

we had just dug them up from the garden outside. First, you'll need an average-size

frying pan. You don't need ❹ _____ large pan because we're not going to

cook too many meatballs at the same time. You know, one thing we pride ourselves

on at this station is that we don't use ❺ _____ expensive equipment or

❻ _____ exotic ingredients. This is real cooking for real people who are

really hungry. OK, in a bowl, beat 5 eggs for 1 minute. Then

add in ¼ cup of chopped parsley, a little salt, and some pepper.

You don't want to add a lot of pepper because meatballs are not

supposed to be ❼ _____ spicy. Now add 1 pound of

lean ground beef. Mix all the ingredients together carefully. Put

this mixture in the refrigerator for about half an hour. We want

nice round meatballs that will hold their shape throughout the

cooking process, and you'll have a better chance of achieving

this with a colder, firmer meat mixture. If you attempt to form

the balls now, you won't end up with ❽ _____ nice

meatballs but rather with little squares perhaps. After the meat

is cold again, go ahead and form the meatballs. Put some

butter or oil on your hands. I know your hands won't feel

❾ _____ nice with all this grease on them, but this is

for your creation! Go ahead and form small meatballs about the size of a half-dollar.

Cover the bottom of a frying pan with vegetable oil, heat it, and then add about

10 meatballs to the pan at a time. As soon as one part of the meatballs is slightly

browned, turn them so that all sides can brown evenly. Fry them for about 6–7

minutes, and then you'll have some delicious meatballs. Now see? That wasn't

⑩ _____ hard recipe today, was it?

Exercise 9.   Change the sentences with *so* to sentences with *such* and those
with *such* to *so*. Follow the example.

1. James Naismith, the inventor of basketball, is not so well known.

   James Naismith, the inventor of basketball, is not such a well-known

   person.

2. Michael Jordan is so good at playing basketball.

   _____

3. I don't know if I can afford to go to the game.
   Those are such expensive tickets.

   _____

   _____

   _____

4. Playing basketball well is such a difficult thing.

   _____

   _____

   _____

5. He had such big hands that he could balance two basketballs on one hand.

   _____

6. The U.S. and Russian Olympic hockey teams are so good that they often win the gold
   or silver medals.

   _____

Adverb Clauses of Purpose

Common adverbs that introduce adverb clauses of purpose are

so that   George added sugar to the coffee <u>so that it would be sweeter</u>.
                     I'm making this salad <u>so that you will have something for lunch</u>.
                     I made this salad <u>so that you would have something for lunch</u>.

in order that   <u>In order that we understand the lesson better</u>, the professor asked us to
                     write a summary of each part of the unit.

CAREFUL! Do not make these common mistakes.

1. In speaking or informal writing, the word **that** is often omitted from the connector
   so that. In any case, do not use a comma with this connector.
   wrong: I took a picture of the party, so I could remember it forever.
   informal: I took a picture of the party so I could remember it forever.
   formal: I took a picture of the party so that I could remember it forever.

2. Avoid using a verb after **so that.** Use a **modal + VERB.** Possible combinations
   include **can + VERB** for present tense and **could + VERB** for past tense.

Exercise 10. Match the main clauses on the left with the best adverb clause of result by putting the letter of the matching clause in front of the appropriate main clause.

___ 1. I'm going to study as much as I can tonight

___ 2. He added more sugar to the cookie dough

___ 3. Cats' whiskers are as wide as their bodies

___ 4. I bought six extra drinks

___ 5. Adult male penguins have an extra fold of skin

___ 6. She saved up all her extra money for a year

___ 7. We arrived at the airport three hours early

___ 8. Animals often gain more weight just before winter

___ 9. Some people have to wear glasses

___ 10. I bought you a medium

A. so they can see well.

B. so that we would not miss our flight.

C. so that they can keep their young warm.

D. so that it would be as sweet as possible.

E. so that she could buy herself a digital camera.

F. so we would be sure to have enough for everyone.

G. so that they will have enough nutrition for their bodies.

H. so that they can judge how wide an opening is before entering.

I. so that I don't have so much studying to do tomorrow night.

J. so it would fit you for sure.

Adverb Clauses of Manner

Common adverbs that introduce adverb clauses of manner are

as   He answered the phone <u>as any native speaker would</u>.
as if   He answered the phone <u>as if he were a native speaker</u>.
as though   He looks <u>as though he is sad</u>.
in that   The two tickets differ <u>in that the first one is business class</u>.

Note: Adverb clauses of manner come after the main clause.

CAREFUL! Do not make these common mistakes.

Do not use regular verb forms with **as if** or **as though** for unreal situations. When the action after **as if** or **as though** is unreal, the verb must be in subjunctive mood. (This resembles simple past tense for a present action and past perfect tense for a past action.)

wrong: (Joe is not rich.) Joe likes to act as if he is rich.
correct: (Joe is not rich.) Joe likes to act as if he were rich.
wrong: (Joe does not have a headache.) Joe looks as though he had a headache.
correct: (Joe does not have a headache.) Joe looks as though he has a headache.

Exercise 11.   Underline the correct verb form in these sentences. Follow the example.

1. *Situation:*   Claudia is from Venezuela.

   Statement: Claudia is from Venezuela, but she speaks as if she (is, <u>were,</u> had been) Colombian.

2. *Situation:*   Kevin eats three regular meals a day as well as some snack food.

   Statement: Kevin is eating so fast! He's eating as if he (never sees, never saw, never seen, had never seen) food before!

3. *Situation:*   Mary does not know Sue at all, but she always speaks very highly of her.

   Statement: It's as though Sue actually (knows, knew, had met) Mary.

4. *Situation:*   Bill is 23 years old, but he still acts like a child sometimes.

   Statement: Bill sometimes behaves as though he (is, were, had, had been) 10 years old.

5. *Situation:*   Kathy had a very hard day at work today. She is really tired.

   Statement: Kathy looks as if she (is, were, had been) exhausted.

6. *Situation:*   Gregory is not an expert on plant care, but I heard him give Ken some advice about his plants.

   Statement: Gregory talks as though he (knew, knows, had known) plants inside and out.

7. *Situation:*   Paula is usually a very calm person. Right now her face is white because she isn't feeling well.

   Statement: "Paula, what's wrong with you? You look as though you (saw, had seen, see) a ghost."

8. *Situation:*   Kim and Lee do not know the flavor of the dessert. It does not have nuts in it, though.

   Statement: This dessert tastes as if it (has, had, had had) nuts in it.

Exercise 12.   Complete these original sentences with a clause that begins *in that.* Follow the example.

1. English and Arabic are different in that *they are written in different directions.*

   _____

2. Coffee and tea are similar in that _____

   _____

3. A jet and a helicopter differ in that _____

   _____

4. A potato is like a carrot in that _____

   _____

5. _____ and _____ are different in that _____

   _____

6. _____ and _____ are similar in that _____

   _____

Speaking Activity

Exercise 13.   Speaking Activity

Part 1.   Preparation. Read this true story. Then write out your answers to the final question. Then use the adverb clause markers to write six to ten sentences explaining or supporting your answers to the question.

On July 18, 1984, a lone gunman walked into a McDonald's restaurant in San Ysidro, California, and opened fire. When the shooting stopped, twenty-one people were dead. Because McDonald's has come to be such a well-known restaurant chain as well as an integral part of American culture, this senseless killing was even more shocking.

In the press reports and stories that followed, the name *McDonald's* appeared right next to words such as *massacre, tragedy,* and *disaster.* The executives had to act extremely quickly to counteract this incredibly horrible publicity. To this end, they took three steps. *Question:* What do you think the three steps were?

When you write your answers, try to use as many of these as possible.

Adverb Clauses of Time

after	whenever	as long as
before	since	once that
when	until	by the time that
while	till	
as	as soon as	

Adverb Clauses of Reason

since	so that	now that
because	inasmuch as	
as	given that	

Adverb Clauses of Opposition

although	though	in spite of the fact that
even though	despite the fact that	

Adverb Clauses of Direct Contrast
while
whereas

Adverb Clauses of Condition

if	whether or not	in case
only if	unless	in the event that
even if	provided that	

Adverb Clauses of Place

anywhere	where
everywhere	wherever

Adverb Clauses of Result

so (adjective) that
such (ADJECTIVE + NOUN) that

Adverb Clauses of Purpose

so that
in order that

Adverb Clauses of Manner

as	as though
as if	in that

Question: What do you think the three steps were? Write at least two reasons for each of your answers. In your sentences, include adverb clauses using the connectors.

Step 1. _____

_____

Reason a: _____

_____

Reason b: _____

_____

Step 2. _____

_____

Reason a: _____

_____

Reason b: _____

_____

Step 3. _____

_____

Reason a: _____

_____

Reason b: _____

_____

Part 2.   Speaking. Work with a partner or in small groups. Take turns presenting
             your ideas for the three steps that the McDonald's executives took as
             well as your reasons. As you are listening to others' ideas, pay special
             attention to adverb clauses.

Exercise 14.   Multiple Choice. Circle the letter of the correct answer.

1. I'm a tennis fanatic! _____ I am tired, I usually have enough energy to play tennis.

   (A) Only if   (C) Since

   (B) Even if   (D) Now that

2. By the time Beethoven reached the young age of 10, he _____ several impressive

   musical works.

   (A) already wrote   (C) already writes

   (B) had already written   (D) will already write

3. _____ the assignment is due tomorrow, it is imperative that we finish it today.

   (A) Unless   (C) So that

   (B) Everywhere   (D) As

4. I can't believe you are having trouble lifting that box. You are acting as if it _____

   really heavy.

   (A) is   (C) had

   (B) had been   (D) were

5. _____ singer left the stage after singing another incredibly beautiful song, but no
one wanted to leave the auditorium.

    (A) When the   (C) In order that the

    (B) Although the   (D) The

6. Given that _____ , your grade for the class is an F.

    (A) you worked so hard in this   (C) your final exam in the course was so bad
          course

    (B) the book for this course was   (D) you were not absent a single day in this
          fairly easy   course

7. She is an excellent teacher who has taught in four schools. _____ she has taught,
she has received wonderful evaluations from her principals.

    (A) Everywhere   (C) Inasmuch as

    (B) Where   (D) In such good schools that

8. The bus driver waited at the stop for an extra minute so that the old man _____
on the bus.

    (A) could get   (C) got

    (B) will get   (D) had gotten

9. Although we tend to think that they are basically the same animal, dolphins,
porpoises, and fish are not alike. Despite how similar they might seem, these three
animals _____ dolphins and porpoises are mammals while fish are not.

    (A) different in that   (C) differ in that

    (B) different so that   (D) differ so that

10. As soon as I _____ at my apartment, I promise that I will call you up to let you
know that I have arrived safely.

    (A) arrive   (C) will arrive

    (B) arrived   (D) arriving

Exercise 15.   Review Test

Part 1.   Read these sentences and underline the correct adverb clause connector.

❶ Last night my cousin and I went to an Italian restaurant (because, whereas, so that) we wanted to eat pasta. ❷ Broadway Eatery has (so, such, such a) good food that we decided to spend thirty minutes driving there (even though, as if, in that) it's so far away. ❸ (Whenever, Wherever, However) I go to Broadway Eatery, I order chicken parmesan. It is by far my favorite dish there! ❹ The food took a little while, so my cousin and I sat telling jokes to each other (as soon as, till, while) we were waiting.

❺ (Whereas, Though, In the event that) I had not eaten all day, I was doing OK (even though, provided that, because) I knew that my favorite dish would soon be in front of me. ❻ (The, Although the, If the) food finally arrived, and we started eating! One thing that I really like about this restaurant is that the food always comes covered with extra cheese

❼ (unless, in that, whether or not) you ask for it. ❽ (Despite, In spite, Because) the fact that my plate was incredibly full, I managed to eat everything on my plate. What a great meal we had!

Part 2.   Read each sentence carefully. Look at the underlined part. If the underlined part is correct, circle the word *correct*. If it is wrong, circle the word *wrong* and write the correct form above the error.

correct   wrong   1. <u>Whenever that I have</u> a headache, I take two aspirin with a large glass of water.

correct   wrong   2. The price of airline tickets is going to go up <u>as soon as the current summer season will end</u>.

correct   wrong   3. <u>Giving that her car had</u> over 100,000 miles on it, Cecilia decided that is was probably time to sell it.

correct   wrong   4. The employees <u>got their paychecks so they went</u> to the bank to

cash them.

correct   wrong   5. I can't play tennis tomorrow because I have to work. <u>Even the</u>

<u>weather is perfect</u>, with sunny skies and no wind, I still can't play.

correct   wrong   6. The passengers look tired because <u>there were such a noisy children</u>

<u>on the plane that</u> hardly any of them could sleep.

correct   wrong   7. <u>Although the invention of the electric lightbulb ushered in a new</u>

<u>era in architectural design</u>, but many people were at first afraid to

have electricity in their homes and offices.

Extra Writing Practice

Situation: Write a paragraph or short essay in which you compare or contrast two things or two people. Some possible topics include two vacation destinations, two famous politicians, two languages, two typical dishes, two careers, and two fast-food restaurants. Underline all the adverb clauses in your writing and circle the initial connecting word so that your teacher can see what you are trying to practice.

Unit 6

Noun Clauses

Discover Grammar

1. Read the following passage. Each group of words in bold letters is a noun clause.

Some people believe **that a goat herder in Ethiopia discovered coffee about 1,500 years ago.** According to legend, he had noticed **that his goats became more frisky after eating coffee berries.** He wondered **what effects the berries might have on humans,** so he decided **that he would try some himself.** Consequently, he was pleased **that he, too, became more energetic and alert.**

Whether or not this legend is true remains uncertain. However, it is widely known **that coffee has stimulating effects.**

2. Work with a partner to answer the following questions so that you can discover the grammar of noun clauses.

   a. Make a list of the words that begin each noun clause.

      _____ .

   b. Write the word and its part of speech (verb or adjective) that comes immediately before the clause.

      _____

      _____ .

   c. Why do you think that the clause beginning with *whether* comes at the beginning of the sentence?

      _____

      _____ .

   d. You have already learned that adjective clauses modify nouns and that adverb clauses modify verbs or main clauses. Can you guess the function of noun clauses?

      _____ .

   [Check page 120 for the answers.]

Noun Clauses: Form and Function

A noun clause, like other clauses, has both a subject and verb. A noun clause is a dependent clause and needs to be connected to an independent clause.

   independent clause: Libby forgot
   noun clause: that a *mocha latte* is made with chocolate syrup.

   Libby forgot that a *mocha latte* is made with chocolate syrup.

A noun clause functions like a noun in these positions:
   object of a verb, object of a preposition, subject, subject complement, or following an adjective

In the above example, the noun clause functions as the object of the verb **forget.** To test this theory, exchange the noun clause with a noun.

> *example:*   Libby <u>forgot</u> <u>Jane's cell-phone number</u>.
>   verb   noun

Noun clauses begin with **that, wh-** words, and **if/whether.**

Exercise 1.   Underline the noun clause in these sentences.

1. *Miki:*   For several years Fumiko has hoped that she could finish her education in

     the U.S.

2. *Juri:*   Do you know where she wants to study?

3. *Miki:*   Where she wants to study is not the problem.

4. *Juri:*   I guess that I misunderstood you.

5. *Miki:*   The problem is whether she can save enough money.

Usage 1: Noun Clauses as Embedded Statements—*That* Clauses

Noun clauses that state information often appear in the object position of an independent clause. This type of noun clause *always* begins with **that.**

> Marshall believes **that** vitamin supplements are necessary.

In conversation, the word **that** may be omitted.

> Sally believes a proper diet will provide all the vitamins you need.

Noun clauses in the object position follow verbs of mental state such as

agree	explain	notice
believe	forget	pretend
claim	guess	promise
demonstrate	hear	realize
deny	hope	remember
determine	imagine	see
discover	indicate	show
dislike	know	suggest
doubt	learn	think
estimate	means	understand

In conversation, a **that** clause can be replaced by *so* when you are answering **yes** to a question about which you are almost certain. The verbs used for affirmative answers are **think, believe, hope,** or **guess.**

> examples: Lisa: Are we having a test tomorrow?
>
> Jen: I think <u>so</u>. (OR) I guess <u>so</u>.
>
> (I think <u>that we are having a test tomorrow</u>.)
>
> Dan: Will the park open early tomorrow?
>
> Sue: I believe so. (OR I hope so.)

Noun clauses beginning with **that** can also follow the expression **it is a fact.**

> example: It is a fact that Brazil grows most of the world's coffee.

Exercise 2. Use these facts to create noun clauses. The subject, verb, and tense for the main clause are in parentheses. Follow the example.

1. Mt. Etna erupted in July 2000. (Mario / remember [present])

   Mario remembers that Mt. Etna erupted in July 2000.

   _____

   _____

   _____ .

2. The lava on Mt. Etna flowed at a rate of 50 meters per hour.
   (Scientists / estimate [simple past])

   _____

   _____

   _____

   _____

   _____

   _____ .

3. Penguins are birds that cannot fly. (Yesterday the children / learn [simple past])

_____

_____

_____ .

4. Penguins can swim underwater at a speed of 15 miles per hour.
   (I / hear [present perfect])

_____

_____

_____ .

5. One mile equals approximately 1.6 kilometers. (It is a fact [present])

_____

_____

_____ .

6. Penguins swim underwater at 24 kilometers per hour. (Using this conversion
   we / can determine [present])

_____

_____

_____ .

Speaking Activity (( ))

Exercise 3a.   Speaking Activity: Crossword Puzzle, Student A

Two students, A and B, work to complete this puzzle. Student A works on the first crossword puzzle (on p. 95) while student B works on the second crossword puzzle (on p. 96). Do NOT look at your partner's puzzle at any time. First use the clues beneath the puzzle to fill in as many of the words as possible. Then take turns asking each other questions about the information that is missing from your puzzle. When giving an answer to your partner, be sure to use a complete sentence with the noun clause as provided in the clue. (*Hint:* Use words from the list on p. 92.)

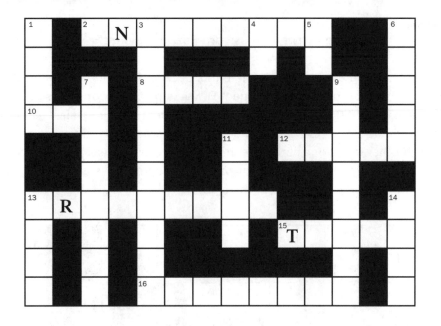

Clues for Student A

Across

2. Einstein's theory _____ that time is relative to speed of movement

8. to seem, appear, demonstrate (present)

12. Marco Polo _____ that Kublai Khan had the greatest empire on Earth.

15. grammar term used to show the time of an action

16. Georgia O'Keeffe _____ being asked to explain her paintings.

Down

3. In 1929, Alexander Fleming _____ that penicillin killed bacteria.

5. Will we ever have clean energy for our cars? I hope _____ .

7. Copernicus _____ that the earth revolved around the sun.

11. The Spanish Conquistadors never _____ that Machu Picchu existed.

13. The Smiths always _____ that they will take a special trip on their anniversary.

14. to refuse to believe (present)

Speaking Activity

Exercise 3b.   Speaking Activity: Crossword Puzzle, Student B

Two students, A and B, work to complete this puzzle. Student A works on the first crossword puzzle (on p. 95) while student B works on the second crossword puzzle (on this page). Do NOT look at your partner's puzzle at any time. First use the clues beneath the puzzle to fill in as many of the words as possible. Then take turns asking each other questions about the information that is missing from your puzzle. When giving an answer to your partner, be sure to use a complete sentence with the noun clause as provided in the clue.

Clues for Student B

Across

8. By pointing out the success of music and movies we can _____ that entertainment is big business.

10. Physicists _____ that fusion will be a future form of green energy.

13. The Greeks _____ that the Trojan horse was a gift to Troy.

15. unable to relax (adjective)

Down

1. The student handbook _____ that we should apply for graduation by September 30th.

3. to find (past)

4. The student handbook says _____ apply for graduation by September 30th.

6. Gandhi _____ that nonviolent protest would bring world peace.

9. The Wright brothers _____ that they could fly in a machine.

14. Few scientists _____ that global warming is a concern.

Usage 2: Noun Clauses as Embedded Questions—*Wh-* or *Yes-No* Clauses

A noun clause as an embedded question is used to indicate knowledge or lack of knowledge about something.

> I don't know <u>where Sarah and Jim are going for vacation.</u>
> I wonder <u>if they are going to Costa Rica.</u>

An embedded question can also be used to request information in an indirect manner.

> Do you know <u>where Sarah and Jim are going for vacation?</u>
> Do you know <u>if they are going to Costa Rica?</u>

Statement word order (**subject + VERB**) is always used in embedded questions. The main clause can be either in question form, followed by a question mark, or in statement form, followed by a period.

> *question:*   Did you hear <u>what she said?</u>
> *statement:*   I didn't hear <u>what she said.</u>

Embedded questions begin with

> **who, what, when, where, why, which, how** for **wh-** questions

> > *examples:*   I can't remember <u>where</u> my keys are.
> > Do you know <u>where</u> my keys are?

> **if** or **whether** for **yes-no** questions

> > *examples:*   We don't know <u>if</u> it is going to rain tomorrow.
> > Do you know <u>if</u> it is going to rain tomorrow?
> > Do you know <u>whether</u> it is going to rain tomorrow?

> > *Note:*   **Whether** can also be followed by **or not.**

> > I don't know <u>whether or not</u> to buy this shirt.

Although embedded questions can follow many of the verbs listed in usage 1, the most common are

care	**hear**	**remember**	**tell**
explain	**know**	**suggest**	**understand**
forget	**notice**	**see**	**wonder**

The verb **wonder** is used only with embedded questions and never with noun clauses beginning with the word **that.**

> I wonder who invented windshield wipers.

A polite way to request information is to use an embedded question inside a question. This is also called an indirect request.

direct question:	What time is it?
indirect request:	Do you know what time it is? (*more polite*)
	Can you tell me what time it is? (*more polite*)

If the modals **can, could,** or **should** are used in a **wh-** noun clause, it is possible to replace the subject and modal with an infinitive after the **wh-** word. The meaning is the same in both forms.

examples:	Vladimir forgot <u>where he can return</u> his books.
	Vladimir forgot <u>where to return</u> his books.
	The teacher told us <u>how we should study</u>.
	The teacher told us <u>how to study</u>.
Note:	The subject of the noun clause must be stated in the independent clause in order to use an infinitive.
example:	Sally knew when John should stay home.
	wrong: Sally knew when John to stay home.

Infinitives cannot follow an **if** clause.

wrong: I don't know if to buy a new car.
correct: I don't know if I can buy a new car.

CAREFUL! Do not make these common mistakes.

Don't use auxiliary verbs **do, did, does** in the embedded question. Remember to use statement word order (**subject + VERB**) for embedded questions.

wrong:	Can you tell me where is the library?
correct:	Can you tell me where the library is?
wrong:	I didn't hear what did she say.
correct:	I didn't hear what she said.
wrong:	Do you know where are my keys?
correct:	Do you know where my keys are?

Exercise 4.   Read the following sentences and then circle SK, IR, or DQ to indicate if they are statements of knowledge, indirect requests, or direct questions. Underline the noun clauses and label the subject and verb of each noun clause; label these *S* and *V*. Finally, add the appropriate punctuation. Follow the example.

SK (IR) DQ   1. Do you know <u>how many active volcanoes exist in the world today?</u>

SK   IR   DQ   2. What do you know about volcanoes

SK   IR   DQ   3. Could you tell me if Mt. Etna is a dangerous volcano

SK   IR   DQ   4. Many people do not know what causes eruptions

SK   IR   DQ   5. Could you please explain the different types of eruptions

SK   IR   DQ   6. Do you ever wonder if Mt. Rainier, in Washington State, will erupt

Exercise 5.   Answer the following questions with *I don't know* (OR *I forgot*) *who/what/when/where . . .* or *I think that* (subject + VERB COMPLEMENT). Follow the example.

1. Who was Alfred Nobel?

    I forgot who Alfred Nobel was. (OR I don't know who Alfred Nobel was.)

2. What is Colombo?

    _____ .

3. Where is Vanuatu?

    _____ .

4. Who was Sacagawea?

    _____ .

5. Who is on a U.S. five-dollar bill?

    _____ .

6. When did Amelia Earhart make her first flight?

    _____ .

Exercise 6.   Change these direct questions into indirect requests. Be careful: both *yes-no* and *wh-* questions are asked. Follow the example.

1. What is a zeppelin?

   Can you tell me what a zeppelin is?

2. What is the difference between an alligator and a crocodile?

   _____

3. Was Jeannette Rankin really the first woman elected to the U.S. Congress?

   _____

4. What does a *bear market* mean?

   _____

5. Does the bank open at 9:00 or 10:00?

   _____

6. Was pizza invented in Italy or New York?

   _____

7. How do I get to the post office from here?

   _____

8. Who is that man who is speaking?

   _____

9. Excuse me. What time is it now?

   Excuse me.

10. Where is Senator Mitchell's office?

   _____

Exercise 7.   Shorten the noun clause by using infinitives after the *wh-* words. Do not change the meaning. Follow the example.

1. Kelly and Steve don't know where they should go for a vacation.

   Kelly and Steve (OR They) don't know where to go for a vacation .

2. After I had wrecked my car, the insurance agent told me what I should do.

   _____ .

3. Veronica doesn't know whether she should stay in Tampa or go back to Mexico.

_____.

4. Do you know how you can find a new roommate?

_____.

5. Patti and I don't know what we should wear to the graduation ceremony.

_____.

6. I have tried everything to remove the stain from the carpet. I don't know what else I can try.

_____.

Speaking Activity

Exercise 8.　　Speaking Activity: Famous Quotations

Step 1.　Change the order of the letters in the left column to spell the names of capital cities around the Mediterranean Sea.

Step 2.　Then move the letters in the circles to the lines of the missing word in the quotation. Put the letters in the correct order to spell the missing word.

EMRO				◯
				1
ORICA	◯			
	2			
IDDMAR			◯	
			3	
RIAPS		◯		
		4		

"Is sloppiness in speech caused by ignorance or apathy? I don't know and

I don't __ __ __ __ !"

(—William Safire)

(*Note:* William Safire is an opinion columnist for the *New York Times* newspaper.)

Step 3. Work with a partner. Do not look at your partner's book. Take turns asking questions using indirect questions with embedded statements to compare your answers.

> *examples:* Can you tell me what you wrote for the first city?
> I don't know what the first one is.

Step 4. Discuss this quotation with your partner and then check with other classmates. You may need a dictionary. Be sure to practice using noun clause forms including

> Do you know . . . ?
> I don't know . . .
> Can you tell me . . . ?
> I have no idea what . . .
> I'm not sure, but I think . . .

> *examples:* What do you think he means by "sloppiness in speech"?
> What does he indicate the causes might be?
> Can you explain what he means with the answer to his own question?
> Do you understand why this quote is humorous?
> As a language learner, can you suggest other reasons for what he calls "sloppy speech"?

Step 5. After you finish your discussion, write your answers on the lines. Use noun clauses.

_____ .

_____ .

_____ .

_____ .

_____ .

Usage 3: Noun Clauses following *Be* + ADJECTIVE

Noun clauses can follow adjectives of mental state, certainty, or emotion such as the following.

Positive Connotation	Negative Connotation	Certainty of Idea
delighted	afraid	certain
encouraging	angry	clear
excited	annoyed	convinced
exciting	disappointed	doubtful

Positive Connotation	Negative Connotation	Certainty of Idea
glad	ironic	known
happy	sad	obvious
pleased	sorry	positive
relieved	strange	sure
remarkable	too bad	a fact★
surprised	worried	
thankful	a pity★	

★ **a pity** and **a fact** are not adjectives; however, they can take the place of an adjective following the verb **be.**

That clauses can follow **be + ADJECTIVE.**

> *examples:* The farmers <u>are</u> <u>relieved</u> **that** it will rain this week.
>
> ### be + ADJECTIVE + NOUN CLAUSE
>
> The students <u>were</u> <u>happy</u> **that** Ms. Ivone canceled the test.
>
> It <u>is</u> <u>a fact</u> **that** the earth revolves around the sun.

If or **whether** clauses usually follow a **be + negative + ADJECTIVE OF CERTAINTY.** These adjectives (listed in the third column above) are **certain, clear, convinced, doubtful** (already negative), **known, obvious, positive,** and **sure.**

> I am <u>not sure</u> **if** Ruiji will pass the TOEFL.   (**negative attitude + if** or **that** clause)
>
> I am <u>sure</u> **that** Ruiji will pass the TOEFL.   (**positive attitude + that** clause)
>
> I will be <u>surprised</u> **if** Ruiji passes the TOEFL.   (This is a conditional use of **if,** explained in unit 4. Be careful not to confuse this use with the noun clause **if** used to show certainty.)

Wh- clauses usually follow: (1) **be + ADJECTIVE + PREPOSITION**
(2) **be + NEGATIVE + ADJECTIVE OF CERTAINTY**

> *examples:* The farmers are *relieved <u>by</u>* **what** the president said.
> The children are *worried <u>about</u>* **when** the test will be given.
> Jeanine is <u>*not sure*</u> **where** she will spend the holidays.

Exercise 9.   Underline the correct word to complete the sentence.
                     Follow the example.

1. Ms. Mitchell is pleased with (<u>what</u>, that) the students are doing in class.

2. It is a fact (what, that) salt water is more buoyant than fresh water.

3. The management is (certain, not certain) if the employees will have a pay increase

   this year.

4. Angelica was thankful (is, that) she had been able to stay with a host family.

5. We are delighted (that, when) Angelica is coming to visit us next year.

6. We are delighted (that, who) she is coming to visit us.

7. I am (sure, not sure) if we are having a test tomorrow.

Speaking Activity

Exercise 10.   Speaking Activity: About Me

Step 1.   Complete each of the following sentences with a noun clause.

Step 2.   Discuss your sentences with a partner or small group.

1. It is a fact *that I am studying English* _____ .

2. I am thankful _____ .

3. I am worried _____ .

4. I am not sure if _____ .

5. I am excited _____ .

6. I am pleased _____ .

Usage 4: Noun Clauses as Subject of the Sentence

Wh- words and **that** mark the beginning of noun clauses in subject positions.

Whether, but never **if,** can also begin a noun clause in the subject position.

   Whenever a noun clause is used in the subject position, the independent main clause
takes a singular verb.

   examples: <u>How the fire started</u> <u>is</u> not known.
                  <u>That Thomas is interested in Ami</u> <u>is</u> quite obvious.
                  <u>Whether or not Aspen has enough snow to ski</u> <u>is</u> not certain.

These sentences could also appear with the pronoun **it** in the subject position and the noun clause as the subject complement. The more formal use is to put the noun clause in the subject position.

> *examples:*   It is not known how the fire started.
> It is quite obvious that Thomas is interested in Ami.
> It is not certain whether or not Aspen has enough snow to ski.

That clauses in subject positions often begin with **The fact . . .**

> *example:*   The fact that he drives a Ferrari is of no interest to me.

CAREFUL! Do not make these common mistakes.

Be sure that each verb has a subject.

> **wrong:**   You have completed the paperwork before the end of the year is important to being admitted.
>
> **correct:**   That **you have completed** the paperwork before the end of the year is important to being admitted.

Hint:

1. Find the subject and verb within the noun clause and make sure they agree (**you + have completed**).
2. Next, find the main sentence verb (**is**). It, too, requires a subject.
3. Eliminate the phrase "before the end of the year" since it is a preposition; also eliminate the noun **paperwork** since it is the object of **you have completed.**
4. In this case, we are left with the noun clause, which acts as the subject for the main verb; consequently, it must begin with a clause marker, **that.**

Exercise 11.   Write these sentences so that the noun clause is the subject of the sentence. Then circle the verb in the main sentence and underline the subject and verb in the noun clause. Follow the example.

1. It is exciting news that Florida will have a new rail system.

   That Florida will have a new rail system (is) exciting news .

2. It is not yet known whether we will visit all of the theme parks.

   _____ .

3. It is a fact that Florida has very competitive college football teams.

   _____ .

4. It is remarkable that Bill goes to the library every Saturday.

   _____ .

5. It is still uncertain when we will arrive in Tampa.

   _____ .

Exercise 12.   Read each sentence carefully. Look at the underlined part. If the underlined part is correct, circle the word *correct.* If it is wrong, circle the wrong part and write the correct form above. Follow the example.

correct (wrong)   1. That Rob's hair salon has 25 percent more clients *is* (are) encouraging.

correct wrong   2. It is amazing quickly she learned to ride a bicycle.

correct wrong   3. What Lin described to the police was very strange.

correct wrong   4. If the Thai Kitchen uses peanut oil or sesame oil is not specified on the menu.

correct wrong   5. Why Edgar quit such a high-paying job that is his own business.

Usage 5: Noun Clauses to Stress Importance or Urgency (subjunctive mood)

When noun clauses follow verbs or adjectives that express urgency or give advice, the verb in the noun clause is in the base form.

> *examples:*   The doctor insisted that Mary go to the hospital.
> It is important that Mr. and Mrs. Hilburn be at my office at 8 o'clock tomorrow.
> That he take his medicine every day is critical to his improvement.

In these examples, the verbs **go, be, take** are in the base form and are not affected by present, past, or future time, nor are they affected by a singular or plural subject.

A negative verb in the subjunctive is formed by **not + base form of VERB.**

> *example:*   My parents prefer that I not buy a car now.

A passive verb in the subjunctive is formed by **be + VERB -ed.**

> *example:* It is necessary that all windows **be closed** at night.

Main clause verbs that express importance include **advise, ask, demand, insist, order, prefer, require, recommend, suggest.**

Adjectives that express importance include **critical, essential, imperative, important, necessary, urgent.**

The use of these verbs and adjectives has the same effect on the noun clause verb as the modals **must** and **should.**

> *examples:* The doctor says, "Mary *must* go to the hospital."
> *subjunctive:* The doctor *insisted* that Mary go to the hospital.
> It is *important* that Mary go to the hospital.

Exercise 13. Complete these sentences with the correct verb form. Use the subjunctive where it is necessary. Follow the example.

Adviser: Good morning, Lisa. Please ❶ _____*come*_____ (come) in.

Student: Good morning, Dr. Canton. Let me introduce you to my mother. She

❷ _____ (insist) that she ❸ _____ (come) with me

this morning.

Adviser: Please sit down. It is important that everyone

❹ _____ (be included).

Mother: Because of the expenses, it is essential that Lisa

❺ _____ (finish) her education as

soon as possible.

Adviser: ❻ _____ (you, understand) what

❼ _____ (be required) for you to

complete your degree?

Mother: Do you demand that she ❽ _____

(take) a lot of science and math courses?

Adviser: Well, if Lisa **❾** _____ (want) a degree in aeronautical engineering, the department requires that she successfully **❿** _____ (complete) Statics and Dynamics.

Mother: Oh, I hope that she **⓫** _____ (be able) to take a few classes in dance, too. Are you aware that Lisa **⓬** _____ (study) ballet since she was eight years old?

Lisa: Mother, please! I prefer that I **⓭** _____ (dance) on the weekends!

Usage 6: Noun Clauses in Reported Speech

Quoted (direct) speech vs. reported (indirect) speech
quoted: Quote marks are used at the beginning and end of words that are written exactly as they were spoken.

> "I have a dream today," Martin Luther King, Jr., said during his famous 1963 speech.

reported: Words that report what someone said DO NOT have quote marks, and they become part of a noun clause.

> During his famous 1963 speech, Martin Luther King, Jr., said that <u>he had</u> a dream <u>that day</u>.

Tense change
Notice the change in the verb tense in the above two sentences. The verb in the quotation is in the present tense (**have**). However, when the quotation is written as reported speech, the verb is changed to past tense (**had**). When speech is reported, the rule of "sequence of tenses" applies.
(*Note:* More information on sequence of tenses is included on the next few pages.)

Pronoun change
Also notice that the pronoun has changed. In the quote, King says "I," but when it is reported, the pronoun is changed to **he** to refer to King.

Time expression change
One other change has been made in this example. In the quote, King says "today." In the reported speech, it is changed to **that day** to refer to the day he gave the speech.

Reporting verbs
Many of the verbs that have already been used for embedded noun clauses are also used for reported speech. Some of the more common verbs are listed here.

Statements		Questions
add	repeat	ask
announced	report	want to know
claim	say	wonder
confess	shout	
declare	state	
exclaim	suggest	
note	tell	
promise	warn	
remark	write	

Note to Advanced Students: In academic writing you will be asked to report what is written in books, journals, Internet articles, encyclopedias, etc. The rules of reported speech are to be used, but unlike the exercises in this unit, you will be required to paraphrase the author's words. Paraphrasing means that you will write what the author said in a way that is shorter or easier to understand. Nonetheless, the original meaning must stay the same.

CAREFUL! Do not make these common mistakes.

Say and **tell** are both used with reported speech. **Tell** must be followed by an object pronoun, a name, or a noun. **Say** is usually followed by a noun clause.

wrong:	My sister **say me** that this class was difficult.
correct:	My sister **told me** that this class was difficult.
correct:	My sister **said that** this class was difficult.
wrong:	Albert **told that** he would be home tonight.
correct:	Albert **told Gary and Linda** that he would be home tonight.
correct:	Albert **told them** (that) he would be home tonight.
wrong:	Juan **say us** that Mr. Cepko had lived in Slovakia.
correct:	Juan **said that** Mr. Cepko had lived in Slovakia.
correct:	Juan **said Mr. Cepko** had lived in Slovakia.

(Remember that **that** may be dropped in informal speech.)

Sequence of Tenses

To this point in unit 6, you have not needed to use the sequence of tenses rule for one of two reasons.

1. the main clause tense is in the **present tense**.

    I <u>don't know</u> where my keys are.

    He <u>is</u> happy that he passed the TOEFL.

2. the information in the noun clause is a habit, a current truth, or a scientific **fact**.

    I didn't remember that Vanuatu <u>is</u> in the South Pacific.

In reported speech, however, what is being reported is something that was said earlier. Consequently, the main clause verb is past tense, such as **said.** This past tense verb acts to pull the noun clause verb back in time even further.

Quoted Speech	*Reported Speech*
Mike said, ...	
"I <u>eat</u> bananas for breakfast." simple present	He said that he <u>ate</u> bananas for breakfast. simple past
"I <u>am eating</u> a pear <u>now</u>." present continuous	He said that he <u>was eating</u> a pear <u>then</u>. past continuous
"I <u>have eaten</u> plums." present perfect	He said that he <u>had eaten</u> plums. past perfect
"I <u>ate</u> an orange once." simple past	He said that he <u>had eaten</u> an orange once. past perfect
"I <u>was eating</u> when you called." past continuous	He said that he <u>had been eating</u> when I called. past perfect continuous
"I <u>will eat</u> a peach tomorrow." modal	He said that he <u>would eat</u> a peach tomorrow. modal—past

"I <u>may try</u> a mango." modal	He said that he <u>might try</u> a mango. modal—past
"I <u>can't eat</u> gooseberries." modal	He said that he <u>couldn't eat</u> gooseberries. modal—past
"I <u>must</u> try a mango sometime." modal	He said that he <u>had to</u> try a mango sometime. modal—past

Note: Modals that are already in past tense cannot be moved back. For example: **might, should, should have.** Also, verbs in past perfect cannot be pulled back in time any further.

Note to Advanced Students: You may hear someone report what has just been said and not hear the use of sequence of tenses. This is acceptable when the speech is being reported soon after it was spoken and it is still true.

Sequence of tenses is not necessary with reported speech for the same reasons as embedded speech in 1 and 2 on page 110.

1. The main clause is in the **present tense**.

   Jill <u>says</u> she still doesn't know where her keys are.

2. The information in the noun clause is a habit, general truth, or scientific **fact**.

   Jackie said that Benin <u>is</u> in West Africa.
   Richard said that his bank <u>opens</u> at 9 o'clock.

Exercise 14. Lisa is telling Claudia what she missed in class yesterday. Explain why the underlined words have been or have not been changed.

1. *Professor Jones:* The blue whale is the largest known mammal on Earth.

   Lisa: <u>Professor Jones said</u> that the blue whale <u>is</u> the largest mammal known on Earth.

   _____

   _____

   _____ .

2. *Professor Jones:* In order to appreciate its size, <u>you</u> <u>should think</u> of a 10-story building.

   Lisa: He said that in order to appreciate its size, <u>we</u> <u>should think</u> of a 10-story building.

   _____

   _____ .

3. *Professor Jones:* I am amazed that it has a heart nearly the size of a small car.

   Lisa: He said that <u>he</u> <u>was</u> amazed that it <u>has</u> a heart nearly the size of a small car.

   _____

   _____ .

4. *Professor Jones:* In 1931 nearly 30,000 whales were killed for commercial purposes.

   Lisa: He said that nearly 30,000 whales <u>had been killed</u> in 1931.

   _____

   _____ .

5. *Professor Jones:* Today, only around 10,000 blue whales exist in all the world's oceans!

   Lisa: He emphasized that only about 10,000 blue whales <u>exist</u> in all the world's oceans today.

   _____

   _____ .

Exercise 15.   A travel agent, Norm, told you the following information and now you must repeat everything to a friend. Use reported speech to complete the following sentences. Be careful to change the pronouns as needed.

1. Norm said, "A round-trip ticket to New York on any Saturday is $208."

   The agent said that _____ .

2. Norm said, "It will cost $248.00 to travel midweek."

   He also said that _____ .

3. Norm said, "Last month the price was $156.00 round trip."

   He told me that _____ .

4. Norm said, "Your friend should make his reservation soon."

   He said that _____ .

5. Norm said, "There have been some great prices on hotels, too."

   He told me that _____ .

6. Norm said, "Your friend will want to go to the Statue of Liberty."

   He said that _____ .

7. Norm said, "Your friend may like to attend a Broadway show."

   He suggested that _____ .

8. Norm said, "I am also going to New York in a few weeks."

   He told me that _____ .

9. Norm said, "I can pick up some show schedules while I am there."

   He said that _____ .

10. Norm exclaimed, "You are a very nice person to be helping your friend!"

    He concluded that _____ .

Speaking Activity

Exercise 16.   Speaking Activity: Texas Chili Cooking Contest

Situation: By the time the "chili aficionados" were called, more than 40 fiery chili recipes had already been judged. The final judges and chili experts, Mr. Pecos Bill Tailgate and Ms. Providence T. Biscuit, each selected his or her favorite recipe and wrote a review on it.

Step 1.   Student A silently reads the review of the chili from Mr. Pecos Bill Tailgate. Student B silently reads the review of the chili from Ms. Providence T. Biscuit. (You may need to refer to a dictionary.)

Step 2.   Report to your partner what the reviewer said.

Step 3.   Based on the descriptions, you and your partner will now try to determine the winner. You will need to use noun clauses to justify your position.

    examples: Pecos Bill thought that . . .
                   Providence said that . . .
                   Can you imagine what . . .
                   I don't think that . . .

Pecos Bill Tailgate: Without a doubt, my choice is chili number 9. I could smell the pungent habañeros* from five feet back and I could hardly wait to wrap my tongue around that fiery stuff. I grabbed a tall, cold drink and approached this chili like a trapper at a rattlesnake round-up. I took a bite. Its bold and scorching flavor tingled my tonsils and watered my eyes. With the marriage of firm red tomatoes, chunks of tender succulent beef, and a sauce smoother than strawberry cream soda, who could ask for more? I think that number 9 has enough capsicum† to extend the rush for several hours or maybe even days.

Providence T. Biscuit: As I approached chili number 16, the aroma of fresh garlic and cumin drifted pleasantly past my nose. My mouth began to anticipate the flavors. As I placed my spoon into the thick, rich, meaty sauce, I was reminded of the marvelous deep-red hues of the Canyonlands National Park at sunset. The chili sat solidly and proudly on my spoon as I placed that first bite into my mouth. My palate luxuriated in the robust blend of spices, chili peppers, and beef. As I swallowed, the chili pepper flavor began to intensify inside my mouth, yet it was never blisteringly hot. I rate this chili a 10 for highest quality.

*habañeros: a kind of hot chili pepper
†capsicum is what makes chili peppers hot

Reported Questions and Requests

For reported questions, use statement word order and **wh-** or **if** or **whether** clause markers just as you did with embedded questions. Also, apply the sequence of tense rule and make any necessary changes in pronouns, punctuation, and time expressions.

"Will we have a test next week?" Felipe asked.

wrong:	Felipe asked <u>would we have</u> a test next week. (*no clause marker and wrong word order*)
correct:	Felipe asked <u>whether we would have</u> a test next week.

"What did you buy at the mall yesterday?" Sandy asked.

wrong:	Sandy asked what <u>did I buy</u> at the mall. (*no tense change and wrong word order*)
correct:	Sandy asked what <u>I had bought</u> at the mall.

Polite requests (**can, should, could**) are reported the same way or they can also be reported using the infinitive.

Patti to Rod: "Could you play my favorite song?"

with noun clause:	She asked him <u>if he could play</u> her favorite song.
with infinitive:	She asked him <u>to play</u> her favorite song.

Exercise 17.   Pretend that you are reporting these conversations the day *after* they were spoken. Use the verbs in parentheses and pay attention to pronouns or time expressions that may need to be changed. Follow the example.

1. *Sally:*   "Do you plan to go fishing this weekend?"

   (ask) <u>Sally asked John if he planned to go fishing this weekend</u>.

   John: "Do you want to go with me?"

   (wonder) _____ .

2. *Jane:*   "I just got back from a trip to Colorado!"

   (exclaim) _____ .

   Lana: "Oh—what did you do while you were there?"

   (ask) _____ .

   Jane: "I went skiing every day."

   (tell) _____ .

   Lana: "How long were you there?"

   (want to know) _____ .

3. *Student:*   "Can you explain reported speech to me?"

   (ask) _____ .

   Teacher: "Can you come to my office at 4 o'clock?"

   (wonder) _____ .

   Student: "Yes, I will be there."

   (say) _____ .

Exercise 18. Review of Punctuation. You have been reading sentences and questions in quotation marks (direct speech). Check what you have learned about punctuation by observing these patterns. Add the missing punctuation and quotation marks to the following.

"I'm going to the store now," Marshall announced.   Is there anything that I can get for you

Yes   there is   Debbie answered.   Could you please pick up a quart of milk

Is that all   Marshall asked   I am happy to get what you need

Debbie thanked   him   and   told   him   that   she couldn't   think of anything else

Speaking Activity

Exercise 19.   Speaking Activity: Gossip

You can do this activity with your entire class if it's not too large. An ideal group number is ten to fifteen.

Step 1. Form a circle with the group members. Choose one student, student A, to begin the activity.

Step 2. Student A selects one of the messages from page 121 or creates his or her own and whispers it in the ear of the person to his or her left. Student B then reports to the student to his or her left, and so on. Each time the information is repeated, the student must begin with, "He said that . . . ." or "She told me that . . . ."

Step 3. When the last person has heard the message, he or she reports to the entire class what was just said. The final message is often very different from the beginning message. This is a good illustration of how stories change when people choose to gossip about others.

Exercise 20.   Multiple Choice. Circle the letter of the correct answer.

1. Do you know _____ at sea before he landed in the Americas?

    (A) how many days Columbus was   (C) how many days was Columbus

    (B) was Columbus how many days   (D) Columbus was how many days

2. _____ in 37 days is the common belief.

   (A) Columbus reached America   (C) That Columbus reached America

   (B) That Columbus reaches America   (D) Columbus reached that America

3. _____ that a Viking named Leif Ericksson had already been to North America 400 years before Columbus.

   (A) Most historians claim   (C) That most historians claim

   (B) Most historians who claim   (D) What most historian claim

4. Barry asked _____ first discovered America.

   (A) who do you think   (C) who thought I had

   (B) who I thought had   (D) do I think who had

5. I often wonder _____ .

   (A) what happened to the Taino Indians   (C) how many Tainos were living when Columbus arrived

   (B) that the Taino Indians were a healthy society   (D) whether or not did the Tainos die from disease

6. *Sada:* Did he say if you can practice before tomorrow's match?

   Ari: Yes. He said _____ practice at Feather Sound.

   (A) if to   (C) that could I

   (B) me to   (D) I could

7. *Gaby:* Do you know whether we are going to go to Disney World tomorrow?

   Pachi: I _____ .

   (A) think that   (C) so know

   (B) guess so   (D) realize that

8. The insurance agent _____ until she gets her driver's license.

   (A) recommended that Jane didn't drive   (C) recommended that Jane not drive

   (B) recommended that Jane drive not   (D) recommends that Jane doesn't drive

9. The flight attendants are not sure about _____ .

(A) if the airline will give them a   (C) when will the airline give
      pay increase   them a pay increase

(B) whether will they get a pay   (D) when the airline will give them a pay
      increase   increase

10. *Paul to Linda:* "I called the hotel for my reservations today."

Linda to June two days later: "Paul said he _____ reservations."

(A) had called the hotel for his   (C) was calling the hotel for his

(B) had called the hotel for our   (D) called the hotel for my

---

Exercise 21.   Review Test

Part 1.   Complete the following conversation with the information provided in
             parentheses.

Gale: _____ (you/know) no person had ever

           been able to go up the Salmon River until my dad made that trip in 1963?

Albert: Sure. Everyone was amazed _____

           (when/he/do that).

Gale: He told me _____

           _____

           _____ .

           (early pioneers be able/float barges down the river,/but they/can not return

           upstream/through the fierce rapids)

Albert: That's right, and that is _____

           (why/be called/it) the River of No Return.

Part 2.   Change each of the following direct questions to an indirect form.

1. What time is it?

   _____

2. How can I open a checking account?

   _____

3. Where is St. Joseph's Hospital located?

_____

4. Why do I have to wait for a refund?

_____

5. Will Kazuki be my roommate?

_____

Part 3. Error Identification. If the underlined portion of the sentence is correct, write *correct* on the line. If it has an error, circle the error and write the correction on the line.

How Important is Grammar in Learning a Second Language?

A great many second-language learners believe ❶ that knowledge about grammar is the most important component of learning a second language. For every educator who might agree with this idea, there is another educator who is completely against the teaching of grammar rules in the second-language classroom. ❷ Grammar is important in learning a second language is true. However, I do not believe that knowing the grammar of a language is the single most important aspect of learning a second language. ❸ Why I say this is not because I am against the study of grammar. Indeed, ❹ what does makes a second-language learner sound intelligent in a second language is a good grasp of vocabulary and a solid knowlege of grammar. Without good grammmar, a second-language speaker would be lost. However, I do not accept ❺ that any one aspect of language learning is more important than another. To me, all of the skills or pieces of a language are important in general. There are numerous aspects of second-language learning that equally influence ultimate success or failure in learning a second language well.

1. _____

2. _____

3. _____

4. _____

5. _____

Extra Writing Practice

Choose one of the following to write about. Use at least five noun clauses. Be sure to underline all of the noun clauses in your writing.

A legend from your culture
A report on someone who gives good advice
A report on a current article in a magazine or newspaper
A regional, national, or international problem and a discussion of some of the possible solutions to the problem

Answers to DISCOVER GRAMMAR on page 91:

(a) that, that, what, that, that, whether, that
(b) believe (verb), noticed (verb), wondered (verb), decided (verb), pleased (adjective), known (adjective)
(c) The clause beginning with *whether* fills the subject position of the sentence and the adjective *uncertain* follows the singular form of *be*.
(d) Noun clauses function like nouns within sentences as subjects, objects of verbs, objects of prepositions, and complements following adjectives.

Messages for Gossip Activity from page 116.

1. Margaret Thatcher, Great Britain's first female prime minister, who won every election by a landslide margin until she resigned, actually began her career as a research chemist. However, chemistry is not why she was known as the Iron Lady; instead, it was because of her convictions and inability to be moved on political issues.
2. Michael Jordan, who won six NBA championships in thirteen years for the Chicago Bulls, retired in 1998. That year his salary was $33,000,000. He then played minor league baseball for two years for the Scottsdale Scorpions and the Birmingham Barons. In 2001, he returned to basketball playing for the Washington Wizards with only a $1,000,000 contract. That same season he became one of four players in NBA history to have scored over 30,000 points.
3. Cher was born in California in 1946. Her father was an Armenian truck driver named John Sarkisian. Her singing and television career began in the 1960s with Sonny Bono, but after their divorce in 1977, her own music career took off. By 2001, Cher had produced nearly fifty albums or CDs. Besides being known as a TV celebrity and singer, Cher has also performed in more than twelve movies, including *Moonstruck* for which she won an Academy Award for Best Actress in 1988. When she is not recording music or making movies, you might find her with Sir Elton John performing for the Queen of England.
4. Starbucks Coffee, with more than 4,000 shops in over 23 countries, is one of the fastest growing companies in the U.S. It originated in Seattle, Washington. The CEO is Howard Schultz. Schultz, an example of the American Dream, was born into a poor family in Brooklyn, N.Y,. and later worked for a company that made coffee machines. During a sales trip to Seattle, he discovered a little coffee shop and saw what great potential it had.

Unit 7

Reduction of Clauses

1. reduction of adjective clauses (including appositives)
2. more (advanced) reduction of adjective clauses
3. reduction of adverb clauses
4. prepositional phrases as reductions of adverb clauses

Reduction of Adjective Clauses (including appositives)

Many adjective clauses (adj cl) can be reduced to a phrase. A clause has a subject and a verb while a phrase does not. (See unit 8 in *Clear Grammar 3* for a review of adjective clauses.)

Clause → Phrase

adj cl: The book <u>that is on the table</u> is green.

phrase: The book <u>on the table</u> is green.

Grammar Rule for Reducing the Clause

You can omit **who, that, which + be** when it is followed by a prepositional phrase.

---

adj cl: The student <u>who is absent from class the most</u> is Jason.

adj cl: The student <u>absent from class the most</u> is Jason.

You can omit **who, that, which + be** when you have **be + ADJECTIVE.**

---

adj cl: George Washington, <u>who was the first U.S. president,</u> died in 1799.

adj cl: George Washington, <u>the first U.S. president,</u> died in 1799.

You can omit **who, that, which + be** when you have **be + NOUN.** This reduced phrase has a special name: appositive. Note that appositives and their original adjective clauses are always set off by commas.

---

adj cl: The box <u>that was stolen yesterday</u> had a red cover.

phrase: The box <u>stolen yesterday</u> had a red cover.

You can omit **who, that, which + be** when you have passive voice.

---

adj cl: The bird <u>that is sitting on the top</u> branch is a crow.

phrase: The bird <u>sitting on the top</u> branch is a crow.

You can omit **who, that, which + be** when you have a progressive tense.

Clause → Phrase	Grammar Rule for Reducing the Clause
adj cl: The people <u>who live in that area</u> are mostly farmers.	You can usually change **who, that, which + VERB to VERB + –ing.**
phrase: The people <u>living in that area</u> are mostly farmers.	

CAREFUL! Do not make these common mistakes.

1. Do not try to reduce a clause that cannot be reduced.

   wrong: The book that Bob brought is on the table.
   → The book brought is on the table.

   correct: No reduction is possible because we do not have **who, which,** or **that** plus a verb. Here we have **that + subject (Bob) + VERB (brought).** There is another subject in the sentence (**Bob**), which we cannot just discard!

2. Do not use appositives in conversation or in informal writing. Appositives are very common in formal writing.

   unusual: Sue said, "My father was born in Sacramento, the capital of California."

   usual: Sue said, "My father was born in Sacramento. That's the capital of California." (*Note:* In conversation, speakers tend to use shorter sentences. People do not use appositives in natural, everyday conversation.)

3. Do not think that the reduced verb form is the verb of the sentence. When you have a reduced clause with a present participle form (**–ing**) or a past participle form (**-ed, -en, -ne,** etc.), you must remember that this is not the main verb, so you must be sure to include a main verb.

   wrong: People living in that specific area of the city.★

   correct: People living in that specific area of the city have poor mail service.

   wrong: People chosen as extras in the movie.★

   correct: People chosen as extras in the movie will receive $200 per day.

★These two wrong examples are called *fragments.* A *fragment* is a sentence that does not have a complete subject-verb relationship. This is a common error in composition for some writers.

──────

Exercise 1.   Underline the adjective clauses in these sentences. If these
               adjective clauses can be reduced, rewrite the reduced phrase below
               the clauses. If they cannot be reduced, write *no change possible.*
               The first one has been done for you.

1. Perhaps the monument <u>that is most frequently visited in Paris</u> is the Eiffel Tower.

   Perhaps the monument most frequently visited in Paris is the

   Eiffel Tower.

2. The number of tourists who visit this Parisian site each year is more than five

   million. _____

   _____

3. In fact, the number of tourists who have
   visited this site since it opened in 1889 is
   approximately two hundred million.

   _____

   _____

4. Construction of the tower, which was begun in
   1887, lasted for over two years.

   _____

   _____

5. Eiffel, the name that we most obviously
   associate with the tower, is actually the name
   of the owner of the construction company that
   built this landmark.

Photo courtesy of Chris Young

   _____

   _____

6. Maurice Koechlin and Emile Nouguier, who were the engineers for this project, are
   not nearly as well known as Eiffel.

   _____

   _____

7. The number of steps that the Eiffel Tower has is 1,665.

   _____

   _____

8. When the tower was first proposed, many people who were well known throughout Europe spoke vehemently against it.

   _____

   _____

9. The "Protest against the Tower of Mr. Eiffel," which was published in the newspaper *Le Temps,* included protests by many people whose names we recognize today, including Guy de Maupassant and the junior Alexandre Dumas.

   _____

   _____

10. The Eiffel Tower, which received two million visitors alone during the World's Fair of 1889, quickly proved to be a popular addition to the Paris skyline and not the monstrosity that many had feared it would be.

    _____

    _____

Exercise 2.   Complete these sentences by putting an appositive after the subject with the correct punctuation and then adding an appropriate verb phrase. You may need to consult a reference book or the Internet for some of these questions. The first two have been done for you.

1. George Washington, *the first president of the U.S., was from Virginia.*

   _____

2. The Statue of Liberty, *a popular tourist attraction, is visited by two million people each year.*

3. Princess Diana _____

   _____

4. Los Angeles _____

   _____

5. Wimbledon _____

_____

6. The children in Mrs. Gordon's class are learning about the Concorde _____

_____

7. The Olympics were held in Sydney _____

_____

8. Jane Addams _____

_____

9. The most famous female entertainer in history is Madonna _____

_____

10. The conference will be held in Rabat _____

_____

Exercise 3.   If the sentence is correct, put a *C* on the line. If the sentence is not complete, write an *X* on the line and then add the missing words. Correct sentences should have a reduced phrase instead of an adjective clause.

__ 1. The letter mailed to the bank needed to have an extra stamp on it.

__ 2. The first president of the United States.

__ 3. According to the map, the cities are located near the coast are closer together.

__ 4. Damaged by bombs, many of the buildings in Berlin had to be rebuilt after the war.

__ 5. Living high in the treetops of the Costa Rican rain forest.

__ 6. The amount of money is required for the trip should be reduced.

__ 7. People who driving long distances from home to work should carpool.

__ 8. Invented by a Canadian, basketball has certainly caught on all over the world.

__ 9. Abraham Lincoln, the sixteenth president of the U.S., was killed in 1865.

__ 10. Reports that typed on a typewriter over twenty years ago are sometimes difficult to read.

Exercise 4.   If the underlined verb form is correct, write *C* on the line. If not,
                 write *X* on the line and correct the error.

___ 1. Without a doubt, people <u>living</u> near the coast pay more for home insurance.

___ 2. Cars <u>purchasing</u> more than forty years ago used a different kind of gasoline.

___ 3. <u>Developing</u> by the company in New York, the new camera costs only $19.

___ 4. <u>Written</u> from a woman's point of view, Ann Helmsley's novel *Teresita* reflects the
         political tensions of that era.

___ 5. <u>Written</u> from a woman's point of view, Ann Helmsley composed an incredible
         work.

___ 6. Some medicines <u>selling</u> in the United States can be purchased in Mexico.

___ 7. <u>Reducing</u> by 50% due to the lack of demand, those coats are a great buy.

___ 8. Some of the birds <u>flown</u> over my yard yesterday were actually owls.

More (advanced) Reduction of Adjective Clauses

As you have seen, certain adjective clauses can be reduced to adjective phrases. These
phrases, like the original clauses, follow the nouns that they modify. However, when an
adjective clause (adj cl) is set off by commas,* the corresponding adjective phrase may
come either after or before the noun. In technical or academic writing, the reduction very
often appears before the noun.

adj cl:	The Eiffel Tower, which was finished in 1889, is a marvel of human construction.	This is the regular position of an adjective clause.
phrase:	The Eiffel Tower, finished in 1889, is a marvel of human construction	This is the regular position of a reduced phrase.
phrase:	Finished in 1889, the Eiffel Tower is a marvel of human construction.	This style is more advanced. Note that the sentence *appears* to begin with past tense (but it does not!).
adj cl:	The Eiffel Tower, which received two million visitors alone during the World's Fair of 1889, proved to be a popular addition to the Paris skyline.	This is the regular position of an adjective clause.

phrase:	The Eiffel Tower, receiving two million visitors alone during the World's Fair of 1889, quickly proved to be a popular addition to the Paris skyline.	This is the regular position of a reduced phrase.
phrase:	Receiving two million visitors alone during the World's Fair of 1889, the Eiffel Tower quickly proved to be a popular addition to the Paris skyline.	This style is more advanced. Note that the subject of the sentence *(the Eiffel Tower)* does not start the sentence but rather has eleven words before it.

*Adjective clauses set off by commas are called *nonrestrictive clauses.* This kind of adjective clause has information that is considered extra or not necessary to identifying the noun. For example, here when we say *Eiffel Tower,* everyone knows what we are talking about, so any information that we give will be extra. This is true of adjective clauses that follow proper nouns since the proper noun identifies the person or object sufficiently. If we had said just *the structure* instead of the Eiffel Tower, then the information would have been considered necessary, would not have had commas, and could not have been moved to the beginning of the sentence.

Exercise 5.   Rewrite these sentences twice, first with a reduced phrase after the subject (as in exercise 1) and then with the reduced phrase before the subject.

Photo courtesy of Chris Young

1. The Eiffel Tower, which lies in the heart of the City of Light, is perhaps the best-known monument in the world.

   _____

   _____

   _____

2. Construction of the Eiffel Tower, which was begun in 1887, lasted for over two years.

_____

_____

_____

3. Maurice Koechlin and Emile Nouguier, who were the engineers for this project, are not nearly as well known as Eiffel.

_____

_____

_____

4. The "Protest against the Tower of Mr. Eiffel," which was published in the newspaper *Le Temps,* was endorsed by Guy de Maupassant and the junior Alexandre Dumas.

_____

_____

_____

5. The Eiffel Tower, which received two million visitors alone during the World's Fair of 1889, quickly proved to be a popular addition to the Paris skyline and not the monstrosity that many had feared it would be.

_____

_____

_____

Reduction of Adverb Clauses

Like adjective clauses, many adverb clauses can be reduced to a phrase. (See unit 5 in *Clear Grammar 3* for a review of adverb clauses.)

	Clause ⟶ Phrase	*Grammar Rule for Reducing the Clause*
adv cl:	<u>When she is at work</u>, she wears very elegant clothes.	When there are two different subjects, no reduction is possible. You can reduce adverb clauses ONLY when the two subjects are the same.
phrase:	Ø	

Clause ⟶ Phrase	*Grammar Rule for Reducing the Clause*
adv cl: <u>When she is at work</u>, she wears very elegant clothes.	You can omit **subject + be.**
phrase: <u>When at work</u>, she wears very elegant clothes.	**ADVERB + PREPOSITIONAL PHRASE**
adv cl: <u>While I am eating</u>, I never answer the phone.	(present action)
phrase: <u>While eating</u>, I never answer the phone.	**ADVERB + PRESENT PARTICIPLE (-ing)**
adv cl: <u>While I was running on the beach</u>, I fell and hurt my knee.	(past action)
phrase: <u>While running on the beach</u>, I fell and hurt my knee.	**ADVERB + PRESENT PARTICIPLE (-ing)**

Note: The idea of **while + -ing** can also be expressed without the word **while.**

phrase: Running on the beach, I fell and hurt my knee.	This is the same meaning as above.
adv cl: <u>When I was injured</u>, I had to go to the emergency room.	(**ADVERB + passive voice**)
phrase: <u>When injured</u>, I had to go to the emergency room.	**ADVERB + PAST PARTICIPLE**
adv cl: <u>When I was absent from class</u>, I missed a lot of exams.	(**ADVERB + be + ADJECTIVE**)
phrase: <u>When absent from class</u>, I missed a lot of exams.	**ADVERB + ADJECTIVE**

CAREFUL! Do not make these common mistakes.

1. Do not try to reduce an adverb clause that has a subject that is different from the subject of the main clause.

   wrong: After <u>the passengers</u> got off the plane, <u>the workers</u> removed their bags.
                    subject   subject

        → After getting off the plane, the workers removed their bags.

        The subjects are different, so the adverb clause cannot be reduced.

        The current sentence means that the <u>workers</u> (not the <u>passengers</u>) got off the plane and removed their bags.

correct: After <u>the passengers</u> got off the plane, <u>they</u> walked to the baggage claim.
subjectsubject
→ After getting off the plane, the passengers walked to the baggage claim.

The subjects refer to the same people, so the adverb clause can be reduced.

The current sentence means that the <u>passengers</u> got off the plane and then the <u>passengers</u> walked to the baggage claim.

2. Do not think that the reduced verb form is the verb of the sentence. When you have a reduced clause with a present participle form (**-ing**) or a past participle form (**-ed, -en, -ne,** etc.), you must remember that this is not the main verb, so you must include a main verb.
wrong: When departing on a late night flight.★
correct: When departing on a late night flight, you will not be served dinner.
wrong: After having finished all of the novels.★
correct: After having finished all of the novels, Ginnie needed to buy a few more.

★*Note:* These two wrong examples are called *fragments. A fragment* is a sentence that does not have a complete subject-verb relationship. This is a common error in composition for some writers.

3. Do not try to use reduced adverb phrases for phrases that begin with **because.** Possible adverb connectors in reduced phrases include **after, although, before, if, though, unless, until, when,** and **while.** Instead of using **because** in the phrase, use the verb alone. For clauses that have **because + subject + be,** a phrase with **being** is possible.
wrong: Because the pilot was tired, he turned the plane over to the copilot.
→ Because being tired, the pilot turned the plane over to the copilot.
→ Because tired, the pilot turned the plane over to the copilot.
correct: → Being tired, the pilot turned the plane over to the copilot.

Exercise 6. Underline the adverb clauses in these sentences. If these adverb clauses can be reduced, rewrite the reduced phrase below the clauses. If they cannot be reduced, write *no change possible.* The first one has been done for you.

1. <u>When Maria flew from LA to New York recently,</u> she traveled with her cat.
   When flying from LA to New York recently, Maria traveled with her cat.

2. Before Maria entered the plane, her cat had to be put in its cage.

_____

_____

3. After the cat was put in its cage, it began to meow loudly.

_____

_____

_____

4. Although Maria tried to calm the cat down, she was unsuccessful.

_____

_____

_____

5. When Maria could not make the cat be quiet, a flight attendant helped her.

_____

_____

_____

6. Once the cat was held by the flight attendant, it got amazingly quiet.

_____

_____

_____

Prepositional Phrases as Reductions of Adverb Clauses

Many adverb clauses can be reduced to prepositional phrases. Certain prepositions have meanings that are similar to some of the adverb clause connectors.

Adverb Connector	Preposition	Examples
because since	because of due to on account of	Because the weather was bad, tennis was canceled. Because of the bad weather, tennis was canceled.
although even though	in spite of despite	Although I paid a lot for the ticket, I really enjoyed the concert. Despite paying a lot for the ticket, I really enjoyed the concert.
whether or not	regardless of	Whether or not we start on time, we will finish late. Regardless of the start time, we will finish late.
when	during	When it was coffee break, I called my wife. During the coffee break, I called my wife.

Exercise 7.   Underline the adverb clauses in these sentences. Then change the adverb clause to a prepositional phrase.

1. Because there was fog, all flights were canceled.

   _____

   _____

2. When it was storming last night, the rain was pounding the roof so hard that I couldn't sleep.

   _____

   _____

3. Marc entered the class and sat in the front row even though he was late.

   _____

   _____

4. When he was a child, Albert Einstein, perhaps the smartest man ever, was not a very good student.

   _____

   _____

5. Since the meeting in Detroit lasted so long, I missed my connecting flight to Houston.

_____

_____

6. Your taxes for next year will increase whether you have a new car or not.

_____

_____

Speaking Activity

Exercise 8.   Speaking Activity

Part 1.   Preparation. Read these English proverbs. Decide if the underlined part is an adjective clause (adj cl), reduced adjective phrase (adj phr), an adverb clause (adv cl), or a reduced adverb phrase (adv phr). Then write in your own words what you think the proverb means.

1. Don't close the barn door <u>after the horse runs away</u>.

_____   _____

_____

2. Justice delayed is <u>justice denied</u>.

_____   _____

_____

3. Those <u>who cannot remember the past</u> are condemned to repeat it.

_____   _____

_____

4. <u>Something well begun</u> is <u>something already half done.</u>

_____   _____

_____

5. <u>When in Rome,</u> do as Romans do.

_____   _____

_____

6. <u>When the cat's away,</u> the mice will play.

_____   _____

_____

7. Let's cross that bridge <u>when we come to it</u>.

_____   _____

_____

8. <u>A friend in need</u> is a friend indeed.

_____   _____

_____

Part 2. Speaking. Work with a partner or in small groups. Take turns presenting your answers for the proverbs. Try to use adjective and adverb clauses and reduced phrases in your discussion.

Exercise 9.   Multiple Choice. Circle the letter of the correct answer.

1. A friend _____ a friend indeed. (proverb)

   (A) who in need is   (C) is in need

   (B) is who is need   (D) in need is

2. The people _____ in the accident were taken to a nearby hospital emergency room for treatment.

   (A) involved   (C) who involved

   (B) involving   (D) who involving

3. Before entering its cage, _____ .

   (A) the cat began to meow loudly   (C) the owner had to give the cat some food

   (B) the loud meow of the cat   (D) the food was given to the cat by
       could be heard   the owner

4. During the coldest part of the winter, certain animals such as black bears _____ in specially constructed "winter homes" until they are ready to emerge from their long winter rest.

   (A) sleeping   (C) sleep

   (B) slept   (D) that sleep

5. Written in central Canada in the early part of the twentieth century, _____ , depicts

   life in Manitoba.

   (A) *The Midnight Sun* was Victor   (C) which was Victor Frank's
       Frank's last novel   last novel, *The Midnight Sun*

   (B) Victor Frank's last novel was   (D) *The Midnight Sun,* which was Victor
       The Midnight Sun   Frank's last novel

6. _____ lasted for over two years.

   (A) Beginning in 1887,   (C) Construction of the tower,
       construction of the tower   which beginning in 1887

   (B) Begun in 1887, construction   (D) Construction of the tower,
       of the tower   which begun in 1887

7. Taken from a previously unknown plant found only in a remote part of the Amazon

   rain forest, _____ .

   (A) scientists may be able to   (C) a cure for cancer might come
       develop a new cure for cancer   from this new medicine
       from it

   (B) it is possible that scientists may (D) the new medicine might be
       be able to develop a new cure   a cure for cancer
       for cancer from it

8. _____ the interviews in Boston lasted so long, I missed my connecting flight to

   New York.

   (A) Due to   (C) Since

   (B) When   (D) Despite

9. _____ two million visitors alone during the World's Fair of 1889, the Eiffel Tower

   quickly proved to be a popular addition to the Paris skyline.

   (A) Receiving   (C) It received

   (B) Received   (D) The Eiffel Tower that received

10. Because of all the taxes and additional fees that _____ to the base price of the car, the final price tag was much higher than anyone expected it to be.

(A) were added   (C) were adding

(B) added   (D) adding

Exercise 10.   Review Test

Part 1.   Read these sentences and underline the correct words.

1. (Whenever, Although, As soon as) the dessert looked good, I decided to pass.

2. I decided to do this (regardless, because, in spite of) my doctor said that I need to cut down on sweets.

3. (Since, After, While) I love desserts more than any other food, this order from the doctor is a tough one to follow.

4. I am a good, obedient patient, and I try to follow all of the suggestions (to give, giving, given) by my dentist.

5. (While I walking, While was walking, While walking) up the stairs to my office the other day, I noticed that I was having a hard time breathing, which tells me that it's time to get in shape!

6. As a result, foods (have, had, having) a high number of calories are now on my list of foods to avoid.

7. It's a tough thing to do, but (to walk, walked, walking) up the stairs the other day convinced me of the need to watch my health for sure.

Part 2.   Read each sentence carefully. Look at the underlined part. If the underlined part is correct, circle the word *correct*. If it is wrong, circle the word *wrong* and write the correct form above the error.

correct   wrong   1. <u>Before go</u> to bed last night, I took two aspirins with a large glass of water.

correct   wrong   2. The menu was quite difficult to read <u>because</u> the small type size.

correct   wrong   3. <u>Building</u> this hotel in less than a year, the workers had to work overtime on most of the days.

correct   wrong   4. The boxes <u>that stolen</u> from the store had mostly canned goods.

correct   wrong   5. <u>7-11, one of the most popular convenience store chains in the</u>
                         <u>United States,</u> has a new and bigger selection of sandwiches.

correct   wrong   6. The police reported that <u>goods worth</u> $5,000 were stolen.

correct   wrong   7. According to the latest weather report, heavy rains will continue
                         tonight <u>despite that we had such great weather</u> most of the day.

Extra Writing Practice

Situation: Write a paragraph or short essay in which you tell in your own words a well-known or popular folk tale or children's story. This kind of writing will naturally have many adjective clauses and adverb clauses. When you write this, try to include adjective and adverb clauses as well as adjective and adverb phrases. Put one line under all the adjective and adverb clauses and two lines under the adjective and adverb phrases so that your teacher can see what you are trying to practice. Be sure to skip a line in your writing so you will have room to underline.

Unit 8

Past Modals

1. *may have, might have*
2. *could, be able to, could have*
3. *would, used to, would have*
4. *should have, ought to have*
5. *had to, must have, had to have*
6. *be supposed to, be going to*

Modal	Meaning
could, be able to	ability
could have	suggestion; slight possibility
would, used to	repeated action in the past
would have	unreal condition
should have, ought to have	advice or suggestion; strong certainty
had to, must have, had to have	strong certainty
be supposed to, be going to	planned intention or expectation

1. Generally, most past modals are formed by using the **MODAL + have + PAST PARTICIPLE.** To form a negative sentence using a past modal, insert **not** between the modal and **have.** Questions are formed by moving the modal to the front.

    I **might have seen** that movie, but I'm not really sure.

    He **could not have called** at a better time. His timing was perfect!

    Should they **have made** reservations for dinner at 8:00?

2. Some past modals do not require *have* or a past participle. To form negative sentences, add *not* or *did not* to the verb. Questions are formed by moving the modal to the front or using *did* or *was/were*.

    I **could read** when I was six years old. I **couldn't ride** a bike though. **Could** you **read** when you were six?

    I **was able to read** when I was six years old. I **wasn't able to ride** a bike though. **Were** you **able to read** when you were six?

    I **would watch** cartoons on Saturday mornings when I was young. I **wouldn't watch** scary movies. **Would** you **watch** cartoons on Saturdays?

    I **used to watch** cartoons on Saturday mornings when I was young. I **didn't use to watch** scary movies. **Did** you **use to watch** cartoons on Saturdays?

    I **had to study** hard to get into the university. I **didn't have to work** while I was a student. **Did** you **have to pay** your own tuition?

    I **was supposed to meet** my friends here at 6:00. They **weren't supposed to leave** without me. **Were** you **supposed to meet** them, too?

    I **was going to meet** my friends here at 6:00. They **weren't going to leave** without me. **Were** you **going to meet** them, too?

3. Past modals can also be used in the progressive form. Use the **MODAL + have + been + VERB + -ing.**

    They **could have been** on their way to the mall when we saw them.

    I **should have been studying** for this exam instead of watching TV.

CAREFUL! Do not make these common mistakes.

1. Do not put **to** between the modal and **have.**
   wrong: He may to have gone home already.
   correct: He may have gone home already.

2. Do not use contracted forms for **may.**
   wrong: He mayn't have paid his bill on time.
   correct: He may not have paid his bill on time.

May Have, Might Have

May have and **might have** are used to express the possibility that something occurred in the past. Both modals express the same meaning.

> *A:*   There's a restaurant. I'm hungry. Did you bring any money with you?
> *B:*   Let me check. I **may have brought** a few dollars along.

> *A:*   The floor's all wet! Didn't we close all the windows when it started raining?
> *B:*   I thought we did, but we **might have** accidentally **left** one open.

Might have is sometimes used to express a complaint.

> I've been waiting for you for over an hour. You **might have called** to let me
> know you were running late.

Exercise 1.   Use *may have* or *might have* plus a past participle to complete the
                sentences. Follow the example.

1. *A:*   Your neighbor Judd just quit his job.

   B: He _may have won_ _____ (win) the lottery.

2. *A:*   I'm looking for Peter. Is he still here? I don't see him anywhere.

   B: He _____ already _____

         (go) home.

3. *A:*   Did you go to the party at Chris and Mike's last Saturday?

   B: Yes, and I waited all night for you to come! You _____

         (tell) me you weren't going to be there.

4. *A:*   Bev is waiting to find out if she got the job she interviewed for.

   B: Has she checked her answering machine? They _____

          (leave) her a message.

5. *A:*   I'm starving. Let's stop at Café Italiano for spaghetti.

   B: Let me call home first. My roommate _____ (make)

          dinner already.

6. *A:*   I can't believe you've agreed to take on more responsibility at work.

   B: I know. I _____ (bite) off more than I can chew!

7. *A:*   Eric, I'd like to introduce you to Natali Andrade, our new accounting manager.

   B: Natali, you look familiar. I think we _____ (met) years

          ago at a conference in Denver.

8. *A:*   I tried calling Sami last night, but her line was busy for over an hour.

   B: She _____ (be talking) to her sister in Toronto.

9. *A:*   It's 10:00. Why isn't the news on?

   B: I think the baseball game _____ (go) into extra

          innings.

Exercise 2.   Read the sentences below and offer a possibility to explain the
                    situation. Use *may have* or *might have* plus a past participle in your
                    answers. Follow the example.

1. Taki didn't go to work this morning. *He might not have been feeling well.*

2. The students didn't have class yesterday. _____

3. The bus driver wouldn't let him on the bus. _____

4. On the test this morning, Erica left five answers blank. _____

5. Ariadne didn't eat any dessert. _____

6. There's a finance charge on my credit card bill. _____

Could, Be Able to, Could Have

Could and **be able to** are used to express past ability. **Could** and **be able to** are used for a repeated action or an action that happened over a period of time in the past.

As a doctor, my mother **could treat** us at home.

As a doctor, my mother **was able to treat** us at home.

Only **be able to** is used in the affirmative to express a single action or event that occurred in the past.

Last night, I **was able to finish** the 600-page book I've been reading.

However, both **could** and **be able to** can be used in the negative to express a single action or event that occurred in the past.

This morning I **couldn't find** my car keys anywhere.

This morning I **wasn't able to find** my car keys anywhere.

Could have is used to offer suggestions about what was possible in the past but which didn't happen, and is often used in conditional sentences. **Could have** is also used to express the slight chance or small possibility that something happened. Like **might have,** it can also be used to express a complaint.

We **could have had** eggs for breakfast, but we didn't.

If I had known you were going to the concert, we **could have gone** together.

I'm pretty sure I turned off the iron, but I **could have left** it on.

You **could have told** me that you didn't have time to help me.

Couldn't have is used to express the belief that it was impossible for an action or event in the past to have happened or to indicate the strong possibility that a situation didn't occur. For some situations, usually related to the present or recent past, **can't have** and **couldn't have** are used interchangeably to indicate emphasis.

He **couldn't have taken** the car. I was driving it!

That **couldn't have been** Ali in the library. He told me he had to work till 10:00 tonight, and it's only 7:30.

I **can't have lost** my passport. I just had it a minute ago!

You **couldn't have misplaced** your house keys. I saw you put them on the counter when you walked in.

Exercise 3.   Read each sentence below. Look at the underlined part. If it is correct, circle the word *correct*. If it is wrong, circle the word *wrong* and the part of the sentence that makes it wrong. Follow the example.

correct (wrong)   1. (Last night) I <u>could fall</u> asleep in the chair.

correct   wrong   2. Six years ago, I <u>could run</u> a mile in four and half minutes.

correct   wrong   3. This morning I <u>was able to run</u> a mile in six minutes.

correct   wrong   4. Yesterday morning I <u>couldn't run</u> a mile in five minutes.

correct   wrong   5. This morning I <u>could run</u> a mile in six minutes.

correct   wrong   6. Yesterday morning I <u>wasn't able to run</u> a mile in five minutes.

Exercise 4.   Change the underlined part of the sentence to *could have* plus the past participle of the verb. Then complete the sentence using *but*. Follow the example.

1. I <u>chose not to take</u> the job in Savannah.

    I could have taken the job in Savannah, but I chose not to.

2. Sung Wook <u>didn't send</u> her a birthday card.

    _____

3. The study group <u>didn't invite</u> Frank to go along.

    _____

4. The neighbor woman <u>refused to call</u> the police.

    _____

5. You <u>didn't ask</u> me for help with your chemistry homework.

    _____

6. Joann's boyfriend <u>decided not to move</u> to Wyoming.

    _____

7. A shopping <u>cart didn't make</u> the dent in your car.

    _____

8. They <u>didn't spend</u> over $150 on books and CDs.

    _____

Exercise 5.   Read the conversation below. Fill in the blanks with *could have, couldn't have,* or *can't have* plus the past participle of the verb given.

1. *A:*   What's wrong? You look panic-stricken!

   B: I can't find my homework assignment—the one that's due in 15 minutes. I

           _____ (lose) it. I had it just a few minutes ago.

2. *A:* _____ you _____ (leave) it in your car?

   B: No, I _____ (do) that. It was in my hand on the way into the building. I remember that.

3. *A:* Well, it _____ (walk) away! It has to be around here somewhere.

   B: Before I came into the room, I decided to clean out my backpack. I _____ (throw) it in the recycling bin by mistake.

4. *A:* Let's go look.

   B: Oh no—the bin's empty!

   A: The maintenance people _____ (get) too far. Let's go find them.

   B: Wait a minute. Look! Here it is—it was inside my *Clear Grammar 4* textbook.

5. *A:* You are *so* lucky. You _____ (spend) hours looking through those recycling bins and never have found it.

   B: Or I _____ (tell) my instructor I had done the assignment and thrown it away by mistake and then hoped for the best!

Exercise 6.   Read each sentence. Write a sentence of your own using *could have* to offer an explanation of what happened. Use *couldn't have* for an event or situation that didn't occur. Follow the example.

1. I wonder why Jana left class early today. (appointment)

   She could have had an appointment with her adviser.

2. I don't understand why all my plants died. (cold weather)

   _____

3. My dog has been in the house all day. (chase your cat)

   _____

4. I just deposited my paycheck in the bank. (overdraw my account)

   _____

5. Mom said she'd call back right away, but she didn't. (get busy)

   _____

6. Jason wanted to see the same movie you did. (together)

_____

7. Klaus looked at the sky and decided to go flying today. (weather better)

_____

Would, Used to, Would Have

Would and **used to** are both used to express repeated actions in the past. **Used to** is often used to introduce the past actions or to begin a story, and **would** for the follow-up sentences. When used to express repeated actions in the past, **would** and **used to** have the same meaning. They may be used in the negative and in questions.

> As children, my brother and I **used to spend** summers visiting our grandparents. We **would ride** the train all by ourselves. Our aunt **would meet** us at the train station. At the end of summer we **would take** the train back home.

> Their parents **wouldn't let** them ride their bikes in the street.
> She **didn't use to cook** many dishes from scratch.
> **Would** your parents **allow** you to stay up late on Saturday nights?
> **Did** you **use to play** a musical instrument?

Used to is also used to express a situation in the past. In this case, **would** is *not* used.

> He **used to live** in Milwaukee, but he moved to Chicago in 1993.
> Lydia **used to own** a health food store but sold it in 1997.

Would have plus a past participle is used to express an unreal condition in the past. See unit 4 on conditionals for more information on using **would have.**

> If we had known you were coming, we **would have met** you at the airport.

Exercise 7.   Fill in the blanks with *would* or *used to* and the correct form of
the verb.

Here's a story my mother ❶ _____ (tell) me whenever I

❷ _____ (complain) about my life. "When I was a young

girl, about 10 years old, I ❸ _____ (get) up early in order to

catch the bus to school. My brothers and sisters and I ❹ _____

(wait) at the corner for the bus to come. The ride ❺ _____

(take, not) more than 20 minutes, but it seemed like hours during the winter. After I

got home from school, I ❻ _____ (take) care of my baby

sister while my mother **7** _____ (fix) supper. My brothers

8 _____ (help, not) with the dishes, so I **9** _____

(do) them by myself after supper. Then I **10** _____ (sit) at our

big kitchen table and do my homework. Sometimes my dad **11** _____

(help) me with math. I **12** _____ (go) to bed about 9:00."

For a few weeks after I listened to her story, I **13** _____

(stop) complaining!

Exercise 8. Study the following groups of three sentences. Identify the ones that are wrong and correct them.

1. I used to take my dog for a walk every day after work.
2. My dog wouldn't eat canned dog food. It would only eat fresh food.
3. I would own a poodle.

4. I would live near the west coast of Florida.
5. It would rain there every afternoon, but it wouldn't cool off.
6. It used to get unbearably hot and humid during the summer months.

7. My grandfather would tell me stories when I visited him.
8. "Life is hard," he used to say to me.
9. He would work in a machine repair shop before he retired.

10. Stefan would drive a Corvette years ago.
11. He would always drive at least 15 miles over the speed limit.
12. He used to get speeding tickets regularly.

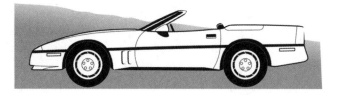

Speaking Activity

Exercise 9.   Speaking Activity

Plan a short (two to three minutes) presentation that describes (1) a special memory you have as a child or young adult, or (2) how you celebrated a holiday or special day in your country. Try to include as many past modals as you can: *would, used to, could, be able to,* etc. Make your presentation in a small group of three or four of your classmates.

Should Have, Ought to Have

Should have and **ought to have** plus a past participle are used to express advice or give suggestions about an action or event in the past. The advice or suggestions are given after the action or event has occurred and so do not express what happened, but what did not happen. Thus, they are commonly used to express regret. They are also used to state strong certainty about an event or situation. **Should have** is used more often than **ought to have. Ought to have** is rarely used in negative sentences or in questions.

> We had a wonderful time last night. You **should have come** with us.
> Liz **ought to have thought** about applying to school earlier.
> I heard the sale was unbelievable. I **should have gone** shopping with you.
> Ms. Kim **should have done** well on the test. She studied hard for it.
> You **shouldn't have waited** so long to ask for help.
> **Should I have called** ahead for an appointment?

Exercise 10.   Fill in the blanks with *should have* or *ought to have* plus the past participle of the verb given. Follow the example.

1. *A:* We didn't plan this project very well. We _should have expected_ (expect) complications.

   B: The walls look horrible. We _____ (paint, not) them this color.

2. *A:* But the color on the chart looked lighter. _____ we _____ (try) painting a small test area first?

   B: What a great idea. You _____ (suggest) that about four hours ago, before we got this far along.

3. *A:* Well, you _____ (stop) me about three and a half hours

ago, after I'd painted one wall.

B: I'm sorry. I _____ (lose) my temper. It's not your fault.

We _____ (spend) more time planning this project.

Haste makes waste and all that, you know.

4. *A:* I know. I _____ (snap) at you, either. I'm just really

disappointed in the way things turned out. Let's start over, okay?

B: OK. And next time, let's both say something if we think we've made a mistake!

Exercise 11. Match each event in the first column with the correct advice from the second column.

___ 1. They missed the parade.

___ 2. He ran his car off the road.

___ 3. They had a fight.

___ 4. It was her birthday.

___ 5. He moved back in with his parents.

___ 6. I missed a pop quiz today.

___ 7. He stayed up late, cramming.

___ 8. The 3:00 A.M. shuttle launch was spectacular.

___ 9. They lost $10,000 in a lottery scam.

A. He shouldn't have quit his job.

B. He should have been preparing all week.

C. You should have gotten up to see it.

D. They shouldn't have gone shopping first.

E. He should have sent her flowers.

F. He should have been paying attention.

G. He shouldn't have mentioned her weight.

H. They ought to have known better than to expect something for nothing.

I. You ought to have expected one.

Had to, Must Have, Had to Have

The past tense form of the modal **must** is **had to,** which in the affirmative or questions is used to express obligation or necessity. The negative of **had to, didn't have to,** however, implies there is a choice, and thus expresses a lack of obligation or necessity.

Scott **had to start** his new job right away.

Did he **have to** start right away? Yes, he did. He had no choice. He left his old job on Friday and started the new one on the following Monday.

Scott **didn't have to start** his new job right away.

He had a choice. He could take time off in between his old job and his new one.

Must have and **had to have** plus a past participle are used to express strong certainty about an action or event that happened in the past. The evidence for believing the action occurred is very strong. **Must have** is more commonly used than **had to have.** Both are used in the affirmative, but only **must have** is used in the negative. Neither form is commonly used to make questions.

The kids **must have made** themselves a snack. There are dirty dishes in the sink.

The butler **had to have been** the killer. His fingerprints were on the weapon.

She hardly ate anything. She **must not have been** very hungry.

Exercise 12.   Underline the correct form in each sentence.

1. *A:*   I'm sorry I couldn't go to your party. I (had to, didn't have to) work late.

    B: Don't apologize. It was a spur-of-the-moment party. You (had to, didn't have to) come.

2. *A:*   Well, I'm sorry I missed it. Knowing you, the party (must have been, didn't have to be) a lot of fun.

    B: Why do you say that? What makes you think it (had to have been, had to be) fun?

3. *A:*   Every single party of yours that I've ever gone to has been a success. This one certainly (must have been, didn't have to be) the same.

    B: I appreciate the compliment, but if my party was a success, it (must be, had to have been) due to the right combination of people who came!

Exercise 13.   Fill in the blanks to show the correct form of *had to, must have,* or *had to have.* Follow the example.

1. The police had followed him for one and a half miles before he pulled his car over. He *must not have seen* _____ (see, not) the flashing lights in his rearview mirror.

2. The invitation read "black tie optional," so he _____ (rent, not) a tuxedo. He wore his suit.

3. I had no choice. I _____ (pay) the late registration fee.

4. Can you believe it? They paid cash for their new beach house! They _____ _____ (saving) their money for quite some time to pay cash.

5. Jeanine went skydiving for the first time last Saturday. That _____ _____ (be) thrilling for her.

6. He's really upset. He lost all the data on his disk. How could that have happened? He _____ (close, not) the program before he took the disk out of the drive.

7. My paycheck is a nice one this week, but I _____ (put) in a

   lot of overtime to get it.

8. Candy—how thoughtful of you! You _____ (bring, not)

   anything to the party.

9. Greg's not here, but his car keys are. He _____ (take) the bus

   to work this morning.

10. The thieves broke down the front door to get in. I can't believe the neighbors didn't

    call 911. They _____ (hear) something, don't you think?

Be Supposed to, Be Going to

Be supposed to is used to express an obligation or expectation in the past which was not fulfilled or did not happen. It can be used in affirmative and negative sentences and in questions.

> You **were supposed to stop** at the grocery store on the way home. Did you
>   forget?
> I **was supposed to get** a FedEx package in the mail today, but it didn't come.
> We **weren't supposed to arrive** until 6:20, but the plane was early.
> **Was** Bradley **supposed to cut** the grass before he went to the game?

Be going to is used to express a plan or intention for the future that was made in the past but which was not fulfilled or carried out. It can be used in affirmative and negative sentences and in questions.

> We **were going to go** to Thailand on vacation, but we changed our minds.
> I **wasn't going to do** the laundry today, but I ran out of clean clothes.
> **Was** April **going to finish** the quilt she started a year ago?

Exercise 14. Fill in the blanks with the correct form of *be supposed to* or *be going to*. Be sure to use *be supposed to* for actions that express or imply obligation.

1. We _____ (go) on a picnic, but it rained.

2. Les and Sharon _____ (meet) me for lunch, but they stood

   me up!

3. I _____ (move) into a new apartment, but construction is

   still going on.

4. It _____ (snow) last night, but it did.

5. _____ you _____ (leave) for Japan

last week? What happened?

6. Jeff _____ (report) for work at 3:00, but he didn't show up.

7. Don and Linda _____ (take) me to the airport, but I took a

taxi instead.

8. The car _____ (be) ready by noon, but it wasn't.

9. What time _____ we _____

(meet)?

Exercise 15

Part 1.   Write three sentences listing things you were expected or obligated to do
at home or work or in class but that you didn't do. Use *be supposed to.*

1. _____

2. _____

3. _____

Part 2.   Write three sentences listing things you were planning or intending to do
but didn't. Use *be going to.* When you finish, share your sentences from
parts 1 and 2 with a classmate.

1. _____

2. _____

3. _____

Exercise 16.   Speaking Activity

Choose a partner. After reading the following scenario, discuss with your partner
what you think happened. Create a story about what happened to present to your
classmates. Use as many of the past modal forms from this unit as you can: *may
have, might have, could have, should have, ought to have, must have,* etc.

Situation: A man and a woman are sitting across from one another at a table
in a very nice restaurant. The tables are covered with white linen
tablecloths, and fresh flowers decorate each table as well. The man

and woman are talking quietly, but they are not smiling or laughing. Suddenly, the woman gets up from her chair, puts on her coat, and walks out of the restaurant. The man remains seated at the table for a moment, calls over the server, pays the bill, puts on his coat, and then leaves the restaurant.

To get you started: The couple may have been married. They could have been fighting about money. The husband . . .

Exercise 17.   Multiple Choice. Circle the letter of the correct answer.

1. *Donna:* Have you ever seen the movie *Always?*

   Debbie: I'm not sure. I _____ it on TV last summer.

   (A) was going to see   (C) may have seen

   (B) would have seen   (D) used to see

2. I'm so tired I can hardly stay awake today. I guess I _____ have had that espresso at 10:30 last night and stayed up so late.

   (A) should   (C) must not

   (B) shouldn't   (D) could

3. I'm a nervous wreck. We applied for a mortgage loan last week, and they _____ let us know this morning if it was approved.

   (A) were supposed to   (C) might have

   (B) would have   (D) must have

4. You're such a wonderful painter. You _____ have taken lessons from an expert!

   (A) would   (C) ought to

   (B) must   (D) shouldn't

5. This scale has to be wrong. I _____ have gained that much weight in only two months!

   (A) might not   (C) would

   (B) could   (D) can't

6. At the last place Gary worked, they _____ an annual company picnic. All the
   employees _____ bring their families along and spend the day at a nearby park. It
   was great.
   (A) had to have/had to   (C) would have/didn't have to
   (B) used to have/couldn't   (D) used to have/would

7. My in-laws _____ New Year's on a cruise ship, but they changed their minds.
   (A) shouldn't have celebrated   (C) can't have celebrated
   (B) were going to celebrate   (D) had to celebrate

8. If we'd known you liked Alison Kree's music, we _____ have invited you to come
   to the concert with us.
   (A) must   (C) would
   (B) wouldn't (D) shouldn't

9. Leslie's upset. She invited about 20 people to her house for a party and then no one
   showed up. The least they _____ have done was to call to say they _____ to
   come.
   (A) might/ were going   (C) might/weren't supposed
   (B) could/weren't going   (D) should/were going

10. He _____ have won the tournament if he hadn't sprained his ankle. He _____
    have felt terrible about dropping out.
    (A) should/could   (C) might/had to
    (B) must not/ought to (D) had to/couldn't

11. No one _____ have predicted that one day she would run for public office.
    (A) must   (C) can't
    (B) might   (D) could

12. You _____ have been trying to call me. I was home all day and the phone never
    rang. You _____ have dialed the wrong number.
    (A) could/might not   (C) must not/couldn't
    (B) might/should   (D) couldn't/must

Exercise 18.   Review Test

Part 1.   Fill in the blanks with a past modal and the correct form of the verb in parentheses.

Dear Personnel Adviser:

I'm writing to ask your advice about a work situation. I probably ❶ _____

_____ (write) to you months ago, but I ❷ _____

(be). I hope it's not too late for your help.

When I was hired at this company, I ❸ _____ (have) a

review after six months. Well, it's now been a year. If I had had a review, I ❹ _____

_____ (get) a raise. My wife and I ❺ _____

_____ (visit) Nashville to celebrate my six months with the company and

❻ _____ (use) my raise to pay for the trip.

In my previous job, my supervisors ❼ _____

(schedule) my review. We ❽ _____ (discuss) my performance

and set goals. But so far, at my new job, nothing has happened. My supervisor

❾ _____ (forget) to schedule my review. My dilemma is

that if I remind my supervisor, she may think I'm telling her she's not doing her job.

This ❿ _____ (happen) at a worse time. The company

is laying people off, and I don't want to look like a complainer. I only want what I

⓫ _____ (receive) six months ago. Any advice?

Sincerely,

Afraid to Ask

Part 2.   Read each sentence carefully. Look at the underlined part. If the underlined part is correct, circle the word *correct*. If it is wrong, circle the word *wrong* and the part of the sentence that makes it wrong. Then write the correct form above it.

correct   wrong   1. I <u>would live</u> in Berlin, Germany, and study at the university.

correct   wrong   2. Where are the kids? They <u>should have been</u> here by now, but

they're not.

correct   wrong   3. He <u>must to cancel</u> all his credit cards when his wallet was stolen.

correct   wrong   4. Whenever my dad sings to my mom, "You <u>must have been</u> a beautiful baby, 'cause, baby, look at you now," she laughs.

correct   wrong   5. They <u>weren't going to drive</u> to Florida for the winter, but they changed their minds after the first snowstorm.

correct   wrong   6. You <u>shouldn't have shaved</u> off your mustache. Why did you do it?

correct   wrong   7. It was the most wonderful wedding I've ever attended. The bride <u>could have looked</u> more beautiful!

correct   wrong   8. As children, my sister and I <u>would set</u> up a lemonade stand in front of our house at least once every summer.

Extra Writing Practice

Situation: We all make choices during our lives, including choosing where we work, live, and study. Write about some of the choices you have made in your life. Start with what you had planned or were expected to do, and then tell what you did. End by telling some of the things you could have, might have, or would have done or been able to do if you had made different choices. Underline the past modals in your life story so the teacher can see what you are trying to practice.

Unit 9

Subject–Verb Agreement

1. singular and plural subjects and verbs
2. intervening: *with, along with, in addition to, as well as, including*
3. compound subjects + *each/every*
4. pronouns *-one, -body, any-, either, neither*
5. *or, nor, either . . . or, neither . . . nor*
6. collective nouns
7. nouns plural in form but singular in meaning
8. *there/here* and inverted word order
9. *who, which, that* as subject
10. subjects that are titles and example words

In front of the United Nations in New York, there **ARE** many **FLAGS. EACH** of the flags **REPRESENTS** a different nation. (UN PHOTO 185522/A. Brizzi [JAN95])

Discover Grammar

1. Look at the sentences below. Some subjects and verbs are singular and some are plural. Circle *singular* or *plural* for the underlined subjects and verbs.
2. Work with a partner to understand the grammar rules for these sentences.

1. A <u>flag is</u> a piece of fabric used as a symbol or signaling device. (singular or plural)

2. <u>Flags are</u> usually rectangular, displaying a distinctive design. (singular or plural)

3. In New York, <u>doormen flag down</u> taxies. (singular or plural)

4. A <u>doorman raises</u> his hand and <u>blows</u> a whistle for a taxi to stop. (singular or plural)

5. The <u>flag</u> of the USA as well as the flags of many other countries <u>is</u> red, white, and blue. (singular or plural)

6. The <u>Netherlands and France have</u> red, white, and blue striped flags. (singular or plural)

7. <u>Every symbol and color has</u> special meaning. (singular or plural)

8. <u>Neither</u> of those <u>represents</u> my country. (singular or plural)

9. Our <u>class is studying</u> symbolism. (singular or plural)

10. The <u>news</u> now <u>carries</u> pictures of patriotic Americans waving flags. (singular or plural)

11. Even though the colors are the same, there <u>are differences</u> in meaning. (singular or plural)

12. Of all the flags <u>that are</u> red, white, and blue, the flag of the USA is the only one <u>that is called</u> Old Glory. (singular or plural) (singular or plural)

13. The <u>Stars and Stripes is</u> another name for the flag. (singular or plural)

14. A <u>number</u> of flags <u>are</u> red, white, and blue. (singular or plural)

15. The exact <u>number</u> of flags <u>is</u> not <u>known</u>. (singular or plural)

[Check page 174 for the answers.]

Subject-Verb Agreement

A **verb** is usually an action, and the **subject** is the person/thing doing that action.

> *example:*   Peter <u>plays</u> golf.
> What is the action? —plays (**verb**)
> Who/what is playing? —Peter (**subject**)

Subjects and verbs agree in number: singular subjects require singular verbs, and plural subjects require plural verbs.

1. An **-s** or **-es** ending does opposite things to nouns and verbs: it *usually* makes a noun plural, but it *always* makes a present tense verb singular.

> *examples:* A frog jump**s** high. (singular)
> Many frog**s** jump. (plural)
> That child sing**s** so beautifully. (singular)
> Those child<u>ren</u> <u>sing</u> so beautifully. (plural)

Note: Most noncount nouns take singular verbs.

> *example:* Furniture cost**s** a lot of money. (singular)

Note: Helping verbs sometimes show number and sometimes don't.

   A. When the helping verb is an independent auxiliary (meaning it can also be a main verb, such as **be, do,** or **have**), it agrees with the subject in number.

> *examples:* My **son is studying** for his exam. (singular)
> Many **dogs have flown** on planes. (plural)

   B. When the auxiliary is a modal, it remains the same. (modals: **will, would, can, could, should, may, might, ought to, must**)

> *examples:* **He will graduate** next year. (singular)
> **Maria and Anna might come** for a visit tomorrow. (plural)

2. Subjects and verbs must agree in number even if other words/phrases come between them. A common intervening item is a prepositional phrase.

> *examples:* **Registration** for courses **begins** on Monday. (singular)
> The **assignments** in this course **are** complex. (plural)
> A **jet** with two aisles **is called** a wide-bodied jet. (singular)

3. Compound subjects joined by **and** usually take a plural verb.

> *example:* **Alaska and Hawaii are** the newest states. (plural)

Note A: When the parts of a compound subject form a single idea or refer to a single person or thing, they take a singular verb.

> *example:* **Peanut butter and jelly is** my favorite sandwich. (singular)

Note B: When a compound subject is preceded by **each** or **every,** the verb is usually singular.

> *example:* **Every man and woman has** to show a form of identification before boarding a plane.

Note C : When **each** comes <u>after</u> a compound subject, the verb is usually plural.

> *examples:* The **men and women each have** to go through a metal detector.

4. Singular indefinite pronouns take singular verbs: **-one, -body, any-, either, neither, each.** Plural indefinite pronouns take plural verbs: **both, few, many, several.**

> *examples:* **Anything is** possible. (singular)
> **Somebody loses** his or her keys every day. (singular)
> **Few know** the answer. (plural)
> **Both have** already left. (plural)

Note: The following indefinite pronouns are either singular or plural, depending on the meaning of the word they refer to: **all, any, more, most,** and **some.**

> *examples:* **All** of the <u>money</u> **was stolen.** (singular)
> **Some** of the <u>coins</u> **were retrieved.** (plural)

Note: In formal English, the indefinite pronoun *none* is always singular. However, in informal spoken English *none* often takes a singular or plural verb, depending on the noun that it refers to.

5. When parts of a subject are joined by **or, nor, either . . . or, neither . . . nor,** the verb agrees with the subject nearest to it.

> *examples:* **Either** Pete **or** his **parents are going to** meet you at the airport. (plural)
> The plumber **nor** the **electrician knows** how to repair it. (singular)

6. When a collective noun acts as a unit, it takes a singular verb. When a collective noun acts as individual members of a group, it takes a plural verb. (Some collective nouns examples are **army, audience, class, committee, crowd, family, group, team.**)

> *examples:* The **team practices** every Tuesday. (singular)
> The **team wash** their own uniforms at home. (plural)

Note: When **the** comes before **number,** it is singular. When **a** comes before **number,** it is plural.

> *examples:* **A number** of people **were watching** the game. (plural)
> **The number** of people **wasn't** verified. (singular)

7. Subjects plural in form (ending in **-s, -ics**) but singular in meaning take a singular verb. (Some examples of these nouns are **athletics, acoustics, politics, news, measles, mumps;** course names such as **linguistics, physics,** etc.; place-names such as **United States, Wales,** etc.)

> *examples:* **Mathematics is** a required course for my major. (singular)
> The **news was** not good. (singular)

Note: Some nouns ending in **-ics** are considered singular when they refer to an organized body and plural when they refer to individual items.

> *examples:* **Statistics requires** many hours of study. (singular)
> The **statistics were written** down in the blue notebook. (plural)

8. Subjects and verbs agree in number even when the subject comes <u>after</u> the verb, for example in inverted word order or with **there/here.**

> *examples:*   **Were they invited** to the wedding? (plural)
> Here **is** the **map** you lost. (singular)
> There **are** many **details** to be aware of. (plural)

9. When the subject of the clause is **who, which,** or **that,** the verb agrees with the number of its <u>antecedent</u>.

> *examples:*   Ken is the <u>man</u> **who is wearing** a black shirt. (singular)
> Those are the <u>cars</u> **that are selling** fast. (plural)

> *Note:* Two tricky phrases are: **one of the _____s who** (plural) (The antecedent is the plural noun.)

> **the only one of the _____ s that** (singular)
> (The antecedent is *one.*)

> *examples:*   Rex is one of the <u>dogs</u> **that won** a red ribbon at the show. (plural)
> Rex is the only <u>one</u> of the dogs **that comes** when he is called. (singular)

10. Titles and example words take singular verbs.

> *examples:*   The **Buccaneers is** the football team from Tampa. (singular)
> *We* **is** a subject pronoun. (singular)

CAREFUL! Do not make these common mistakes.

1. Do not use a singular verb with an irregular plural subject.
   wrong: The men was astonished at what they saw.
   correct: The men were astonished at what they saw.

2. Do not use plural verbs with noncount subject nouns.
   wrong: The homework were passed in on time.
   correct: The homework was passed in on time.

3. Do not make modals agree with third person singular.
   wrong: She cans go out tomorrow night.
   correct: She can go out tomorrow night.

4. Do not be confused by count/noncount nouns after indefinite pronouns that can be either singular or plural.
   Count Noun—Plural
   wrong: Most of the facts was misstated.
   correct: Most of the facts were misstated.

Noncount—Singular
wrong: None of the information were correct.
correct: None of the information was correct.

5. Do not use plural verbs with expletive **it.**
wrong: It were gloomy and cold yesterday.
correct: It was gloomy and cold yesterday.

Exercise 1.   Underline the correct answer. Follow the example.

A flag ❶ (is, are) a piece of cloth, usually with a picture or design on it that

❷ (stands, stand) for something. Cloth flags ❸ (was, were) probably first

used in China about 3000 B.C. Those flags ❹ (was, were) made of silk.

Most of the flags that ❺ (was, were) used before the 1700s stood for

people or families. National flags ❻ (is, are) the most recent. Every

national flag ❼ (uses, use) more than one color. A number of colors

❽ (is used, are used). The number of colors ❾ (depends, depend) on the

choice of the government of the country. There ❿ (is, are) seven basic

colors: red, white, blue, green, yellow, black, and orange. The

designs usually ⓫ (represents, represent) something from the history of

the country. It usually ⓬ (symbolizes, symbolize) historical events.

Exercise 2.   This dialogue is between a reporter and Betsy Ross, alleged
seamstress of the first American flag. Fill in the blanks with either
the singular or plural form of the given verbs.

Reporter: Hello, Ms. Ross. I ❶ _____ a reporter for the *Tribune*.
               (be)

               ❷ _____ it all right if I ❸ _____ you some
                  (be)   (ask)

               questions?

Betsy Ross: Hello. It ❹ _____ nice to meet you. No, I ❺ _____
                        (be)   (not mind)

               at all. What ❻ _____ you _____ to know?
                                                (want)

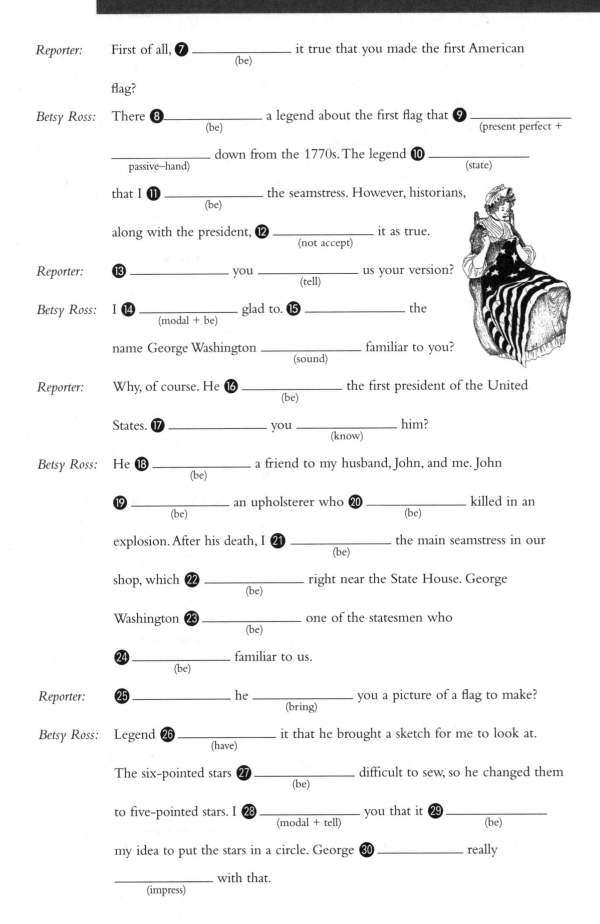

Reporter: First of all, **7** _____ it true that you made the first American
(be)

flag?

Betsy Ross: There **8** _____ a legend about the first flag that **9** _____
(be)   (present perfect +

_____ down from the 1770s. The legend **10** _____
passive–hand)   (state)

that I **11** _____ the seamstress. However, historians,
(be)

along with the president, **12** _____ it as true.
(not accept)

Reporter: **13** _____ you _____ us your version?
(tell)

Betsy Ross: I **14** _____ glad to. **15** _____ the
(modal + be)

name George Washington _____ familiar to you?
(sound)

Reporter: Why, of course. He **16** _____ the first president of the United
(be)

States. **17** _____ you _____ him?
(know)

Betsy Ross: He **18** _____ a friend to my husband, John, and me. John
(be)

19 _____ an upholsterer who **20** _____ killed in an
(be)   (be)

explosion. After his death, I **21** _____ the main seamstress in our
(be)

shop, which **22** _____ right near the State House. George
(be)

Washington **23** _____ one of the statesmen who
(be)

24 _____ familiar to us.
(be)

Reporter: **25** _____ he _____ you a picture of a flag to make?
(bring)

Betsy Ross: Legend **26** _____ it that he brought a sketch for me to look at.
(have)

The six-pointed stars **27** _____ difficult to sew, so he changed them
(be)

to five-pointed stars. I **28** _____ you that it **29** _____
(modal + tell)   (be)

my idea to put the stars in a circle. George **30** _____ really

_____ with that.
(impress)

Reporter: This **31** _____ a great story. Thank you for your time.
                                (modal + make)

Betsy Ross: You **32** _____ welcome.
                                 (be)

Speaking Activity

Exercise 3.   You are going to interview someone from another country. You are
                    going to gather as much information as you can about the flag of
                    his or her country. After asking as many questions as you can think
                    of, try to draw the flag as the person has described it. First, write
                    out your questions, checking for subject-verb agreement for
                    inverted word order.

1. What country _____ you from?
                        (be)

2. What _____ your flag _____ like?
                                              (look)

3. _____

4. _____

5. _____

6. _____

7. _____

8. _____

9. _____

10. _____

This _____ the flag of _____ .
          (be)

Exercise 4.   Multiple Choice. Circle the letter of the correct answer.

1. The colors of the American flag _____ red, white, and blue.

   (A) is   (C) was

   (B) are   (D) were

2. The colors did not have meaning for the Stars and Stripes when it _____ adopted.

   (A) is   (C) was

   (B) are   (D) were

3. The Stars and Stripes _____ one of the names of the flag.

   (A) is   (C) was

   (B) are   (D) were

4. The stars and six stripes _____ white.

   (A) is   (C) was

   (B) are   (D) were

5. The background for the stars _____ blue.

   (A) is   (C) was

   (B) are   (D) were

6. Purity and innocence _____ by the color white.

   (A) is represented   (C) can represent

   (B) will represent   (D) are represented

7. Red _____ hardiness and valor.

   (A) signifies   (C) signifier

   (B) is signified   (D) was signified

8. Vigilance, perseverance, and justice _____ by the color blue.

   (A) is characterized   (C) been characterized

   (B) are characterized   (D) being characterized

9. A symbol of the heavens _____ the star.

    (A) is   (C) do

    (B) are   (D) does

10. Thus, on flags that _____ one or more stars, this design _____ the heavens.

    (A) has . . . symbolizes   (C) have . . . symbolizes

    (B) has . . . symbolize   (D) have . . . symbolize

11. The stripes of the flag _____ symbolic of the rays of light that _____ from the

    sun.

    (A) is . . . emanate   (C) are . . . emanate

    (B) is . . . emanates   (D) are . . . emanates

12. One of the stars in the sky _____ our sun.

    (A) has   (C) will

    (B) does   (D) is

13. The seven red stripes and six white stripes _____ the original thirteen colonies.

    (A) representing   (C) represents

    (B) had represented   (D) represent

14. There _____ 50 states, so there _____ 50 stars.

    (A) is . . . is   (C) are . . . is

    (B) is . . . are   (D) are . . . are

15. _____ there any places where the flag _____ 24 hours a day?

    (A) Is . . . fly   (C) Has . . . flew

    (B) Are . . . flies   (D) Does . . . flown

Exercise 5.   Underline the subjects and verbs in each sentence. Look for subject-verb agreement in number. Correct the mistakes.

❶ Today, the colors of red, white, and blue each has meaning even though the Continental Congress didn't leave any record to show why they chose those colors.

❷ In 1777, Congress passed a resolution that the flag should have thirteen stars; however, each of the stars were not assigned to a particular state. ❸ Symbolizing a "new constellation," every one of the white stars were placed on the blue background. ❹ Every red and white stripe in the American flag have exact

measurements established by the government. ❺ The height, width, and length each has to be proportionately the same on every flag made. ❻ The red and white stripes is a representation of the original thirteen colonies. ❼ The top and bottom stripes is red. ❽ Every stripe in between these two alternate in color.

Exercise 6.   Read each sentence carefully. Underline the pronoun. Fill in the blank with the correct form of the verb. Follow the example.

1. Almost <u>everyone</u> _____*likes*_____ (like) to watch a parade.

2. Several _____ (watch) to see the floats, bands, costumes, and flags.

3. Some of the flags _____ (stand for) the towns or bands while others _____ (represent) countries.

4. All of the entertainment _____ (present passive–appreciate) by applause.

5. None of the floats _____ (go) by unrecognized.

6. Most of the people _____ (salute) when the American flag passes by.

7. Many _____ (put) their right hands over their hearts.

8. All _____ (show) a sign of respect.

Exercise 7.   Combine the two sentences using: **or, nor, not . . . nor, cannot . . . nor, either . . . or,** or **neither . . . nor.**

1. Maria will be the flag bearer in the parade.
   Her sister, Anna, will be the flag bearer in the parade.

   _____

   _____

2. The flag is not big. The flag is not heavy.

   _____

   _____

3. They can use the black flagpole. They can use the gold flagpole.

   _____

   _____

4. The flag cannot be flown in the rain. The flag cannot touch the ground.

   _____

   _____

5. The flag can be made of paper. The flag can be made of cloth.

   _____

   _____

6. The flag is not flown after dusk. The flag is not flown before sunrise.

   _____

   _____

7. Students salute the flag at the beginning of the school day.
   Students salute the flag at the end of the school day.

   _____

   _____

8. The flag cannot be folded haphazardly. The flag cannot be stored irreverently.

   _____

   _____

Exercise 8.   Put the following sentences in the correct order. Look for
               antecedents. Write the sentence on the line, following the example.

1. who work for him / should listen to / the people / the manager

   The manager should listen to the people who work for him.

   _____

2. who first called the U.S. flag the Star-Spangled Banner / was / the person / Francis
   Scott Key

   _____

   _____

3. that became the national anthem / wrote / Key / the poem

   _____

   _____

   _____

4. who was a sea captain / Old Glory / gave / William
   Driver / the name / the flag

   _____

   _____

   _____

5. which is the most popular name / the national flag / the Stars and Stripes / of the
   United States / is

   _____

   _____

6. who was president / during the Civil War / refused to have / Abraham Lincoln / of
   the southern states / taken off the flag / the stars

   _____

   _____

7. which was fought between the North and the South / five years / the Civil War /
   lasted

   _____

   _____

8. who were known as Yankees / who were from the South / the Northerners / the Confederates / and / different flags / carried

_____

_____

9. that was known as the American flag / carried / the Yankees / the flag

_____

_____

10. that was known as the Confederate flag; / a flag / the Southerners / carried / it was also red, white, and blue

_____

_____

_____

_____

Speaking Activity

Exercise 9.   Speaking Activity

Work in groups of three to five students. Each person should find out information about the flags of three different countries. (In other words, if there are four people in your group, you will discuss information about flags from twelve different countries.) Each person should research information about each flag including the design of the flag, the colors of each flag, what the colors mean (if possible), what any symbols in the flag mean, and when the flag was designed. When you have done your research, meet in a group to tell each other your information. Everyone should pay attention here to subject-verb agreement. Most of the verbs in this exercise will be in simple present tense because you are describing a current fact. Any information about the history of the flag will not be in present tense. _Remember:_ Listen carefully for subject-verb agreement in your group members' oral reports.

Exercise 10.   Multiple Choice. Circle the letter of the best answer for each sentence.

1. Linguistics _____ one of the required courses for ESL teachers.

    (A) is   (C) are

    (B) am   (D) been

2. All of the food _____ before we got to the picnic.

   (A) gone   (C) was gone

   (B) going   (D) were gone

3. *The Klumps* _____ one of the funniest movies I _____ seen.

   (A) is . . . have   (C) is . . . has

   (B) are . . . have   (D) are . . . has

4. There _____ so much work that I have to do now!

   (A) is   (C) are

   (B) am   (D) have

5. Thanks to the post office, our mail _____ on time every day.

   (A) arriving   (C) arrive

   (B) arrives   (D) to arrive

6. Measles _____ a childhood disease that _____ almost eradicated.

   (A) are . . . have been   (C) is . . . have been

   (B) is . . . has been   (D) are . . . has been

7. Peterson Associates _____ the winners of the contest every Thursday.

   (A) announce   (C) announces

   (B) that announce   (D) that announces

8. Here _____ the answers to your questions.

   (A) they are   (C) are

   (B) it is   (D) is

9. The only one of the actors who _____ the lines _____ not here today.

   (A) know . . . is   (C) knows . . . are

   (B) know . . . are   (D) knows . . . is

10. Something _____ fishy around here.

   (A) smell   (C) smelling

   (B) that is a smell   (D) smells

> **CHALLENGE** Read number 10 again carefully. What does this sentence mean? *Hint:* It is an idiom. It does not mean that there is old, smelly fish around here. What do you think it means? If you do not know, ask a native speaker or consult a good dictionary.

Exercise 11. Review Test

Part 1.   Fill in the correct form of the verb in parentheses.

1. The job applicants each (type) _____ fifty words a minute.

2. Where (be) _____ those bright lights coming from?

3. None of my students (disrespect) _____ the principal.

4. The cassette or the CD (cost) _____ too much money; I can't buy both.

5. Each dollar I spend on entertainment (mean) _____ less I have for bills.

6. A kite (fly) _____ higher than a glider.

7. Kites and gliders (need) _____ a strong wind to keep them flying.

8. A flock of geese (fly) _____ overhead yesterday when a loud noise (scare) _____ them.

9. A truck driver or a motorcyclist (need) _____ a special license.

10. There (be) _____ many statistics to verify that statement.

Part 2.   Read each sentence carefully. Look at the underlined word. If the underlined word is correct, circle the word *correct*. If it is wrong, circle the word *wrong* and write the correct form above the underlined word.

correct   wrong   1. None of the countries in Asia that we discussed in our last class meeting <u>produces</u> much oil for export.

correct   wrong   2. Of all the books that Jalstony wrote in the eighteenth century, perhaps the best known of those <u>are</u> *When Birds Fly Wildly.*

correct   wrong   3. Though there are many good runners, only the best <u>is</u> going to win the race.

correct   wrong   4. Neither the pilots who are working for lower wages at the current time nor the president of the company <u>are</u> ready to agree to the new salary arrangement.

correct   wrong   5. They <u>were</u> going to drive to Florida for the winter, but they changed their minds after the first snowstorm.

correct   wrong   6. I have dozens and dozens of folders of documents that we have to look over as soon as possible, and here <u>are</u> your folder with two hundred documents.

correct   wrong   7. If the team sincerely <u>want</u> to win more games, the players are going to have to practice harder and be more committed.

correct   wrong   8. After the fire at the antique store, some of the rare coins <u>were</u> recovered; however, some of the rare paper money <u>was</u> destroyed completely.

Situation: Now that you know so much about the American flag, we would like to know about the national flag of another country. Research its history. When did the concept first appear in that country's history? Who was the originator? How has it evolved since then? What are the colors, and what do they represent? Are there any other insignia or emblems on the flag? What do they stand for? Is there a flag code for how to handle the flag? When can it be displayed? Write a descriptive essay about this flag.

   Pay attention to subject-verb agreement. Underline each verb two times and each subject one time.

Answers to DISCOVER GRAMMAR on page 159:

1. singular   2. plural   3. plural   4. singular   5. singular   6. plural   7. singular
8. singular   9. singular   10. singular   11. plural   12. plural, singular   13. singular
14. plural   15. singular

Unit 10

Review of Prepositions

1. time and space: *at, on, in*
2. possessive: *of*
3. adverbs of manner: *by, with*
4. *to, in order to* vs. *for*
5. VERBS + PREPOSITIONS
6. ADJECTIVES + PREPOSITIONS
7. ADJECTIVES/PARTICIPLES + PREPOSITIONS
8. idioms (throughout the unit)

Are you *AT the end OF your rope???* Well, *hang ON!* I've got something *UNDER my hat* that will help you with PREPOSITIONS.

Time and Space: *at, on, in*

at . . . is like a point in time
- at 5 o'clock—use with exact time
- at noon—use with part of a day considered a point in time
- at lunchtime—use with words compounded with time

at . . . is like a point in space
  • at 235 Elm Street—use for addresses with numbers
  • at school—use to refer to a point in a general area

on . . . is like a line in time with a beginning and an end
  • on Saturday—use with a day of the week
  • on June 20th—use with a day of the month
  Note: Informally, **on** can be omitted. I saw him Saturday.

on . . . is like a line (one-dimensional) or a surface (two-dimensional) in space
  • on the street—use to indicate line (as on a map) or surface (as on an actual street)
  • on the table—use to indicate surface

in . . . is like a three-dimensional area in time
  • in May—use with a month (any time within that month)
  • in 1976—use with a year (any time within that year)
  • in the morning—use with part of the day (any time within that morning)
  • in the summer—use with a season (any time within that season)

in . . . is like a three-dimensional area of space
  • in the drawer—use with an enclosed area
  Note: Inside is similar to *within*, meaning the interior.

Be careful with the verb *arrive!*

Arrive at refers to a place *smaller* than a city or town.

   example: She arrived **at the theater** very early.

Arrive in refers to a place *larger* than a city or town.

   example: He arrived **in Italy** on Tuesday.

Note: For a city or town, **in** is used more often, but **at** is also acceptable.
   example: The train **arrived in** Atlanta on time.
             The train **arrived at** Atlanta on time.

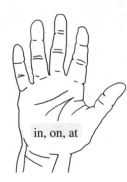

in, on, at   in, on, at

ON the one hand there's *space*   ON the other hand there's *time*

Speaking Activity

Exercise 1.   Work with a partner.

Ask your partner the questions about space and fill in his or her answers after the prepositions. Then switch roles and your partner will ask you the questions about time and fill in your answers after the prepositions.

1. What country do you live in?

   in _____

2. Where in (country) _____ ?

   in _____

3. Where in (city) (OR What street) ____ ?

   on _____

4. Where on (street) _____ ?

   at _____

1. At what time did your plane arrive in the USA?

   at _____

2. What was the date?

   on _____

3. What day was that?

   on a _____

4. What month?

   in _____

5. What year?

   in _____

6. What century?

   in _____

With your partner, compare your answers. Do your answers range from most specific to most general or from most general to most specific? Which triangle best depicts your answers? Why?

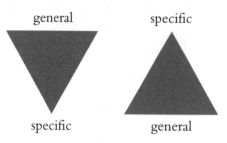

general   specific

specific   general

Exercise 2.   Time and Space: *in, on, at.* Complete the following sentences.

I had better set my alarm, so that I can get up really early. I want to *get a jump on* my co-worker. I guess I'll get up at ❶ _____ . Last week, Bill was late three days in a row. I wonder why he's been so *out of it* lately. He looks like *he's on his last legs.* On ❷ _____ he has to give a presentation. I hope he is on ❸ _____ . If Bill is late for or misses that meeting, he'll *be in hot water* with the boss. If he's not coming in, he had better call in ❹ _____ , so the boss can reschedule the meeting.

Bill missed the meeting, so now his job *is on the line.* The boss told him he had to get to work at ❺ _____ . The boss was so angry at Bill that he told Bill to *shape up or ship out!* Embarrassed, Bill apologized and reassured the boss that he would be in ❻ _____ on ❼ _____ at ❽ _____ every day from now on.

CHALLENGE   Work with a partner to *figure out* what each of these idioms means.
- get the jump on
- be on one's last legs
- be in hot water
- be on the line
- shape up or ship out
- be out of it

Did you get up on the wrong side OF the bed?

Exercise 3.   Possessive: *of.* Find the eight mistakes and correct them.

Jane got up late for work, so she had to hurry. The breakfast of Jane consisted of a

glass of juice and a granola bar. As she ran out the door, her shoe's heel got caught in

the sidewalk's crack. She had to go back inside for another shoe's pair. The only ones

she could find were navy blue, which didn't go with her outfit. Therefore, she had to

change her clothes to match her shoes. Then she jumped in the car's front seat and

drove off to work. She didn't have time to read the newspaper of the morning, so she

didn't know that it was supposed to rain. By the time she arrived at work, her navy

shoes' tops were so wet that they were squeaking. On her lunch hour, she had to buy

a new pair of navy shoes to go with her outfit's color.

Exercise 4.   Adverbs of Manner: *by, with.* Read each sentence carefully.
                    Write *by,* which tells means, method, or how something is done,
                    or write *with,* which is used with an instrument.

After getting to work late, Jane saw a pile of work on her desk. She had to

respond to a customer ❶ _____ email, but the computers were down. She

thought she could save time ❷ _____ calling, but he wasn't in, so she had to leave a message. She realized that she had forgotten to send an order ❸ _____

_____ fax. She typed in the number ❹ _____ her right hand and held

the phone ❺ _____ her left hand. She couldn't open the file cabinet

❻ _____ her set of keys. ❼ _____ borrowing keys from the

secretary, she was able to access the files. She introduced herself to a new client

❽ _____ a handshake. She was able to get away from the office for a while

❾ _____ offering to take the client to lunch. She paid for the meals

❿ _____ a check and wrote it into her expense account. ⓫ _____

keeping an accurate account, she is able to stay on budget. This makes her boss very

pleased ⓬ _____ her accounting.

Different strokes FOR different folks.

Exercise 5.   *to, in order to* vs. *for.* Write three possible answers to the following
                    questions. Use *to, in order to,* and *for.*

1. Why are you reading this book?

   _____

   _____

   _____

2. Why do adults go to work every day?

   _____

   _____

   _____

3. Why do some adults bring a lunch to work?

_____

_____

_____

4. Why do some people take the bus to work?

_____

_____

_____

5. After eating in a restaurant, why do customers leave money on the table?

_____

_____

_____

Exercise 6.   VERBS + PREPOSITIONS. Fill in the blanks with the appropriate verbs and *of* from the word bank. Use tenses appropriate to the situations.

---

approve of   consist of   remind _____ of   think of

Note: **of** is used for reason/cause/origin, material, characterized by.

Jane had to get her boss to ❶ _____ _____ a new ad campaign.
She ❷ _____ _____ some ideas that were very unconventional. She
didn't know how her boss would react to them. One of the ideas ❸ _____
_____ using a laser light show as a backdrop. However, she decided not to use
that idea after a co-worker ❹ _____ her _____ how conservative their
boss is.

| belong to | give to | happen to | listen to | look forward to |
| speak to | talk to | write to | | |

Note: **to** is used for direction, movement, position, contact, purpose, result, addition.

The office was in a festive mood. They were ❺ _____ _____

holiday music over the intercom. A lot of employees were congregating at the water

cooler talking about how they were ❻ _____ _____ the upcoming

company holiday party. Jane was ❼ _____ _____ her secretary about

the new outfit she had bought for the occasion. Ruth ❽ _____ _____

pass by and heard Jane ❾ _____ _____ her secretary. The outfit Jane

was describing sounded just like the one she had just purchased. Rather than

interrupt their conversation, Ruth decided to ❿ _____ an email _____

Jane asking about the outfit.

| ask for | look for | thank _____ for | wait for |

Note: **for** is used for reason/cause, purpose.

Bill's car was in the shop, so he had to ⓫ _____ a co-worker _____

a ride to work. Time passed by slowly. It seemed as if he had been ⓬ _____

_____ hours. He kept ⓭ _____ out the window _____ his

ride. Because of a traffic jam, they got to work late. Bill hopped out of the car,

⓮ _____ his co-worker _____ the ride, and went straight to

his office.

Exercise 7.   Multiple Choice: ADJECTIVES + PREPOSITIONS. Circle the letter of
the correct preposition.

1. Steve is crazy _____ his new car.

   (A) from   (C) about

   (B) with   (D) for

You are almost *out OF the woods* WITH these prepositions!

2. He was ashamed _____ how his old car looked.

    (A) for

    (B) with

    (C) from

    (D) of

3. Whenever he drove it to work, he parked in back of the building because he was

    tired _____ the frowns on his co-workers' faces.

    (A) of

    (B) from

    (C) for

    (D) about

4. Steve was fed up _____ their looks.

    (A) for

    (B) with

    (C) of

    (D) from

5. He decided he was ready _____ a new car anyway.

    (A) by

    (B) about

    (C) with

    (D) for

6. He was very curious _____ the new SUVs.

    (A) about

    (B) of

    (C) for

    (D) with

7. When he went to the dealer, all of the salespeople were polite _____ him.

(A) with   (C) to

(B) for   (D) about

8. They explained how the SUVs are known _____ their versatility.

(A) to   (C) at

(B) of   (D) for

9. Steve was satisfied _____ its performance, so he told the salesperson that he was

interested _____ buying one.

(A) for . . . about   (C) in . . . for

(B) with . . . in   (D) about . . . with

10. Now his co-workers are jealous _____ his new car.

(A) for   (C) with

(B) from   (D) of

Exercise 8.   Timed Speaking Activity: ADJECTIVES/PARTICIPLES
                  + PREPOSITIONS

Preparation: Write ten to fifteen of the following ADJECTIVES + PREPOSITIONS
                  on separate strips of paper. Put the strips of paper in a hat or bowl.

accustomed to	acquainted with	afraid of
angry at	bad at	bored with/by
composed of	confused about	different from
disappointed in/with	excited about	familiar with
famous for	far from	full of
guilty of	harmful to	innocent of
known for	married to	opposed to
proud of	ready for	related to
responsible for	satisfied with	sick of
sorry about	successful in	surprised at/by
tired from	tired of	worried about

                  Four to six students sit in a circle. The first student pulls a strip of
                  paper out of the hat and reads it aloud. Students have ten seconds
                  to write down the adjective, the preposition, and an object for the
                  preposition. Going around the circle, each member says a complete
                  sentence, which includes the adjective, preposition, and object.
                  The student gets a point for each object and another point for the
                  complete sentence. The person with the most points at the end of
                  the activity wins.

I can't believe my eyes!
You are almost THROUGH the prepositions.

Exercise 9.   Idioms and Expressions. Try to match these idioms and expressions with their meanings.

___ 1. When people say: **You're putting me on** . . .

___ 2. When people say something is **over before you know it** . . .

___ 3. When people say they want to **get rid of** an old coat . . .

___ 4. If people say they **can't get over** how much something costs . . .

___ 5. When people use the expression: "**as I said before** . . ."

___ 6. When people tell you that you should **give up** smoking . . .

___ 7. When people say they are **in the dark** when it comes to clothing fads . . .

___ 8. If people ask if you **"got it?"** . . .

___ 9. When people say that they **bent over backwards for** someone/something . . .

___ 10. When people ask you to **keep an eye on** their pocketbook . . .

A. it means that they are unaware of what is popular right now.

B. it means that they want to know if you understand.

C. it means that they think you should stop or quit.

D. it means that they want you to watch it so that it is safe.

E. it means that they want to throw it away/out.

F. it means that they tried very hard.

G. it means that they can't believe the price.

H. it means that they are repeating.

I. it means that they think you are joking.

J. it means that it happens faster than you thought it would.

CHALLENGE Now that you have *taken the bull by the horns* and gotten through this unit, you must *feel like a million dollars.* At this point in the text, you are *sitting pretty* because you have completed ten units. If you *stick to your guns* and *plow through* the rest of the units, you will soon be able *to kick up your heels.* So, *get the ball rolling* and *give it your best shot.* At the end, *you can toot your own horn.* In your own words, write what you think each of these idioms means.

Exercise 10.   Multiple Choice. Circle the letter of the correct answer.

1. The watch _____ my bureau drawer is my great-grandmother's.

   (A) at   (C) in

   (B) on   (D) into

2. Brenda was late, and she didn't arrive _____ my house until midnight.

   (A) near   (C) in

   (B) at   (D) on

3. Her car broke down _____ Sunday.

   (A) in   (C) at

   (B) from   (D) on

4. American Airlines flight 234 should arrive _____ Puerto Rico _____ noon.

   (A) at . . . by   (C) on . . . in

   (B) in . . . at   (D) by . . . on

5. _____ which area _____ Chicago do you live?

   (A) On . . . near   (C) In . . . of

   (B) At . . . by   (D) From . . . to

6. I live _____ 350 Elm Street.

   (A) at   (C) on

   (B) in   (D) by

7. When I was _____ high school, I had a part-time job _____ McDonald's.

   (A) in . . . in   (C) at . . . in

   (B) at . . . at   (D) in . . . at

8. Are you sick? You look as if you are _____ your last legs.

   (A) in   (C) under

   (B) on   (D) from

Exercise 11.   Review Test

Part 1.   Fill in the blanks with the correct preposition. 介

1. Did you get _____ _____ the wrong side _____ the bed?

2. He had plenty _____ time to do his homework.

3. The top _____ the bookshelf is too high _____ me to reach.

4. That beautiful afghan was made _____ hand.

5. The little girl was playing _____ the dog when it bit her.

6. The upholstery _____ the back _____ the chair was torn =tear

7. They flew _____ helicopter _____ the Grand Canyon.

8. Here are your keys; I found them _____ the floor _____ the table.

Part 2.   Editing. Find at least ten preposition mistakes and correct them.

   Last Saturday I happened of run into Mary in my way home to the supermarket. She was waving by her left hand because she was wearing a cast in her right arm. It reminded me from when we were children. Mary was always a daredevil, and she always got on trouble. Once, she climbed a tree in which a cat that belonged by her neighbor had gotten stuck. When she tried to reach for the cat, it scratched her. She got so nervous that she fell out from the tree. She broke the same arm in which she was wearing a cast today. I can't wait to her to have children!

Extra Writing Practice

Look around the room you are in and focus on one thing that catches your attention. Using this as your main focus, write a spatial order paragraph in which you describe the room (including the contents of the room). Use as many prepositional phrases as you can. Be sure to underline all of the prepositional phrases that you have used.

example:

My kitchen is a nice, bright room with many modern conveniences. A large, white refrigerator is located <u>next to the window</u>. <u>To the right</u> <u>of the refrigerator</u> is the stove. Right now there are two pots <u>on top</u> <u>of the stove</u>. . . .

Unit 11

Review of Verb Tenses

1. regular verbs vs. irregular verbs
2. overview of verb tenses
3. three principal parts: base, past, past participle
4. simple tenses: present, past, future
5. progressive tenses: present, past, future
6. perfect tenses: present, past, future
7. perfect progressive tenses: present, past, future

There are twelve verb tenses in English. Review the examples for regular and irregular verbs in the twelve tenses.

Regular verbs: the past tense and past participle forms end in *-ed (cook, cooked, cooked)*

COOK	Simple	Progressive	Perfect	Perfect Progressive
present	I cook	I am cooking	I have cooked	I have been cooking
past	I cooked	I was cooking	I had cooked	I had been cooking
future	I will cook	I will be cooking	I will have cooked	I will have been cooking

Irregular verbs: the past tense and past participle forms do not end in *-ed (take, took, taken)*

TAKE	Simple	Progressive	Perfect	Perfect Progressive
present	he takes	he is taking	he has taken	he has been taking
past	he took	he was taking	he had taken	he had been taking
future	he will take	he will be taking	he will have taken	he will have been taking

Exercise 1.   Follow the examples to fill in these four verb charts.

WORK	Simple	Progressive	Perfect	Perfect Progressive
present	you	you	you	you
past	you	you	you had worked	you
future	you	you	you	you

EAT	Simple	Progressive	Perfect	Perfect Progressive
present	he	he	he	he
past	he	he was eating	he	he
future	he	he	he	he

HAVE	Simple	Progressive	Perfect	Perfect Progressive
present	I	I	I	I
past	I	I	I	I
future	I	I	I will have had	I

RUN	Simple	Progressive	Perfect	Perfect Progressive
present	she	she	she	she
past	she	she	she	she
future	she will run	she	she	she

Three Principal Parts of a Verb: Base, Past, Past Participle

Because six of the twelve tenses (or half!) make use of the past participle forms, it is imperative that you know these forms perfectly.

B

be	was/were	been
bear	bore	born
beat	beat	beaten/beat
become	became	become
begin	began	begun
bend	bent	bent
bet	bet	bet
bid	bid	bid
bind	bound	bound
bite	bit	bitten
bleed	bled	bled
blow	blew	blown
break	broke	broken
breed	bred	bred
bring	brought	brought
broadcast	broadcast	broadcast
build	built	built
burst	burst	burst
buy	bought	bought

C

cast	cast	cast
catch	caught	caught
choose	chose	chosen
cling	clung	clung
come	came	come
cost	cost	cost
creep	crept	crept
cut	cut	cut

D

deal	dealt	dealt
dig	dug	dug
dive	dove/dived	dived
do	did	done
draw	drew	drawn
dream	dreamed/dreamt	dreamed/dreamt
drink	drank	drunk
drive	drove	driven

E

eat	ate	eaten

F

fall	fell	fallen
feed	fed	fed
feel	felt	felt
fight	fought	fought
find	found	found
fit	fit	fit
flee	fled	fled
fling	flung	flung
fly	flew	flown
forbid	forbade	forbidden
forecast	forecast	forecast
forget	forgot	forgotten
forgive	forgave	forgiven
freeze	froze	frozen

G

get	got	gotten
give	gave	given
go	went	gone
grind	ground	ground
grow	grew	grown

H

hang	hung	hung
have	had	had
hear	heard	heard
hide	hid	hidden
hit	hit	hit
hold	held	held
hurt	hurt	hurt

I

input	input	input

K

keep	kept	kept
kneel	knelt/kneeled	knelt/kneeled
knit	knit/knitted	knit/knitted
know	knew	known

L

lay	laid	laid
lead	led	led
leap	leapt/leaped	leapt/leaped
leave	left	left
lend	lent	lent
let	let	let
lie	lay	lain
light	lit/lighted	lit/lighted
lose	lost	lost

M

make	made	made
mean	meant	meant
meet	met	met
mistake	mistook	mistaken

O

overcome	overcame	overcome

P

pay	paid	paid
prove	proved	proven/proved
put	put	put

Q

quit	quit	quit

R

read	read	read
rid	rid	rid
ride	rode	ridden
ring	rang	rung
rise	rose	risen
run	ran	run

S

say	said	said
see	saw	seen
seek	sought	sought
sell	sold	sold
send	sent	sent
set	set	set
sew	sewed	sewn/sewed

shake	shook	shaken
shed	shed	shed
shine	shone	shone
shoot	shot	shot
show	showed	shown/showed
shrink	shrank/shrunk	shrunk
shut	shut	shut
sing	sang	sung
sit	sat	sat
slay	slew/slayed	slain
sleep	slept	slept
slide	slid	slid
sling	slung	slung
slit	slit	slit
speak	spoke	spoken
speed	sped/speeded	sped/speeded
spend	spent	spent
spill	spilled/spilt	spilled/spilt
spin	spun	spun
spit	spit	spit
split	split	split
spread	spread	spread
spring	sprang/sprung	sprung
stand	stood	stood
steal	stole	stolen
stick	stuck	stuck
sting	stung	stung
stink	stank/stunk	stunk
strew	strewed	strewn
stride	strode	stridden
strive	strove	striven
strike	struck	struck
string	strung	strung
swear	swore	sworn
sweep	swept	swept
swell	swelled	swollen/swelled
swim	swam	swum
swing	swung	swung
T		
take	took	taken
teach	taught	taught
tear	tore	torn
tell	told	told

think	thought	thought
throw	threw	thrown
thrust	thrust	thrust

U

understand	understood	understood
undertake	undertook	undertaken
undo	undid	undone
unwind	unwound	unwound
uphold	upheld	upheld
upset	upset	upset

W

wake	woke/waked	woken/waked
wear	wore	worn
weave	wove	woven
weep	wept	wept
win	won	won
wind	wound	wound
withdraw	withdrew	withdrawn
wreak	wreaked/wrought	wreaked/wrought
wring	wrung	wrung

Exercise 2.   Practice with Verb Forms. Fill in the first blank with the base form of the verb, the second blank with the past tense, and the third blank with the past participle form.

	base	*past*	*past participle*
1.	become	_____	_____
2.	_____	_____	bitten
3.	bring	_____	_____
4.	_____	caught	_____
5.	_____	chose	_____
6.	deal	_____	_____
7.	eat	_____	_____
8.	_____	_____	fed
9.	_____	_____	found
10.	_____	fit	_____

base	past	past participle
11. _____	got	_____
12. _____	_____	given
13. hide	_____	_____
14. _____	_____	hit
15. _____	_____	input
16. _____	_____	known
17. lend	_____	_____
18. _____	_____	let
19. _____	_____	meant
20. _____	_____	quit
21. ride	_____	_____
22. _____	_____	sought
23. _____	_____	shaken
24. shed	_____	_____
25. slit	_____	_____
26. _____	_____	stuck
27. _____	took	_____
28. _____	threw	_____
29. _____	understood	_____
30. _____	_____	woven

Exercise 3.   Practice with Verb Forms

Step 1. For each of the twenty items, fill in *one* of the blanks with the base form, past tense form, or past participle form of a verb.

Step 2. Exchange textbooks with another student. Without looking at the reference list, fill in the two missing verb forms for each item.

Step 3. Return the book to its owner, who will check your answers.

base	past	past participle
1. _____	_____	_____
2. _____	_____	_____
3. _____	_____	_____

4. _____　　　_____　　　_____

5. _____　　　_____　　　_____

6. _____　　　_____　　　_____

7. _____　　　_____　　　_____

8. _____　　　_____　　　_____

9. _____　　　_____　　　_____

10. _____　　　_____　　　_____

11. _____　　　_____　　　_____

12. _____　　　_____　　　_____

13. _____　　　_____　　　_____

14. _____　　　_____　　　_____

15. _____　　　_____　　　_____

16. _____　　　_____　　　_____

17. _____　　　_____　　　_____

18. _____　　　_____　　　_____

19. _____　　　_____　　　_____

20. _____　　　_____　　　_____

Exercise 4.　　　Repeat exercise 3 on a separate sheet of paper. Because these verb forms are so important to having better English, it is recommended that students quiz each other several times on this topic.

Simple Tenses

Tense	Usage	Example
SIMPLE PRESENT In general, the simple present is used for situations that always or usually exist. The form for simple present tense consists of a verb or **VERB + s** (for **he, she, it**).	(a) a fact that is true now	(a) The U.S. <u>has</u> 50 states. (a) Kaylin <u>speaks</u> six languages.
	(b) a recurring event	(b) The people <u>vote</u> for president every four years.
	(c) state or condition	(c) He <u>seems</u> very angry.
Question: **do/does + subject + VERB** Negative: **don't/doesn't + VERB**	(d) a future action (with a future time word)	(d) The meeting <u>is</u> tomorrow. (d) This plane <u>leaves</u> in an hour.

Tense	*Usage*	*Example*
SIMPLE PAST The simple past is used for an action that happened in the past. The action began and ended in the past. The form consists of **-ed** added the base form of the verb. Question: **did + subject + VERB** Negative: **didn't + VERB**	(a) a completed action (b) an activity that took place regularly in the past (c) a completed condition	(a) I <u>lived</u> in Brownsville in 2000. (b) In the 1990s, I <u>took</u> the bus to work almost every day. (c) The weather <u>was</u> not good yesterday.
SIMPLE FUTURE The simple future expresses an action that will take place in the future. The form for simple future consists of **will + VERB** Question: **will + subject + VERB** Negative: **won't + VERB**	(a) a prediction about a future event (b) a decision at the time of speaking (not planned in advance) (c) an agreement to do something	(a) The price of gasoline <u>will go</u> up. (b) (The phone suddenly rings when you are visiting your friend's house.) "I<u>'ll answer</u> it." (c) If you <u>will go</u> to the store for me, I <u>will cook</u> dinner for us.

Exercise 5. This is an interview between a TV reporter and Dr. Gibson, a famous scientist. Write the correct verb tenses (present, past, future) using the words in parentheses. Use the context to decide if you should use affirmative or negative forms.

TV Reporter: Dr. Gibson, when ❶ _____ (you, begin) your

career as a scientist?

Dr. Gibson: Well, let me see. I'd like to give you a simple, direct answer to your

question, but ❷ _____ (it, be) not so simple.

You see, ❸ _____ (I, be) always good at science

in junior high and high school, but ❹ _____

(I, become) really interested in science when ❺ _____

(I, be) a student at the University of Texas at Brownsville in 1980.

❻ _____ (I, have) a professor ❼ _____

(who, spark) a certain curiosity in me **8** _____

(that, make) me choose a serious career as a scientist.

TV Reporter: So **9** _____ (this teacher, play) an important

part in your decision to become a scientist?

Dr. Gibson: Yes, **10** _____ (that, be) correct. My original

11 _____ (plan, be) to be a teacher, but because

of that professor, **12** _____ (I, change) my career

path. **13** _____ (my parents, want) me to become

a teacher, but to tell you the truth, **14** _____

(I, really, want) to teach. My **15** _____ (goal, be)

to create things, to experiment, to use my hands.

TV Reporter: Many of your current research **16** _____

(reports, deal) with work with animals, so **17** _____

(be, biology) your main area of specialization?

Dr. Gibson: Actually, no. **18** _____ (you, be) correct that

the last two reports that **19** _____ (I, wrote)

20 _____ (be) about research dealing with

animals. However, the reports before those two **21** _____

(have) anything to do with animals.

TV Reporter: Can you tell us anything about your next research report?

Dr. Gibson: There **22** _____ (some things, be) that I cannot

discuss with you right now, but I can tell you that the **23** _____

_____ (report, be publish) in the next issue of *World Science*

Today. **24** _____ (I, be) sure that your

25 _____ (listeners, be) intrigued by this

upcoming research report.

TV Reporter: Well, Dr. Gibson, **26** _____ (I, be) afraid that

27 _____ (we, have) any more time, so

28 _____ (we, be) able to go into any more

details at the current time. Thank you so much for agreeing to be on our

show today.

Dr. Gibson: Thanks, it was my pleasure. I hope that I can come back again some time.

Progressive Tenses*

Tense	Usage	Example
PRESENT PROGRESSIVE Present progressive is used for an action that is happening right now. The form consists of two parts: **am/is/are + VERB + -ing.** Question: **am/is/are + subject + VERB + -ing** Negative: **am not/isn't/ aren't + VERB**	(a) an action that is happening now (b) an action that occurs this week, this month, or this year (c) a future action (with a future time word)	(a) It's <u>raining</u> really hard. (b) I <u>am working</u> at the bank. (c) They <u>are flying</u> to Texas tomorrow.
PAST PROGRESSIVE In general, past progressive is used for an action that began before a second action and that was happening until the second action interrupted. The form is **was/were + VERB + -ing.** Question: **was/were + subject + VERB + -ing** Negative: **wasn't/weren't + VERB**	(a) an action in the past that was interrupted in the past by another action (b) a repeated past action (an activity that took place in the past but for a long time)	(a) I <u>was living</u> in Japan when my mom died. (b) We <u>were planning</u> our wedding for many months.
FUTURE PROGRESSIVE Future progressive describes a longer action that will be happening in relation to another future action. The form is **will be + VERB + -ing.** Question: **will + subject + be + VERB + -ing** Negative: **won't be + VERB + -ing**	An action that begins before another action and will be happening at a point of time in the future.	You <u>will be sleeping</u> when I get off work tonight, so I'm not going to call you up.

*Progressive tenses are also referred to as continuous tenses. Progressive tenses express the idea that an action is in progress during a particular time. Note that verbs of perception do not usually occur in progressive tenses. For example, you cannot say "I'm owning" or "he was believing." (Common verbs that do not usually occur in progressive include *appreciate, believe, belong, care, consist, contain, dislike, doubt, exist, feel, hate, have, hear, know, like, look like, love, matter, mean, need, owe, own, possess, prefer, realize, resemble, seem, smell, sound, want.*)

Exercise 6.   Answer these questions in complete sentences. Pay close attention to the verb tenses.

1. Think of three of your classmates. What are your classmates doing right now?

    _____

    _____

    _____

    _____

    _____

2. What were you doing today before you opened this book?

    _____

    _____

    _____

    _____

    _____

3. Think about an important event in world news such as the attack on the World Trade Center in 2001 or the death of Princess Diana in 1997. What were you doing when you heard the news about this event?

    _____

    _____

    _____

    _____

    _____

4. Try to predict the future. What will you be doing one year from now?

    _____

    _____

    _____

    _____

    _____

Perfect Tenses*

Tense	Usage	Example
PRESENT PERFECT Present perfect is used for several different situations. The form consists of two parts: **have/has + PAST PARTICIPLE.** Question: **have/has + subject + PAST PARTICIPLE★** Negative: **haven't/hasn't + PAST PARTICIPLE★**	(a) an action that happened at a past unspecified time (b) a recent action that is important to the current situation or conversation (c) an action that began in the past but continues in the present (d) repetition of an action before now	(a) *Jo:* I wonder what sushi is like. *Sue:* I've eaten it before. It's pretty good. (a) <u>Have</u> you ever <u>flown</u> on the Concorde? (b) *Ann:* "Wow, it's hot in here." *Liz:* "Well, <u>I've turned</u> on the air conditioner. Just wait a minute." (c) We <u>have been</u> here since noon. (d) <u>I've traveled</u> to Asia many times.
PAST PERFECT Past perfect is used when one action finished before another action. The form is **had + PAST PARTICIPLE.** Question: **had + subject + PAST PARTICIPLE** Negative: **hadn't + PAST PARTICIPLE**	(a) a past action that occurred before another past action or time *Note:* With **before** or **after,** it is not necessary to use past perfect because the order of the actions is obvious.	(a) I <u>had eaten</u> dinner when my mom called. (a) By midnight, we <u>had watched</u> three movies.
FUTURE PERFECT Future perfect describes a future action that will take place before another (future) action. This tense is formed by combining **will have + PAST PARTICIPLE.** Question: **will + subject + have + PAST PARTICIPLE** Negative: **won't have + PAST PARTICIPLE**	(a) a future action that will take place before another particular future action (or time)	(a) By next Friday, we <u>will have finished</u> the first two units in this book. (a) When you reach home tomorrow night, I <u>will have spoken</u> to Jim about the problem.

★The word *perfect* comes from the Latin word *perfectare,* which means to complete. Because the verbs in the perfect tenses are being compared to other verbs, the perfect tense verbs are therefore being compared (in time) to other verbs. Present perfect tense is covered in depth in *Clear Grammar 3,* unit 4. Past perfect tense is covered in depth in this book, *Clear Grammar 4,* unit 2. You use the past perfect when you're writing or talking about two events that happened in the past but you want to indicate that one of them is further in the past than the other.

Exercise 7.   How Well Can You Predict the Future? Use the prompts to write predictions with future perfect tense. For numbers 5 through 8, write original predictions.

1. by the year 2020 / English / become / the first language in every country

_____

2. by the year 2100 / doctors / discover / a cure for AIDS

_____

3. by the time people can live on the moon / people / learn to live under the ocean

_____

4. by next year / McDonald's / add at least one hundred new restaurants

_____

5. _____

6. _____

7. _____

8. _____

Perfect Progressive Tenses

Tense	Usage	Example
PRESENT PERFECT PROGRESSIVE Present perfect progressive is similar to present perfect but has more emphasis on the duration of the action. In some cases, there is very little difference in meaning between these two tenses. The form consists of three parts: **have/has + been + VERB + -ing.** Question: **have/has + subject + been + VERB + ing** Negative: **haven't/hasn't + been + VERB + -ing**	(a) an action that began in the past, has continued into the present, and may continue into the future (with an emphasis on the duration of the action) (b) a general action in progress recently for which no specific time is mentioned (c) an action that began in the past and has just recently ended	(a) "Why are you so late? I have been waiting here for almost an hour." (b) *Ken:* "Wow, your tennis game is really good now!" *Kay:* "I've been practicing a lot recently." (c) *Jim:* "There's green stuff in your hair." *Dan:* "Oh, don't worry. I've been painting my house. It will come out with a little soap and water."

Tense	Usage	Example
PAST PERFECT PROGRESSIVE Past perfect progressive is similar to past perfect but has more emphasis on the duration of the action. This tense consists of three parts: **had + been + VERB + -ing.** Question: **had + subject + been + VERB + -ing** Negative: **hadn't + been + VERB + -ing**	(a) an activity that occurred before another action in the past (with emphasis on the duration) (b) a long action occurring recently before another action in the past	(a) The pilot <u>had been flying</u> the plane for over an hour before he noticed that there was a problem with the engine. (b) *Greg:* "Why didn't you go to the party last night?" *Lisa:* "I was too tired. I <u>had been working</u> all day long."
FUTURE PERFECT PROGRESSIVE Future perfect progressive is similar to future perfect but has more emphasis on the duration of the action. This tense consists of three parts: **will + have + been + VERB + -ing.** Question: **will + subject + have + been + VERB + -ing** Negative: **won't have + been + VERB + -ing**	(a) a long action that is taking place in relation to another future event (with special emphasis on the duration) (b) a long action occurring before another action (or point of time) in the future	(a) By next Friday, we <u>will have been working</u> here five years. (b) *Wes:* "Do you want to go out with us after the party tomorrow night?" *Ben:* "I don't know. By the time of the party, I <u>will have been standing</u> on my feet for eight hours, so I don't know if I'll feel like going to a party or not."

Exercise 8.   Change these verbs in perfect forms to perfect progressive forms.

1. I have studied   I _____

2. she's gotten   she _____

3. they had done   they _____

4. he will have had   he _____

5. you'd written   you _____

6. it will have rained   it _____

7. I've taken   I _____

8. I had flown   I _____

9. I'll have worked   I _____

10. we have stood   we _____

Exercise 9.   Underline the correct verb forms to complete this true story.

In 1984, Bernard McCummings and two other men ❶ (had attacked, attacked, have attacked) and ❷ (had robbed, have robbed, robbed) Jerome Sandusky, a 72-year-old man, in a New York subway station. They ❸ (hit, had hit, will have been hitting) and ❹ (choked, had choked, will have been choking) him and ❺ (pinned, had pinned, will have been pinning) him to the ground. Fortunately for Sandusky, two policemen ❻ (have worked, will have been working, worked, were working) nearby and ❼ (were hearing, will hear, heard, had been hearing) his cries for help. One of the policemen, Manuel Rodriguez, ❽ (shot, has shot, has been shooting) Bernard McCummings as he and the other two men

❾ (have been trying, were trying, try) to escape from the crime scene. One of the bullets ❿ (is hitting, had hit, was hitting, hit) McCummings in the spine, and now he cannot walk. He ⓫ (is, was, had been) paralyzed from the chest down.

New York police guidelines ⓬ (were stating, will state, state, had been stating) that police can only use guns defensively. They cannot be used to stop a fleeing criminal "unless there ⓭ (had been, was, is) probable cause to believe a felon ⓮ (will use, has been using, uses) deadly force."

McCummings ⓯ (pleads, has been pleading, was pleading, pleaded) guilty to the mugging and ⓰ (will serve, will have been serving, served) 32 months in jail. McCummings is not new to the jail system. He ⓱ (had previously spent, had previously been spending, previously spends) two years in prison on another robbery conviction.

McCummings then ⓲ (sued, had sued, had been suing) the government for $4.3 million. He claimed that excessive force ⓳ (will be, were, was) used and this ⓴ (resulted, results, has been resulting) in his being paralyzed.

If you were the judge, what would you do? ㉑ (Was McCummings deserving, Did McCummings deserve, Had McCummings deserved) money from the city? ㉒ (Did the police officers act, Do the police officers act, Were the police officers acting, Had the police officers been acting) wrongly?

[Discuss this with your classmates and then read the judge's decision in exercise 13.]

Adapted from K. Folse and J. Ivone, *First Discussion Starters* (Ann Arbor: University of Michigan Press, 2002).

Exercise 10.   Underline the correct verb form to complete this true story.

In 1991, an Akita dog named Taro ❶ (bites, had bitten, was biting, bit) a young girl on her lip. The girl ❷ (had been, was, will be, will have been) a niece of Taro's owner, so the dog ❸ (had seen, had been seeing, saw, was seeing) the girl before. In 1987, the state of New Jersey passed a new law that said that owners of pit bulls, another breed of dog, ❹ (had, were having, will have) to restrain or control their dogs.

The wound that Taro ❺ (causes, will have caused, caused) was not so serious. However, Taro was found guilty of biting the girl, which was true, and was sentenced to death under this 1987 law.

Brigitte Bardot, the famous French actress who became an international animal rights activist, ❻ (begs, begged, had begged) for the New Jersey state governor to be lenient and not kill Taro. Taro's owner ❼ (will have spent, will have been spending, spent) thousands of dollars on lawyers for the dog. Even the Japanese government ❽ (had been asking, asked, has asked) for leniency and offered to let Taro live in Japan. This is because Akitas ❾ (were, are, had been) a breed that ❿ (will originate, has originated, originated) in Japan.

The man who first ⓫ (has suggested, has been suggesting, suggested) this dog law, Joseph Azzolina, said that Taro should live. He said that the court's decision was "as ridiculous as it is unbelievable, since my law was meant to affect only vicious pit bulls and other dogs that ⓬ (attack, were attacking, had attacked) humans."

If you were the judge, what would you do? ⓭ (Was Taro deserving, Does Taro deserve, Had Taro deserved) to die? ⓮ (Did Taro do, Does Taro do, Was Taro doing, Had Taro been doing) something so wrong that he should be killed?

[Discuss this with your classmates and then read the judge's decision in exercise 14.]

Adapted from K. Folse and J. Ivone, *First Discussion Starters* (Ann Arbor: University of Michigan Press, 2002).

Exercise 11. Fill in the blanks with the correct tenses of the verbs in parentheses to complete these math problems. Then use your math skills to solve each problem. Write your final solution in the boxes.

a. Karen ❶ _____ (take) a trip to Mexico City two months ago. She ❷ _____ (stay) at the Hotel Del Angel for $40 a night. This price ❸ _____ (include) breakfast, but it ❹ _____ (negative include) lunch or dinner. She ❺ _____ (spend) about $10 for each of these meals. The airfare from Miami to Mexico City on United Airlines ❻ _____ (be) $390. She ❼ _____ (take) four tours, and each tour ❽ _____ (cost) her $25. She ❾ _____ (be) there for a total of four full days and nights. How much money

10 _____ (she / spend) for everything? ⌸

b. Mrs. Hanks **11** _____ (invite) five people to come to her house for

dinner tonight. Each person at the table **12** _____ (have) two glasses of

milk. A carton of milk **13** _____ (have) about six glasses of milk in it.

How many cartons **14** _____ (she / need) to buy when she goes to the

store this afternoon? ⌸

c. Mr. and Mrs. Dalton have four children. Each of their children **15** _____

(be) married, and each of their children **16** _____ (have) two children.

Every Christmas the Daltons **17** _____ (buy) presents for all their

children, their sons-in-law, their daughters-in-law, and their grandchildren.

By Christmas, their oldest daughter **18** _____ (give) birth to another

grandchild. How many presents **19** _____ (they / have) to buy this

Christmas? ⌸

d. Jack **20** _____ (live) in Sacramento, California. By 2020, he will have

lived there for thirty years. When **21** _____ (he begin) living in

Sacramento? ⌸

e. Steven **22** _____ (arrive) at the bus stop at ten minutes to one. Right

now he **23** _____ (wait) for the bus for twenty minutes. If he waits until

1:30, he **24** _____ (wait) for forty minutes. What time is it now?

⌸

Problems a., b., and c. adapted from K. Folse, *Beginning Reading Practices* (Ann Arbor:
University of Michigan Press, 1993).

Exercise 12.   Fill in the blanks with the correct tense of the verbs in parentheses to complete this true story.

Today the official language of the United States and most of Canada ❶ _____

_____ (be) English. However, French almost ❷ _____ (become) the

official language because of a war.

The French and Indian War ❸ _____ (be) fought between 1754 and

1763. The name of this war is not accurate because the war was actually between

England and France. The Indians ❹ _____ (fight) on the side of the French.

At this time, France and England ❺ _____ (try) to gain control

of North America. France ❻ _____ (hold) Canada, and England

❼ _____ (hold) part of what ❽ _____ (be) now the United

States. However, France tried to expand its land by moving southward into New York,

Pennsylvania, Ohio, and Virginia. When the French ❾ _____ (build) a fort

on the Ohio River, the residents in Virginia ❿ _____ (send) George

Washington to attack the fort in 1754. However, the French ⓫ _____

(defeat) Washington.

The French, aided by the Indians, ⓬ _____ (outsmart) the English and

⓭ _____ (win) many early battles. Later, the British began to do well

against the French. In the final battle in Quebec, Canada, General Wolfe of England

⓮ _____ (face) General Montcalm from France. Both generals

⓯ _____ (die) in this battle, but the English ⓰ _____ (outlast)

the French and ⓱ _____ (win) the battle. Thus, most of the continent of

North America today ⓲ _____ (have) English culture and

⓳ _____ (speak) the English language.

Adapted from K. Folse, *Intermediate Reading Practices,* rev. ed. (Ann Arbor: University
of Michigan Press, 1993).

Exercise 13.   Underline the correct verb forms to complete the story.

Here ❶ (will be, will have been, was, is) the answer for the case of McCummings
and the police. The case ❷ (was, will be, has been) decided by a jury. The jury found
that McCummings should receive the money because the policeman should not have
fired a gun since there was no probable cause to believe that McCummings ❸ (is,
will be, was, has been) going to use deadly force. He ❹ (is, was, will be) in fact
running away at the time.

The New York City Transit Authority ❺ (does not agree, did not agree, has not
agree) with this decision, so they ❻ (had appealed, have been appealing, appealed) it
to a higher court. The New York State Court of Appeals found that it could not
reverse the decision. The court ❼ (will say, has been saying, was saying, said) that it
"could not avoid what may seem to some to be an unacceptable resolution of the
factual disputes." The court agreed that the Transit Authority had to pay McCummings
4.3 million dollars.

The Transit Authority ❽ (is still not, was still not, has still not been) satisfied and
appealed the case to the U.S. Supreme Court. However, the Supreme Court ❾ (will
have agreed, will be agreeing, will agree, agreed) with the lower courts' decisions and
❿ (ordered, had ordered, had been ordering) the Transit Authority to pay the $4.3
million.

Adapted from K. Folse and J. Ivone, *First Discussion Starters* (Ann Arbor: University of
Michigan Press, 2002).

Exercise 14.   This is the solution to the case of Taro, the dog who bit a young girl.
Underline the correct verb forms to complete the solution.

The result: The dog ❶ (was not, had not been, will not have been) killed.

The real story: Taro was a 115-pound Akita that "scratched" the owner's
niece over the holidays. There were no formal complaints, but when the police heard
about it, they ❷ (entered, enter, were entering, had been entering) the picture. The
girl was not seriously hurt, and it ❸ (had been, was, is, will be, will have been) a

family matter. If Taro had been a vicious dog, the little girl would have been killed. After much controversy, then-governor Christine Whitman ❹ (had released, will have released, has been releasing, released) Taro as property to his owner, but she said that the dog could no longer live in the state of New Jersey. Despite predictions of more Taro terror to come, the dog ❺ (had been living, had lived, lived, was living) out the rest of his uneventful life in upstate New York and ❻ (died, had died, was dying, has been dying) peacefully several years ago. Assemblyman Azzolina, who introduced the first law, later ❼ (revised, will have been revising, had revised) the law to prevent further incidents like this one.

Adapted from K. Folse and J. Ivone, *First Discussion Starters* (Ann Arbor: University of Michigan Press, 2002).

Speaking Activity

Exercise 15.   Speaking Activity

Working with a partner or two, write a dialogue that uses as many verb tenses as possible. Here are some possible situations for the dialogue.

a. A police officer is talking to two drivers who just had a car accident.
b. A teacher is talking to two students who were cheating on a test.
c. Three roommates are talking about moving to a new apartment.

When you finish, practice your dialogue in your small groups. Then the groups should take turns presenting their dialogues to the entire class.

Exercise 16.   Multiple Choice. Circle the letter of the correct answer.

1. Have a good time playing tennis! When you get back here, I _____ your tax papers for you so all you'll have to do is sign them.

    (A) will have finished   (C) will have been finishing

    (B) will finish   (D) have finished

2. During the time that the plane _____ from Boston to Dallas, the pilot did not notice anything strange with the aircraft.

    (A) flies   (C) was flying

    (B) has been flying   (D) has flown

3. The party can be a great success if you _____ your famous cheese sandwiches.

   (A) had made   (C) had been making

   (B) make   (D) will have been making

4. *Karen:* "You've lost a lot of weight."

   Bruce: "Well, _____ doing a lot of exercise lately."

   (A) I'm   (C) I'd been

   (B) I was   (D) I've been

5. When I get off the train, I am sure that my family _____ for me at the station.

   (A) was waiting   (C) will wait

   (B) had been waiting   (D) will be waiting

6. Gina's only trip to Greece was back in 1991. She _____ there before.

   (A) did not go   (C) had not been going

   (B) was not going   (D) had not gone

7. The house _____ for almost fifteen minutes before the fire trucks arrived.

   (A) will have been burning   (C) will burn

   (B) had been burning   (D) burns

8. Much to the happy surprise of many pet shop owners, the preparation, maintenance and enjoyment of freshwater and marine aquariums _____ increasingly popular hobbies in the U.S. so that many families have an aquarium now.

   (A) had been becoming   (C) have become

   (B) were becoming   (D) become

9. "Sir, can you please drive faster? I have to get to the airport as soon as possible. My flight for Turkey _____ in an hour."

   (A) has been leaving   (C) leaves

   (B) will have been leaving   (D) left

10. The Barbie doll, which was introduced in 1959, quickly caught on so that by 1963,

    total sales _____ five million dolls.

    (A) had been reaching   (C) will have reached

    (B) had reached   (D) reached

Exercise 17.   Review Test

Part 1. Complete this true story by filling in the blanks with the correct tense of
          the verbs in parentheses.

    It is common for companies to promote their products by having some sort

of competition with large prizes. For example, a company might have a contest to

see who can come up with the best slogan to promote a certain product. Another

company might ask contestants to write in approximately fifty words why they

❶ _____ (prefer) a particular product.

    Soft-drink companies often have competitions that involve both small amounts

of money and other prizes. However, Pepsi, a leading soft-drink company, recently

❷ _____ (have) a competition with a very rich prize. To participate in

this contest, people ❸ _____ (have) to buy a bottle of Pepsi and look

under the cap on the bottle. Customers could win prizes ranging from a free soft

drink to one million dollars!

Because of this contest, two workers in a health foods store recently had a problem regarding a Pepsi. Judy Richardson bought a Pepsi, which she ❹ _____ _____ (leave) unopened in the refrigerator at work. Sindy Allen, a co-worker who worked the night shift, ❺ _____ (see) the soft drink in the refrigerator and ❻ _____ (decide) to drink it. After opening it, Allen discovered that the bottle cap ❼ _____ (have) the $1,000,000 prize.

Richardson says that the Pepsi was hers and that the million-dollar prize should be hers. Allen says that she found the Pepsi in the refrigerator at work and that there is no way to prove that it is Richardson's drink. She said that she ❽ _____ (clean) the refrigerator when she found the Pepsi and asked if it ❾ _____ (belong) to anyone. Richardson has no receipt for the soft drink. Former co-workers at the store testified that Richardson was practically addicted to Pepsi and that the area where Richardson left the soft drink was the spot where she usually kept her bottles of Pepsi.

Allen offered to split the money with Richardson, but Richardson ❿ _____ _____ (refuse). The winner of this contest would not get a lump sum of $1,000,000 but rather an annual payment of $50,000 for twenty years. The two women went to court when they could not resolve this issue amicably.

So what happened in court? The judge listened to both sides and eventually agreed that Richardson should get the money. How does the judge's decision compare with what you would have done in this case?

From K. Folse and J. Ivone, *More Discussion Starters* (Ann Arbor: University of Michigan Press, 2002).

Part 2.   Read each sentence and look at the underlined verbs. If the verbs are correct, circle the word *correct.* If they are wrong, circle the word *wrong* and write the correct forms above the verbs.

correct   wrong   1. Medical science <u>sees</u> an amazing number of new innovations.

correct   wrong   2. One of the most promising <u>involves</u> our chromosomes.

correct   wrong   3. The chromosomes that control our hair color, our height, and our
                        likelihood to develop certain diseases <u>had been identified</u>.

correct   wrong   4. Scientists can alter some of these chromosomes already and <u>will be</u>

able to do so for many others in the near future.

correct   wrong   5. By the beginning of the next century, scientists <u>will</u> probably <u>have</u>

<u>discovered</u> an incredible number of innovations involving

chromosomes.

Extra Writing Practice

Situation: Look at one of the court cases presented in this unit. These are found in exercises 9, 10, and 17. Write a summary of the case and then write your own verdict (as if you were the judge). Double space your writing. Underline at least fifteen of the verbs and write the name of the verb tenses next to them. This will allow the teacher to easily see what you are trying to practice.

Unit 12

Review of Book 4

1. past perfect
2. word forms
3. conditionals
4. adverb clauses
5. noun clauses
6. reduction of adjective and adverb clauses
7. past modals
8. subject-verb agreement
9. prepositions
10. verb tense review

Exercise 1. Past Perfect. Combine the statements using the given time phrases. Change any verbs necessary. Follow the example.

1. How romantic! Nick got down on one knee and proposed to her. Amanda said, "Yes." (after)

   How romantic! Amanda said "yes" after Nick had gotten down on one knee and proposed to her.

216

2. What luck! Khalid was offered a full-time teaching job at Jackson High School. He accepted a part-time one at King High School. (after)

   _____

   _____

3. This is par for the course! I knew it. I gained 15 pounds over the holidays. (before)

   _____

   _____

4. It was the oddest thing! The orchestra was playing. Suddenly, the conductor left the stage. (when)

   _____

   _____

5. It happened again! Brian finished his project. It was too late to go to the movies. (by the time)

   _____

   _____

6. I've never told anyone this! I lived in the U.S. for eight months. I started taking English classes. (before)

   _____

   _____

7. I couldn't believe it! The department store sale ended. I finally found some time to go to the mall. (when)

   _____

   _____

8. What a disappointment! We finished biking all the way to the yacht club. The regatta ended. (by the time)

   _____

   _____

9. What luck! Leslie and Scott just bought their house. Construction began on a six-lane highway two blocks away. (when)

   _____

   _____

10. This is interesting! New elections were held. The government was in power for three months. (after)

_____

_____

11. How sad! She realized it was a scam. The thieves took her life savings. (by the time)

_____

_____

12. This is almost unheard of today! My dad worked for the same retail company for 40 years. He retired in 1997. (when)

_____

_____

Exercise 2.   Word Forms. Match the word with an appropriate ending and write a sentence. Follow the example.

–able	–ance	–en	–ish	–ity	–ness
–al	–ate	–ify	–ism	–ly	–ous

1. light _+ -en = lighten   Painting the walls white will lighten up a dark room._

2. alien _____

3. null _____

4. fool _____

5. child _____

6. danger _____

7. quick _____

8. do _____

9. professional _____

10. selfish _____

11. regular _____

12. attend _____

13. live _____

Exercise 3. Conditionals. Last week, someone stole all four wheels from Brenda and Ron's brand new car. It happened one night while they were sleeping. Brenda told her friends about it and warned them to take precautions to protect their own cars. Read what she said and fill in the blanks with the correct form of the verbs.

"We still can't believe this happened while we were sleeping. If we ❶ _____

_____ (sleeping, not), we ❷ _____ (might,

hear) something. If we ❸ _____ (heard) a noise, we

❹ _____ (called) the police right away. I wish they

❺ _____ (catch) the thieves. ❻ _____

we _____ (have) wheel locks on the car, this never

❼ _____ (happen). If I ❽ _____

(be) you, I ❾ _____ (put) wheel locks on my car. You

know, this wasn't an emergency, so I didn't call 911. If you ❿ _____

(call) 911, the police ⓫ _____ (respond) right away. They

⓬ _____ (catch) the thieves if they ⓭ _____

_____ (leave) clues behind. If thieves ⓮ _____

(wear) gloves, though, they ⓯ _____ (leave, not)

fingerprints. That's what happened in our case—they wore gloves. If we

⓰ _____ (report, not) the theft, we ⓱ _____

never _____ (have) a chance of getting our stolen property back. If they

18 _____ (catch) the thieves, I **19** _____

(feel) so much better. I worry they might still try to come back."

Exercise 4.   Adverb Clauses. Complete the following sentences. Follow the example. After you have finished, share your sentences with a classmate.

1. Since _you live closer to the mall than I do,_ why don't I pick you up on

    the way?

2. Because _____ , he was offered the job.

3. We've decided to go skiing even though _____ .

4. There's no sense in buying a new computer until _____ .

5. Whenever _____ , I start to cry.

6. The instructor prefers multiple choice tests, whereas _____ .

7. Even if you paid me, _____ .

8. They celebrated their 25th wedding anniversary in the city where _____ .

9. What's wrong? You look as though _____ .

10. Unless _____ , the farmers will lose all their crops this season.

11. After _____ , we can head home.

Exercise 5.   Noun Clauses. Read the questions. Then complete the responses to form correct noun clauses. Follow the example.

1. Is this the right answer to question 6? I don't know _if that's the right answer_ .

2. Did they make it to the airport in time? I wonder _____ .

3. How on earth did you do that? You have to tell me _____ .

4. Does she work full time for Microsoft? I have no idea _____ .

5. Who took the last brownie? She's asking _____ .

6. Will she be moving to Seattle with her family? Do we know _____ ?

7. Will Carlos be laid off next month? She doesn't know _____ .

8. Where in Salt Lake City does she work? Do you know _____ ?

9. Will my students enjoy this particular lesson? I'm not sure _____ .

10. When is the final exam for this course scheduled? Could you tell me _____ ?

11. Has this team ever made it to the play-offs? I doubt _____ .

12. Did we need more homework this weekend? Who asked _____ ?

Exercise 6.   Reduction of Adjective and Adverb Clauses. Read the sentences below and reduce the adjective and adverb clauses wherever possible. Make changes in the sentence as necessary. Follow the example.

1. The car that is parked behind yours is mine.

   The car parked behind yours is mine.

2. Those students who qualify for scholarships must attend Monday's orientation meeting.

   _____

3. Although the car is in our price range, it lacks the options we want.

   _____

4. Only employees whom the supervisor recommends receive quality-service awards.

   _____

5. I can't believe I fell asleep while I was watching the news last night.

   _____

6. Students who take risks with the language often make the most progress.

   _____

7. I can't stand movies that contain scenes of extreme violence.

   _____

8. When you're working at a job you enjoy, time seems to fly by!

   _____

9. While I was walking home from the movie, my wallet fell out of my pocket.

   _____

10. Tallahassee, which is the capital of Florida, is halfway between St. Augustine and Pensacola, which were once the capitals of East and West Florida, respectively.

_____

11. Music videos that are targeted to teenagers don't sell as well in small towns as they do in big cities.

_____

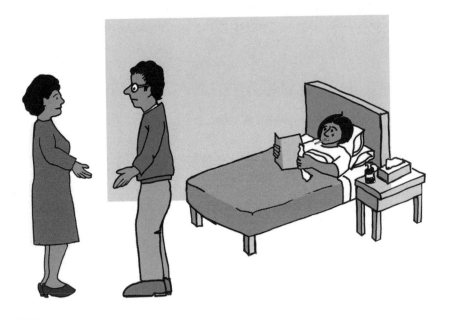

Exercise 7.   Past Modals. Underline the correct modal.

1. *Pat:*   Did you know that Jane was sick three days last week? At first, she thought it

     (might, should) have been a case of food poisoning, but it (would, could)

     have been the flu.

2. *Dale:*   (Could she have seen, Was she able to see) the doctor?

3. *Pat:*   She (could be, was) going to go on Thursday, but she felt better by then.

4. *Dale:*   Well, the doctor (might, must) have been able to give her something.

5. *Pat:*   She stayed home from work and drank lots of water and juice. I remember

     when I was a child and had the flu, my mom (had, used) to give me ginger

     ale to drink. It (would, ought to) make me feel better.

6. *Dale:*   I know. My mom did that, too. Poor Jane. She (had to, should) have felt just

     awful. If I had known she wasn't feeling well, I (was going to take, would

     have taken) her something.

7. *Pat:*   You know Jane. She (should, had to) have called, but she didn't want to

            bother anyone.

8. *Dale:*   Well, she still (ought, had) to have called. I (may, would) have gone over to

            take care of her. It (would, wouldn't) have been any trouble. She (may, must)

            have been miserable.

9. *Pat:*   She was. In fact, she (had, was supposed) to meet me for lunch on Friday, but

            she still wasn't feeling well, so she canceled. I called her this morning,

            though, and she's feeling much better.

Exercise 8.   Subject-Verb Agreement. Read the sentences and underline the verb that agrees with its subject.

1. By the end of the term, each of the students (has, have) to turn in a 15-page research paper.

2. The shrub that I transplanted from the back of the house to the front near my roses (is, are) beginning to sprout new leaves.

3. I can't make up my mind. There (is, are) a dozen new CDs to choose from.

4. What a deal! A dozen disposable pens (cost, costs) just $.89 at the office supply store.

5. A number of students (were, was) unable to access the university library Web site over the weekend. As a result, their homework (were, was) turned in late.

6. My mom, along with two of my sisters, (plan, plans) to visit me over spring break in March.

7. For some reason, politics (interest, interests) me more now than when I was in my 20s.

8. The police (works, work) hard to prevent crime in the community from escalating.

9. Lining the walkway near the university plaza (is, are) dozens of tall royal palm trees.

10. The number of shopping malls within a five-mile radius of my house (have, has) increased dramatically over the past two years. Everyone (say, says) so.

11. Neither of the young men (want, wants) to admit any wrongdoing. Both (feel, feels) it's the other's fault.

12. One of the people I met at the educational conference I attended last month (lives, live) in North Dakota.

Photos courtesy Don Ward

Exercise 9. Prepositions. Read the story about Nina's plans to visit Washington, D.C., and fill in the blanks with the correct prepositions.

I've never been ❶ _____ Washington, D.C. I'm looking forward ❷ _____ going there ❸ _____ vacation. I'm excited ❹ _____ visiting all of the monuments and museums. I'm especially interested ❺ _____ seeing the Capitol and the White House! Perhaps I'll get a glimpse of the president while I'm ❻ _____ the White House. I'll be flying ❼ _____ Washington, D.C., and then renting a car. I've already bought a map of the area so I can become familiar ❽ _____ the streets. I've heard that driving there can be an adventure, and I don't want to get confused ❾ _____ where I'm going and end up lost!

I've also heard that it's expensive to stay ❿ _____ Washington, D.C., and I'm a little worried ⓫ _____ spending too much money while I'm there. I've spoken ⓬ _____ the cost ⓭ _____ people who have been there, and what they say agrees ⓮ _____ what I've heard.

I have a long list of places to visit: the Smithsonian ⓯ _____ its 13 museums and galleries, the Vietnam Veterans Memorial designed ⓰ _____ Maya Lin, and the Lincoln Memorial. . . . I borrowed some books on tape ⓱ _____ the city and its history ⓲ _____ the library, and I've listened ⓳ _____ three of them so far.

When I get back, you can count ⓴ _____ getting a detailed report from me!

Photo courtesy Dale Radak

Exercise 10.   Verb Tense Review. Read the passage about a cultural experience, the U.S. county fair, and fill in the blanks with the correct form of the verb given.

    Every year the county fair ❶ _____ (come) to our small Midwestern town. It ❷ _____ (be) a wonderful event, offering a midway, carnival rides, livestock shows, and music. Last year they even ❸ _____ (have) a horse pull at the fair. A horse pull ❹ _____ (be) a contest to see which horse can pull the most weight piled on a sled hitched to the horse.

    County fairs ❺ _____ (be) a part of U.S. culture for many, many years. At the fair, children ❻ _____ (show) the animals they ❼ _____ (raise) during the past year. People ❽ _____ (display) their homemade pies, cakes, and jams as well as canned fruit and vegetables. Judges ❾ _____ (taste) the items and ❿ _____ (award) ribbons as prizes. If you ⓫ _____ (win) first place, you ⓬ _____ (receive) a blue ribbon.

You **13** _____ (come) to our county fair last year! The county **14** _____ (plan) for a large turnout, and lots of people **15** _____ (show) up. People **16** _____ (be) everywhere! People **17** _____ (walk) up and down the midway, **18** _____ (eat) corn dogs, candied apples, and cotton candy. Children **19** _____ (beg) their parents to let them go on rides. People **20** _____ (throw) balls at wooden bottles. If they **21** _____ (knock) all the bottles over, they **22** _____ (win) a prize, usually a stuffed animal.

In the Midwest, fairs **23** _____ (take) place in the summer. If it **24** _____ (be) too late for you to go to the fair this year, next year there **25** _____ (be) another one. You **26** _____ (have) to come and **27** _____ (experience) it. There **28** _____ (be) nothing else like it!

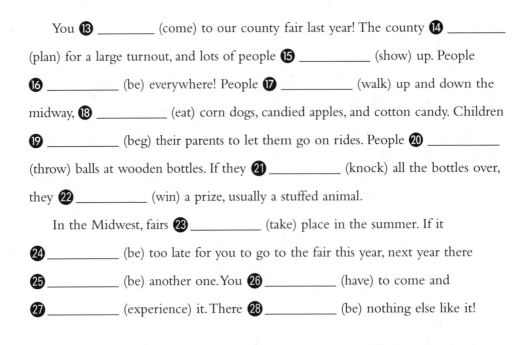

Situation: You have reached the final exercise in the final unit of your grammar book. To get to this point, you have had to learn, study, and practice a lot of rules. Your final activity is to develop a paragraph about all the rules you have learned and used. First, look at the table of contents in this book and choose a variety of grammatical structures. Then, write a sentence about each structure using that structure. For example, if you chose the past perfect, you could write, "I <u>had never used</u> past perfect tense before I studied it in unit 2." Here is an example sentence you could write for word forms, "It was important to <u>memorize</u> the meaning of word forms in order to increase my vocabulary." Underline the grammar point you use so your teacher can see what you are trying to practice.

Answer Key

Unit 1

Ex. 1, p. 1: 1. it up 2. up/back 3. out 4. it in
5. out 6. through 7. across 8. on it 9. through
/over it 10. it out

Ex. 2, p. 3: 1. I 2. F 3. G 4. H 5. D 6. J 7. B
8. E 9. C 10. A

Ex. 3, p. 3: Answers will vary.

Ex. 4, p. 4: 1. they weren't. They were sleeping . . .
2. they weren't. They thought . . . was
getting . . . 3. she wasn't. She was leading . . .
4. she wasn't. She was eating . . . 5. they
weren't. They were asking . . . 6. he wasn't.
He was researching . . .

Ex. 5, p. 5: 1. become 2. forgot 3. bring 4. read
5. wear 6. ran 7. grown 8. say 9. slept
10. drawn

Challenge, p. 6: am, is, are, was, were, been, being

Ex. 6, p. 6: 1. warm 2. famous 3. humorously
4. hardly 5. well 6. quickly 7. suddenly
8. scientifically

Ex. 7, p. 7: look for, approve of, think of, speak to,
ask them for, talked to/with, consist of, forgot
about, concentrate on, thanks for

Ex. 8, p. 7: 1. used to tell 2. was used to talking 3.
used to seeing 4. used to read 5. is used to
seeing 6. used to wait 7. used to waste 8.
used to leave 9. is used to being

Ex. 9, p. 8: Answers may vary. Possible answers:
1. was curious about, were excited about, were
worried about, be confused about 2. were
afraid of (OR were scared of), were aware of,
were afraid of (OR were scared of), were . . .
proud of 3. was only related to, were similar
to, were not relevant to, are accustomed to,
would have been harmful to 4. satisfied
with, was impressed with, was too familiar
with, was bored with, was finished with, was
fed up with

Ex. 10, p. 9: 1. Cloning is researched at the
Roslin Institute in Scotland. 2. Drugs for
human use are being developed. 3. For many
years, animals have been used in research.
4. Dolly was cloned by Dr. Wilmut from the
udder cells of a ewe. (OR Dolly was cloned
from the udder cells of a ewe by Dr.
Wilmut). 5. Adult cells rather than embryonic
cells were being experimented with. 6. A
scientific milestone had been achieved by Dr.
Wilmut and his team when Dolly was

born. 7. A new frontier for the science of
medicine is going to be opened. 8. Because
of these experiments, cures for widespread
diseases might be expected. (OR Cures for
widespread diseases might be expected
because of these experiments.) 9. A remedy
for the common cold could be found.
10. Questions about ethics should be
considered. 11. Human life has to be
prolonged.

Ex. 11, p. 11: Answers will vary.

Ex. 12, p. 11: 1. interested 2. confusing 3. shocking
4. amazed 5. astonishing 6. fascinating
7. frightening 8. satisfying 9. satisfied

Ex. 13, p. 12: 1. Who's (who is) 2. correct
3. whose 4. correct 5. . . . were taken
6. . . . sheep, which was 7. . . . birth were not
aware 8. whose 9. . . . person who
10. . . . which was kept

Ex. 14, p. 12: 1. to cite 2. leaving 3. to use 4. to
write 5. asking 6. to cite 7. to know 8. to
look 9. reading 10. searching 11. going
12. seeing

Ex. 15, p. 13: 1. him to search 2. said, "Look
. . . 3. him to browse 4. to find 5. expect not
to use 6. urged him to use 7. allowed him to
write 8. should have told her 9. to write
10. to look . . . to cite

Ex. 16, p. 14: Answers will vary.

Ex. 17, p. 14: Answers will vary. Possible answers:
1. to search for sources, in order to search for
sources, for sources 2. to ask for help, in order
to ask for help, for help 3. to get information,
in order to get information, for information
4. to experiment, in order to experiment, for
experimentation 5. to keep Dolly safe, in
order to keep Dolly safe, for safety

Ex. 18, p. 15: 1. Dolly Parton is famous, and so is
Dolly, the sheep (OR and Dolly, the sheep, is
too). 2. Dolly Parton does not live in
England, and neither does Dolly, the sheep
(OR and Dolly, the sheep, doesn't either).
3. The Roslin Institute has become well
known because of its cloning experiment, and
so has the MA biotech firm (OR and the MA
biotech firm has too). 4. Dr. Wilmut was not
present for Dolly's birth, and neither was Dr.
Campbell (OR and Dr. Campbell wasn't
either). 5. Dolly had a fear of humans, and so

did the other sheep in the pens (OR and the other sheep did too).

Ex. 19, p. 16: 1. sheep; however, 2. cells; therefore, 3. medicine, so now . . . 4. secret so 5. sheep, but

Ex. 20, p. 16: 1. said . . . to 2. mention . . . to 3. announced . . . to 4. explained/described . . . to 5. repeated . . . to 6. do . . . for 7. open . . . for 8. close . . . for 9. prescribed . . . for 10. changed . . . for

Ex. 21, p. 17: 1. The librarian wished the student good luck. 2. He saved himself a lot of time. 3. He asked his mother a question. 4. The librarian charged him money for an overdue book. 5. It cost him more money than expected.

Ex. 22, p. 17: 1. Dr. Wilmut gave a different pen to Dolly. 2. Dr. Wilmut did a favor for Dolly. 3. He wrote Dolly a dedication in his book. 4. Visitors bought treats for Dolly. 5. They would pass Dolly the treats through the fence.

Challenge, p. 18: Internet, books, magazines, newspapers, journals, interviews, surveys

Unit 2

Challenge, p. 21: The question is about the subject (*who* and *what*) in items 3 and 4; therefore, the subject does not separate the auxiliary *had* and past participle.

Ex. 1, p. 21: had fallen, had fallen, had fallen, had fallen, had closed, had closed, had closed, had closed

Ex. 2, p. 21: 1. When had Linda made her Christmas candy? 2. How many times had Kumiko seen the movie before she read the book? 3. Where had Miki lived before she moved to Tampa? 4. How long had Serhat spent working on his project before it was completed? 5. What had Caroline studied before she got her MBA? 6. Who had eaten all of the cake before Amna came home? 7. What had Mindo read by the end of the semester?

Ex. 3, p. 22: had been sleeping, had been sitting, had been living, had been crying, had been listening, had been planning, had been writing, had been eating

Ex. 4, p. 23: 1. When Mom came in the door, she knew that the kids hadn't been napping. 2. I went skiing yesterday, but I hadn't been on skis since 1994. 3. Dave and Linda hadn't been dating very long when they got married. 4. Brenda told the veterinarian that her cat hadn't eaten for several days. 5. On his way to work, Ray suddenly remembered that he hadn't turned off the coffeemaker. 6. Where

hadn't Marshall traveled before he got married? He is a world traveler.

Ex. 5, p. 24: 1. B 2. B 3. C 4. B 5. B 6. A

Ex. 6, p. 24: 1. Gary had photographed the whale before it dove under the water. 2. The children had already eaten when their father came home. 3. The girls were tired because they had been dancing all morning. 4. The baby had been sick for two days, so Kerri and John decided to stay home. 5. Sally had never used the Internet until John taught her how. 6. I had read the entire trilogy by the time my vacation ended. 7. John Grisham hadn't even written the final chapter when the publisher began to advertise the book. 8. The printing press had been used in China before Gutenberg invented movable type. 9. Susan B. Anthony had taught school before she joined the struggle for women's rights in 1848. 10. Susan B. Anthony had died by the time women received the right to vote in 1920.

Ex. 7, p. 25: 2. he doesn't work, he worked, he didn't work, he had worked, he hadn't worked 3. we don't go, we went, we didn't go, we had gone, we hadn't gone 4. they aren't, they were, they weren't, they had been, they hadn't been 5. they don't live, they lived, they didn't live, they had lived, they hadn't lived 6. you don't have, you had, you didn't have, you had had, you hadn't had 7. it doesn't take, it took, it didn't take, it had taken, it hadn't taken 8. she doesn't have, she had, she didn't have, she had had, she hadn't had 9. I don't see, I saw, I didn't see, I had seen, I hadn't seen 10. you don't do, you did, you didn't do, you had done, you hadn't done

Ex. 8, p. 26: Answers will vary.

Ex. 9, p. 26: 1. got 2. had requested 3. began 4. had been 5. had stood 6. was 7. knew 8. had happened 9. lived 10. never came back 11. had given 12. left 13. had told 14. needed 15. flew

Challenge, p. 28: With the use of the prepositions *before* and *after,* the time relationship between the two actions is made clear. Therefore, the use of simple past has the same meaning as the past perfect.

Ex. 10, p. 28: a. 1. held 2. had been 3. had won 4. turned 5. began 6. had split up. b. 7. Had Julia Roberts ever received 8. starred 9. had had. c. 10. Did you enjoy 11. never heard 12. had been working 13. began 14. had written 15. he worked

Ex. 11, p. 29: 1. B 2. D 3. A 4. C 5. D 6. D 7. B 8. A

Ex. 12, p. 31: Part 1. 1. came 2. is 3. had gone/ went 4. bought 5. got 6. had never bought

7. chose 8. was making 9. started 10. had cooked (OR had been cooking) 11. called 12. were (OR were going to be) (OR would be) 13. was 14. have known 15. invited (past participle without the have) (OR have invited) (OR had invited) 16. had not canceled 17. did not attend 18. turned 19. had 20. had known; Part 2. 1. wrong; change *How long have* to *How long had* 2. wrong; change *had been struggled* to *had been struggling* or *had struggled* 3. wrong; change *had chased* to *had the cheetah chased* 4. correct 5. wrong; change *had landed in* to *landed in* 6. wrong; change *had never saw* to *had never seen* 7. wrong; change *they had been traveling* to *had they been traveling* 8. change *had changed* to *changed*

Unit 3

Ex. 1, p. 34: 1. classify 2. diversify 3. finalize 4. alienate 5. lighten 6. clarify 7. idealize 8. differentiate

Ex. 2, p. 36: 1. sensible 2. perilous 3. classical 4. accurate 5. violent 6. monotonous 7. stylish 8. helpful/helpless

Challenge, p. 36: An *-ing* participial adjective describes the person or thing that makes the action. An *-ed* participial adjective describes the person or thing that receives the action. An *-able* adjective neither makes action nor receives action, but rather it *has* the quality of the verb. Consider the meaning of a comforting chair, a comforted chair, or a comfortable chair. A chair cannot actively give comfort, nor can it receive comfort.

Ex. 3, p. 37: 1. quickly 2. suddenly 3. carefully 4. optionally 5. humbly 6. impulsively 7. heavily 8. constantly

Ex. 4, p. 38: There may be other answers possible. 1. investor 2. conformity 3. impression 4. confidence 5. personality 6. mprovement 7. integration 8. composition

Ex. 5, p. 38: 1. noun 2. verb 3. noun 4. adj 5. noun 6. adj 7. adv 8. adj 9. adv

Ex. 6, p. 39: 1. flexibility 2. reversible 3. denial 4. Victorian 5. darken 6. clarify 7. regularity 8. slowly 9. faithfulness 10. sanitize

Ex. 7, p. 39: Answers will vary.

Ex. 8, p. 40: 1. correct 2. wrong; change *accuracy* to *accurate* 3. wrong; change *preferentially* to *preferential* 4. correct 5. wrong; change *prosecute* to *prosecutor* 6. wrong; change *Politics* to *Political* 7. wrong; change *attraction* to *attractive*

Ex. 9, p. 41:

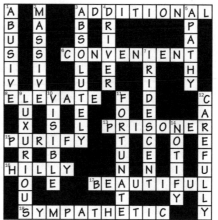

Ex. 10, p. 43: 1. depression 2. regularly 3. confidence 4. hastily 5. realistic 6. slowly 7. enjoyable 8. variety 9. diversify 10. individualize

Ex. 11, p. 43: 1. regression 2. compassionate 3. virtually 4. submission 5. resident 6. appear 7. lovely 8. attribute 9. originate 10. extend

Ex. 12, p. 44: 1. B 2. A 3. A 4. D 5. B 6. D 7. D 8. C 9. A 10. D

Ex. 13, p. 45: Part 1. 1. A 2. A 3. B 4. A 5. A 6. C 7. C 8. B 9. C 10. C; Part 2. 1. recognize 2. correct 3. limited 4. infer 5. able 6. full 7. correct 8. knowledge 9. severely 10. sufficient

Unit 4

Ex. 1, p. 52: 1. spend 2. are 3. rains 4. rakes 5. get 6. will enjoy 7. doesn't put in 8. doesn't rain 9. should ask

Ex. 2, p. 52: 1. If today is Monday, tomorrow is Tuesday. 2. If there are 24 hours in a day, there are 168 hours in a week. 3. If it's summer north of the equator, it's winter south of the equator. 4. If I have free time in the evening, I will/am going to/may/might/can visit you tomorrow. 5. If they vacation in Florida in February, they can eat fresh strawberries. 6. You'll be sorry if you pass up the opportunity this time. 7. He'll get a ticket if the parking meter expires. 8. They won't/aren't going to/may not come if they don't get a personal invitation. 9. He'll star in a movie if the price is right.

Ex. 3, p. 54: 1. If I were you 2. if she truly loved him 3. if she postponed the exam on conditionals 4. If they hurried up 5. If he had the time 6. if I asked you 7. if it didn't star what's-her-name 8. If my VCR worked

Ex. 4, p. 54: 1. weren't 2. would be 3. didn't like 4. would jump 5. stayed 6. would be 7. were 8. would accept 9. were 10. could commute 11. would feel 12. came 13. wouldn't like 14. saw 15. took 16. would have 17. would feel 18. would be 19. meant 20. could/would be 21. weren't 22. wouldn't have

Ex. 5, p. 55: Answers will vary.

Ex. 6, p. 56: Answers will vary.

Ex. 7, p. 57: 1. had seen, would have known 2. would have been, had not missed 3. Would you have gone, had not had 4. would have helped, had asked 5. could/would not have run, had not trained 6. had not invented, would have done 7. had followed, would not have been 8. Could/Would, have avoided, had paid 9. would not have recognized, had not heard

Ex. 8, p. 58: Part 1. 1. I didn't see the paper, so I didn't know about the sale at Macy's. 2. She wasn't on time because she had missed the bus. 3. You didn't go to Daniel's party because you had to work overtime. 4. I didn't help you because you didn't ask me. 5. He ran in the Boston Marathon because he had trained so rigorously for it. 6. Orville and Wilbur Wright invented the airplane, so no one else did. 7. They didn't follow their parents' advice, so Ray and Lisa were in a fix. 8. They didn't/couldn't avoid the fee because they had paid the bill by credit card instead of by check. 9. I recognized you because I heard your voice. Part 2. 1. If I had been hungry, I would have eaten. 2. If he had felt well, he wouldn't have stayed home. 3. If he hadn't retired from his job early, he wouldn't have been able to travel to exotic places. 4. If she had been at home, she would have gotten the package UPS tried to deliver. 5. They wouldn't have skipped the concert if tickets hadn't been outrageously expensive. Part 3. Answers will vary.

Ex. 9, p. 59: Answers will vary.

Ex. 10, p. 59: 1. Had they been able to afford it, they would have bought the car. 2. Cannot invert 3. Were Elaine a true friend, she'd stand by you no matter what. 4. Should any new job openings become available, please let me know. 5. Cannot invert. 6. Cannot invert. 7. Had IBM offered Kari a job anywhere but Chicago, she'd have taken it. 8. Had they grown up in the 1950s, they would know what a hula hoop is. 9. Were she not allergic to them, Dharma would send Smriti roses.

Ex. 11, p. 60: 1. weren't studying, would turn on 2. were snowing, could/would build 3. had been paying, could answer 4. had asked, wouldn't be 5. wouldn't have signed, were

6. hadn't been talking, would/could have understood 7. were, would not have stopped 8. would have been, had been smiling 9. hadn't eaten, wouldn't be

Ex. 12, p. 62: 1. could 2. could call 3. were 4. would 5. knew 6. watched 7. had known 8. had come, had not interrupted 9. had remembered

Ex. 13, p. 62: 1. were 2. could go 3. had studied 4. had listened 5. had enrolled 6. did 7. knew 8. could be 9. would give 10. had listened

Ex. 14, p. 63: 1. C 2. B 3. C 4. B 5. D 6. B 7. B 8. C

Ex. 15, p. 64: Part 1. 1. pours 2. walk 3. grew 4. were 5. had not invented, couldn't OR wouldn't drink OR wouldn't be drinking 6. had been living, would have been 7. were 8. Had not studied, wouldn't know; Part 2. 1. correct 2. correct 3. I volunteered 4. correct 5. If we had bought 6. Had you not been 7. If I weren't taking 8. I had understood 9. correct 10. correct

Unit 5

Ex. 1, p. 68: put commas after the underlined clause in numbers 3, 5, 8, 9, 10; numbers 2, 4, 6, 7 do not have a comma

Ex. 2, p. 70: 1. since 2. While 3. As soon as 4. before 5. till 6. After 7. by the time 8. By the time 9. while 10. whenever

Ex. 3, p. 71: Answers will vary.

Ex. 4, p. 73:

1. *she the* is incorrect; add *is* after *she.* The clause needs to have a verb.

2. *has* is incorrect; change *has* to *is.* The correct verb here should be *is,* from the verb *to be.*

3. *In spite* is incorrect; add *of* after *spite.* We always use *of* with *in spite.*

4. *Even she* is incorrect; add *though* after *Even.* You can use *though* alone or with *even* (even though), but you cannot have the word *even* alone.

5. *brown. Her* is incorrect; change the period to a comma and the upper-case *H* to a lower-case *h.* The expression *despite the fact that +* SUBJECT + VERB is not a complete sentence but rather a fragment. In this case, it can be corrected by connecting it with the following independent clause: Her name is Cocoa.

6. *Although* in addition to *but* is incorrect; cross out *Although* (OR *but*). You cannot have *although* and *but* in the same sentence.

Ex. 5, p. 74: Answers will vary.

Ex. 6, p. 75:

1. *If is* is incorrect; add *it* before *is.* Every verb needs a subject.

2. *no* is incorrect; change *no* to *not*. The correct expression is *whether or not*.

3. *Whether* is incorrect; change *Whether* to *If*. Do not confuse *if* and *whether*.

4. *Even it* is incorrect; add *if* after *even*. *Even* is not a connector, so you want to use *even if* here.

5. *you outdoors* is incorrect; add *are* after *you*. Every clause needs a verb.

6. *Thus* is incorrect; change *Thus* to *However*. However is used for contrasts.

7. *an* is incorrect; change *an* to *the*. *In the event* is a set phrase.

8. *if only* is incorrect; reverse the word order to *only if*. *Only if* is the correct word order in this connector.

9. *are you* is incorrect; reverse the word order to *you are*. After *if*, you need a subject and verb in that order.

10. *not* is incorrect; nothing else is needed here. *Unless* expresses a negative idea already, so you do not need to use a negative verb here after *unless*.

11. *even* is incorrect; add *if* (OR *though*). *Even* alone is not a connector.

12. *that provided* is incorrect; reverse the word order. The correct word order is *provided that*.

Ex. 7, p. 77: 1. wherever 2. where 3. wherever 4. where 5. anywhere

Ex. 8, p. 79: 1. such a 2. so 3. so 4. such a 5. such 6. such 7. so 8. such 9. so 10. such a

Ex. 9, p. 80: 1. James Naismith, the inventor of basketball, is not such a well-known person. 2. Michael Jordan is such a good basketball player. 3. Those tickets are so expensive. 4. Playing basketball well is so difficult. (OR It's so difficult to play basketball well.) 5. His hands were so big that he could balance two basketballs on one hand. 6. The U.S. and Russian Olympic hockey teams are such good teams that they often win the gold or silver medals.

Ex. 10, p. 81: 1. I 2. D 3. H 4. F 5. C 6. E 7. B 8. G 9. A 10. J

Ex. 11, p. 82: 1. were 2. had never seen 3. knew 4. were 5. were 6. knew 7. had seen 8. had

Ex. 12, p. 83: Answers will vary. (In general, check to make sure that every sentence with *in that* is followed by a subject and a verb.)

Ex. 13, p. 84: Answers will vary.

Ex. 14, p. 86: 1. B 2. B 3. D 4. D 5. D 6. C 7. A 8. A 9. C 10. A

Ex. 15, p. 88: Part 1. 1. because 2. such, even though 3. Whenever 4. while 5. Though, because 6. The 7. whether or not 8. Despite; Part 2. 1. wrong; change *Whenever that* to *Whenever* 2. wrong; change *will end* to *ends* 3. wrong; change *Giving* to *Given* 4. wrong; change *paychecks so* to *paychecks, so* 5. wrong;

change *Even* to *Even if* 6. wrong; omit *a* 7. wrong; change *Although the* to *The*.

Unit 6

Ex. 1, p. 92: 1. that she could finish her education in the U.S. 2. where she wants to study 3. Where she wants to study 4. that I misunderstood you 5. whether she can save enough money

Ex. 2, p. 93: 1. Mario remembers that Mt. Etna erupted in July 2000. 2. Scientists estimated that the lava on Mr. Etna flowed at a rate of 50 meters per hour. 3. Yesterday the children learned that penguins are birds that cannot fly. 4. I have heard that penguins can swim underwater at a speed of 15 miles per hour. 5. It is a fact that one mile equals approximately 1.6 kilometers. 6. Using this conversion we can determine that penguins can swim underwater at 24 kilometers per hour.

Ex. 3, p. 94:

Ex. 4, p. 99: 1. IR; <u>how many active volcanoes exist in the world today</u>?; S = volcanoes; V = exist 2. DQ; no noun clause; . . . volcanoes? 3. IR; <u>if Mt. Etna is a dangerous volcano</u>?; S = Mt. Etna; V = is 4. SK; <u>what causes eruptions</u>.; S = what; V = causes 5. IR; no noun clause; . . . eruptions? 6. IR; <u>Mt. Rainier, in Washington State, will erupt</u>?; S = Mt. Rainier; V = will erupt

Ex. 5, p. 99: Answers may vary. Some possible answers are: 1. I forgot who Alfred Nobel was. (OR I don't know who Alfred Nobel was). 2. I don't know what Colombo is. (OR I think that Colombo is the capital of Sri Lanka). 3. I don't know where Vanuatu is. (OR I think that Vanuatu is in the South Pacific). 4. I don't know who Sacagawea was. (OR I think that Sacagawea was a Native American guide for Lewis and Clark in 1805). 5. I don't know who is on the five-dollar bill. (OR I think that President Lincoln is on the U.S. five-dollar bill). 6. I don't know when Amelia Earhart made her first flight. (OR I think that Amelia Earhart made her first flight in 1920).

Ex. 6, p. 100: Answers may vary. Some possible answers are: 1. Can you tell me (OR Do you know) what a zeppelin is? 2. Can you tell me (OR Do you know) what the difference is between an alligator and a crocodile? 3. Can you tell me (OR Do you know) whether or not (OR if) Jeannette Rankin was the first woman elected to the U.S. Congress? 4. Can you tell me (OR Do you know) what a *bear market* means? 5. Can you tell me (OR Do you know) whether (OR if) the bank opens at 9:00 or 10:00? 6. Can you tell me (OR Do you know) whether (OR if) pizza was invented in Italy or New York? 7. Can you tell me (OR Do you know) how I get to the post office from here? 8. Can you tell me (OR Do you know) who that man is who is speaking? 9. Can you tell me (OR Do you know) what time it is now? 10. Can you tell me (OR Do you know) where Senator Mitchell's office is?

Ex. 7, p. 100: 1. Kelly and Steve (OR They) don't know where to go for a vacation. 2. After I had wrecked my car the insurance agent told me what to do. 3. Veronica (OR She) doesn't know whether to stay in Tampa or go back to Mexico. 4. Do you know how to find a new roommate? 5. Patti and I (OR We) don't know what to wear to the graduation ceremony. 6. I don't know what else to try.

Ex. 8, p. 101: 1. Rome 2. Cairo 3. Madrid 4. Paris; C A R E

Ex. 9, p. 104: 1. what 2. that 3. not certain 4. that 5. that 6. that 7. not sure

Ex. 10, p. 104: Answers will vary.

Ex. 11, p. 105: Circle *is* as the main sentence verb in each sentence. 1. That <u>Florida will have</u> a new rail system is exciting news. 2. Whether <u>we will visit</u> all of the theme parks is not yet known. 3. That <u>Florida has</u> very competitive college football teams is a fact. 4. That <u>Bill goes</u> to the library every Saturday is remarkable. 5. When <u>we will arrive</u> in Tampa is still uncertain.

Ex. 12, p. 106: 1. wrong; change *are* to *is* 2. wrong; add *how* after *amazing* 3. correct 4. wrong; change *If* to *Whether* 5. wrong; delete *that*

Ex. 13, p. 107: 1. come 2. insisted 3. come 4. be included 5. finish 6. Do you understand 7. is required 8. take 9. wants 10. complete 11. is able 12. has studied 13. dance

Ex. 14, p. 111: 1. Professor Jones said this yesterday. The verb *is* is correct because reporting scientific facts in present tense is correct. 2. *You* is changed to *we* because Professor Jones was speaking to us. The modal verb *should* cannot be changed. 3. Professor Jones said this yesterday, so *I* is changed to *he* and *am*

is changed to *was*. The verb *has* does not need to be changed as the size of a whale's heart is a scientific fact; however, *has* could be changed to *had* without changing the meaning. 4. Past tense *were killed* is changed to past perfect in reported speech. 5. The verb *exist* does not change because the reported sentence adds the word *today.*

Ex. 15, p. 112: 1. a round-trip ticket to New York on any Saturday was $208. 2. it would cost $248 to travel midweek. 3. last month the price had been $156 round trip. 4. you should make your reservation soon. 5. there had been some great prices on hotels, too. (*Note:* the verb *have been* could also be used if the hotel prices were the same now as they were the day you talked to Norm.) 6. you would want to go to the Statue of Liberty. 7. you might like to attend a Broadway show. 8. he was also going to New York in a few weeks. 9. he could pick up some show schedules while he was there. 10. I am a very nice person to have been helping my friend.

Ex. 16, p. 113: Answers will vary.

Ex. 17, p. 115: 1. Sally asked John if he planned to go fishing that weekend. John wondered if Sally wanted to go fishing with him. 2. Jane exclaimed that she had just gotten back from a trip to Colorado. Lana asked her what she had done while she was there. Jane told her that she had gone skiing every day. Lana wanted to know how long Jane had been there. 3. The students asked if the teacher could explain reported speech to him (OR her). The teacher wondered whether (OR if) the student could come to his/her office at 4 o'clock. The student said that he/she would be there.

Ex. 18, p. 116: "Is there anything that I can get for you?" "Yes, there is," Debbie answered. "Could you please pick up a quart of milk?" "Is that all?" Marshall asked. "I am happy to get what you need." Debbie thanked him and told him that she couldn't think of anything else.

Ex. 19, p. 116: Answers will vary.

Ex. 20, p. 116: 1. A 2. C 3. A 4. B 5. C 6. D 7. B 8. C 9. D 10. A

Ex. 21, p. 118: Part 1. Did you know (that); when he did that; that early pioneers had been able to float barges down the river, but they couldn't return upstream through the fierce rapids; why it is called the River of No Return; Part 2. Answers may vary. Some possible answers are: 1. Do you know what time it is? (OR Can you tell me what time it is?) 2. Could you tell me how to open a checking account? 3. Do you know where St. Joseph's Hospital is located? (OR Could you tell me where St. Joseph's Hospital is located?)

4. Do you know why I have to wait for a refund? (OR Can you tell me why I have to wait for a refund?) 5. Do you know if Kazuki will be my roommate? (OR Do you know whether Kazuki will be my roommate? OR Can you tell me whether Kazuki will be my roommate?); Part 3. 1. correct 2. That grammar is important in learning a second language 3. correct 4. what makes a second-language learner 5. correct

Unit 7

Ex. 1, p. 124: 1. <u>that is most frequently visited in Paris</u>, most frequently visited in Paris 2. <u>who visit this Parisian site each year</u>, visiting this Parisian site each year 3. <u>who have visited this site since it opened in 1889</u>, having visited this site since it opened in 1889 4. <u>which was begun in 1887</u>, begun in 1887 5. <u>that we most obviously associate with the tower</u>, no change possible 6. <u>who were the engineers for this project</u>, the engineers for this project 7. <u>that the Eiffel Tower has</u>, no change possible 8. <u>who were well known throughout Europe</u>, well known throughout Europe 9. <u>which was published in the newspaper *Le Temps*</u>, published in the newspaper *Le Temps*; <u>whose names we recognize today</u>, no change possible 10. <u>which received two million visitors alone during the World's Fair of 1889</u>, receiving two million visitors alone during the World's Fair of 1889

Ex. 2, p. 125: Answers will vary. In numbers 3, 4, 5, and 8, there must be a comma after the last noun before each blank, followed by some noun, then another comma, and a main verb. In numbers 6, 7, 9, and 10, there must be a comma after the last noun before each blank, followed by some noun, and then another comma.

Ex. 3, p. 126: Corrections may vary. 1. C 2. X; The first president of the United States was Washington. 3. X; According to the map, the cities located near the coast are closer together. 4. C 5. X; Those animals living high in the treetops of the Costa Rican rain forest are difficult to catch. 6. X; The amount of money required for the trip should be reduced. 7. X; People driving long distances from home to work should carpool. 8. C 9. C 10. X; Reports typed on a typewriter over twenty years ago are sometimes difficult to read.

Ex. 4, p. 127: 1. C 2. X; purchased 3. X; Developed 4. C 5. X; Writing 6. X; sold 7. X; Reduced 8. X; flying

Ex. 5, p. 128: 1. The Eiffel Tower, lying in the heart of the City of Light, is perhaps the best-known monument in the world. Lying in the heart of the City of Light, the Eiffel Tower is perhaps the best-known monument in the world. 2. Construction of the Eiffel Tower, begun in 1887, lasted for over two years. Begun in 1887, construction of the Eiffel Tower lasted for over two years 3. Maurice Koechlin and Emile Nouguier, the engineers for this project, are not nearly as well known as Eiffel. The engineers for this project, Maurice Koechlin and Emile Nouguier are not nearly as well known as Eiffel. 4. The "Protest against the Tower of Mr. Eiffel," published in the newspaper *Le Temps,* was endorsed by Guy de Maupassant the junior and Alexandre Dumas. Published in the newspaper *Le Temps,* the "Protest against the Tower of Mr. Eiffel" was endorsed by Guy de Maupassant and the junior Alexandre Dumas. 5. The Eiffel Tower, receiving two million visitors alone during the World's Fair of 1889, quickly proved to be a popular addition to the Paris skyline and not the monstrosity that many had feared it would be. Receiving two million visitors alone during the World's Fair of 1889, the Eiffel Tower quickly proved to be a popular addition to the Paris skyline and not the monstrosity that many had feared it would be.

Ex. 6, p. 131: 1. When flying from LA to New York recently, Maria traveled with her cat. 2. *Before Maria entered the plane,* no change possible 3. *After the cat was put in its cage,* After being put in its cage 4. *Although Maria tried to calm the cat down,* no change possible 5. *When Maria could not make the cat be quiet,* no change possible 6. *Once the cat was held by the flight attendant,* Once held by the flight attendant, the cat

Ex. 7, p. 133: 1. *Because there was fog,* Because of the fog 2. *When it was storming last night,* During the storm last night 3. *even though he was late,* in spite of being late (OR despite being late) 4. *When he was a child,* During his childhood 5. *Since the meeting in Detroit lasted so long,* Because of the length of the meeting in Detroit (OR Due to the length of the meeting in Detroit OR Due to the fact that the meeting in Detroit lasted so long) 6. *whether you have a new car or not,* regardless of your car (OR regardless of the age of your car)

Ex. 8, p. 134: Part 1. Discussion answers will vary. 1. adv cl 2. adj phr 3. adj cl 4. adj phr, adj phr 5. adv phr 6. adv cl 7. adv cl 8. adj phr Part 2. Answers will vary.

Ex. 9, p. 135: 1. D 2. A 3. A 4. C 5. D 6. B 7. D 8. C 9. A 10. A

Ex. 10, p. 137: Part 1. 1. Although 2. because 3. Since 4. given 5. While walking 6. having 7. walking; Part 2. 1. wrong, Before going 2. wrong, Because of (OR Due to) 3. correct

4. wrong, stolen (OR that were stolen)
5. correct 6. correct 7. wrong, despite the fact that we had such great weather (OR although we had such great weather)

Unit 8

Ex. 1, p. 141: 1. may have won 2. may have already gone (OR might have already gone) 3. might have told 4. may have left (OR might have left) 5. may have made (OR might have made) 6. may have bitten (OR might have bitten) 7. may have met (OR might have met) 8. may have been talking (OR might have been talking) 9. may have gone (OR might have gone)

Ex. 2, p. 142: Answers will vary.

Ex. 3, p. 143: 1. wrong, Last night 2. correct 3. correct 4. correct 5. wrong, This morning 6. correct

Ex. 4, p. 144: 1. I could have taken the job in Savannah, but I chose not to. 2. Sung Wook could have sent her a birthday card, but he didn't. 3. The study group could have invited Frank to go along, but it didn't. 4. The neighbor woman could have called the police, but she refused to. 5. You could have asked me for help with your chemistry homework, but you didn't. 6. Joann's boyfriend could have moved to Wyoming, but he decided not to. 7. A shopping cart could have made the dent in your car, but it didn't. 8. They could have spent over $150 on books and CDs, but they didn't.

Ex. 5, p. 144: 1. can't have lost (OR couldn't have lost) 2a. could you have left 2b. couldn't have done 3. can't have walked (OR couldn't have walked), could have thrown 4. can't have gotten (OR couldn't have gotten) 5. could have spent; could have told

Ex. 6, p. 145: Answers will vary. Possible answers: 1. She could have had an appointment with her adviser. 2. It could have been the cold weather. 3. He couldn't have chased your cat. 4. I couldn't have overdrawn my account. 5. She could have gotten busy. 6. You could have seen it together. 7. The weather couldn't have been better.

Ex. 7, p. 146: 1. used to tell (OR would tell) 2. used to complain (OR would complain) 3. used to get up (OR would get up) 4. would wait 5. wouldn't take 6. would take 7. would fix 8. wouldn't help 9. would do 10. would sit 11. would help 12. would go 13. would stop

Ex. 8, p. 147: 1. correct 2. correct 3. I used to own a poodle. 4. I used to live near the west coast of Florida. 5. correct 6. correct 7. correct

8. correct 9. He used to work in a machine repair shop before he retired. 10. Stefan used to drive a Corvette. 11. correct 12. correct

Ex. 9, p. 148: Answers will vary.

Ex. 10, p. 148: 1. should have expected, shouldn't have painted 2. Should we have tried, should have suggested (OR ought to have suggested) 3. should have stopped (OR ought to have stopped); shouldn't have lost; should have spent (OR ought to have spent) 4. shouldn't have snapped

Ex. 11, p. 150: 1. D 2. F 3. G 4. E 5. A 6. I 7. B 8. C 9. H

Ex. 12, p. 151: 1. had to, didn't have to 2. must have been, had to have been 3. must have been, had to have been

Ex. 13, p. 151: 1. must not have seen 2. didn't have to rent 3. had to pay 4. must have been saving (OR had to have been saving) 5. must have been (OR had to have been) 6. must not have closed 7. had to put 8. didn't have to bring 9. must have taken 10. must have heard (OR had to have heard)

Ex. 14, p. 152: 1. were going to go 2. were supposed to 3. was going to 4. wasn't supposed to snow 5. Weren't you supposed to leave (OR Weren't you going to leave) 6. was supposed to report 7. were going to take 8. was supposed to be 9. were we supposed to meet (OR were we going to meet)

Ex. 15, p. 153: Part 1. Answers will vary. Part 2. Answers will vary.

Ex. 16, p. 153: Answers will vary.

Ex. 17, p. 154: 1. C 2. B 3. A 4. B 5. D 6. D 7. B 8. C 9. B 10. C 11. D 12. D

Ex. 18, p. 156: Part 1. 1. should have written (OR ought to have written) 2. wasn't able to 3. was supposed to have 4. would have gotten (OR could have gotten OR may have gotten OR might have gotten) 5. were going to visit 6. were going to use (OR were supposed to use OR could have used OR would have used) 7. used to schedule (OR would schedule) 8. would discuss (OR used to discuss) 9. must have forgotten (OR had to have forgotten) 10. couldn't have happened 11. should have received; Part 2. 1. wrong, used to live 2. correct 3. wrong, had to cancel 4. correct 5. correct 6. correct 7. wrong, couldn't have looked 8. correct

Unit 9

Ex. 1, p. 163: 1. is 2. stands 3. were 4. were 5. were 6. are 7. uses 8. are used 9. depends 10. are 11. represent 12. symbolizes

Ex. 2, p. 163: 1. am 2. Is 3. ask 4. is 5. don't mind 6. do you want 7. is 8. is 9. has been handed

down 10. states 11. was 12. don't accept
13. Will you tell 14. would be 15. Does . . .
sound 16. was 17. Did . . . know 18. was
19. was 20. was 21. was 22. was 23. was
24. were 25. Did . . . bring 26. has 27. were
28. should/will/must . . . tell 29. was 30. was
. . . impressed 31. will make 32. are

Ex. 3, p. 165: 1. are 2. does . . . look—Answers will
vary.

Ex. 4, p. 166: 1. B 2. C 3. A 4. B 5. A 6. D 7. A
8. B 9. A 10. C 11. C 12. D 13. D 14. D
15. B

Ex. 5, p. 168: 1. <u>colors</u> . . . <u>have</u> meaning,
<u>Continental Congress</u> <u>didn't leave</u>, <u>they</u> <u>chose</u>
2. <u>Congress</u> <u>passed</u>, <u>flag</u> <u>should have</u>, <u>each</u> . . .
<u>was not assigned</u> 3. <u>one</u> . . . <u>was placed</u>
4. <u>stripe</u> . . . <u>has</u> 5. <u>height, width, and length</u>
<u>have</u> 6. <u>stripes</u> . . . <u>are</u> 7. <u>stripes</u> . . . <u>are</u>
8. <u>stripe</u> . . . <u>alternates</u>

Ex. 6, p. 168: 1. <u>everyone</u> likes 2. <u>several</u> watch
3. <u>some</u> . . . stand for, <u>others</u> represent 4. <u>all</u>
. . . has been appreciated 5. <u>none</u> . . . goes
6. <u>most</u> . . . salute 7. <u>many</u> put 8. <u>all</u> show

Ex. 7, p. 169: 1. Maria or her sister, Anna, will be
the flag bearer in the parade. (OR Either
Maria or Anna will be the flag bearer in the
parade.) 2. The flag is neither big nor heavy.
(OR The flag is not big nor heavy.) 3. They
can use the black or the gold flagpole. (OR
They can use either the black or the gold
flagpole.) 4. The flag can neither be flown in
the rain nor touch the ground. (OR The flag
cannot be flown in the rain nor touch the
ground.) 5. The flag can be made of paper or
cloth. (OR The flag can be made of either
paper or cloth.) 6. The flag is neither flown
after dusk nor before sunrise. (OR The flag is
not flown after dusk nor before sunrise.)
7. Students salute the flag either at the
beginning or the end of the school day.
8. The flag can neither be folded haphazardly
nor stored irreverently.

Ex. 8, p. 170: 1. The manager should listen to the
people who work for him. 2. Francis Scott
Key was the person who first called the U.S.
flag the Star-Spangled Banner. 3. Key wrote
the poem that became the national anthem.
4. William Driver, who was a sea captain, gave
the flag the name Old Glory. 5. The Stars and
Stripes, which is the most popular name, is the
national flag of the United States. 6. During
the Civil War, Abraham Lincoln, who was
president, refused to have the stars of the
southern states taken off the flag. 7. The Civil
War, which was fought between the North
and the South, lasted for five years. 8. The
Northerners, who were known as Yankees, and
the Confederates, who were from the South,

carried different flags. 9. The Yankees carried
the flag that was known as the American
flag. 10. The Southerners carried a flag that
was known as the Confederate flag; it was also
red, white, and blue.

Ex. 9, p. 171: Answers will vary.

Ex. 10, p. 171: 1. A 2. C 3. A 4. A 5. B 6. B 7.
C 8. C 9. D 10. D

Ex. 11, p. 173: Part 1. 1. type 2. are 3. disrespects
4. costs 5. means 6. flies 7. need 8. was
flying 9. needs 10. are; Part 2. 1. correct,
scared 2. wrong, is 3. correct 4. wrong, is
5. correct 6. wrong, is 7. wrong, wants
8. correct

Unit 10

Ex. 1, p. 177: Answers will vary.

Ex. 2, p. 178: 1. (a specific time) 2. (a specific day)
3. time 4. the morning 5. (a specific time)
6. the building/his office 7. (a specific day)
8. (a specific time)

Challenge, p. 178: to do something before someone
else does, very sick and getting worse, in
trouble, in danger of losing it, behave properly
or leave; not feeling normal

Ex. 3, p. 179: 1. Jane's breakfast 2. the heel of her
shoe 3. the crack in the sidewalk 4. pair of
shoes 5. front seat of the car 6. the morning's
newspaper 7. the tops of her navy shoes
8. the color of her outfit

Ex. 4, p. 179: 1. by 2. by 3. by 4. with 5. with
6. with 7. By 8. with 9. by 10. with 11. By
12. with

Ex. 5, p. 180: Answers will vary. Some possible
answers: 1. to learn grammar, in order to learn
grammar, for grammar 2. to earn a living, in
order to earn a living, for earnings/money
3. to eat a homemade meal, in order to eat a
homemade meal, for a homemade meal 4. to
save money, in order to save money, for savings
5. to tip the server, in order to tip the server,
for a tip

Ex. 6, p. 181: 1. approve of 2. thought of
3. consisted of 4. reminded . . . of 5. listening
to 6. looking forward to 7. speaking to (OR
talking to) 8. happened to 9. speaking to
(OR talking to) 10. write . . . to 11. ask . . .
for 12. waiting for 13. looking . . . for
14. thanked . . . for

Ex. 7, p. 182: 1. C 2. D 3. A 4. B 5. D 6. A 7. C
8. D 9. B 10. D

Ex. 8, p. 184: Answers will vary.

Ex. 9, p. 185: 1. I 2. J 3. E 4. G 5. H 6. C 7. A
8. B 9. F 10. D

Challenge, p. 186: You make a decision in a difficult
situation; feel wonderful; in a fortunate
position; maintain your position; work 100%;

celebrate; get going, initiate action; try hard; boast about how well you did

Ex. 10, p. 186: 1. C 2. B 3. D 4. B 5. C 6. A 7. D 8. B

Ex. 11, p. 187: Part 1. 1. up, on, of 2. of 3. of, for 4. by 5. with 6. on, of 7. by, over/to/near 8. on, under/near/by; Part 2. 1. happened to 2. on my way 3. home from 4. with her left hand 5. on her right arm 6. reminded me of 7. in/into trouble 8. belonged to 9. fell out of 10. on which 11. wait for

Unit 11

Ex. 1, p. 190:

WORK	Simple	Progressive	Perfect	Perfect Progressive
present	you work	you are working	you have worked	you have been working
past	you worked	you were working	you had worked	you had been working
future	you will work	you will be working	you will have worked	you will have been working

EAT	Simple	Progressive	Perfect	Perfect Progressive
present	he eats	he is eating	he has eaten	he has been eating
past	he ate	he was eating	he had eaten	he had been eating
future	he will eat	he will be eating	he will have eaten	he will have been eating

HAVE	Simple	Progressive	Perfect	Perfect Progressive
present	I have	I am having	I have had	I have been having
past	I had	I was having	I had had	I had been having
future	I will have	I will be having	I will have had	I will have been having

RUN	Simple	Progressive	Perfect	Perfect Progressive
present	she runs	she is running	she has run	she has been running
past	she ran	she was running	she had run	she had been running
future	she will run	she will be running	she will have run	she will have been running

Ex. 2, p. 195: 1. became, become 2. bite, bit 3. brought, brought 4. catch, caught 5. choose, chosen 6. dealt, dealt 7. ate, eaten 8. feed, fed 9. find, found 10. fit, fit 11. get, gotten 12. give, gave 13. hid, hidden 14. hit, hit 15. input, input 16. know, knew 17. lent, lent 18. let, let 19. mean, meant 20. quit, quit 21. rode, ridden 22. seek, sought 23. shake, shook 24. shed, shed 25. slit, slit 26. stick, stuck 27. take, taken 28. throw, thrown 29. understand, understood 30. weave, wove

Ex. 3, p. 196: Answers will vary.

Ex. 4, p. 197: Answers will vary.

Ex. 5, p. 198: 1. did you begin 2. it is 3. I was 4. I became 5. I was 6. I had 7. who sparked 8. that made 9. did this teacher play 10. that is 11. plan was 12. I changed 13. My parents wanted (OR My parents had wanted) 14. I really did not want 15. goal was 16. reports deal 17. is biology 18. You are 19. I wrote 20. are (OR were OR have been) 21. did not have 22. are some things 23. report will be published 24. I am 25. listeners will be (OR listeners are going to be) 26. am 27. we do not have 28. we will not be (OR we are not going to be)

Ex. 6, p. 201: Answers will vary.

Ex. 7, p. 203: 1. By the year 2020, English will (OR will not) have become the first language in every country. 2. By the year 2100, doctors will (OR will not) have discovered a cure for AIDS. 3. By the time people can live on the moon, people will (OR will not) have learned to live under the ocean. 4. By next year, McDonald's will (OR will not) have added at least one hundred new restaurants. 5–8. Answers will vary.

Ex. 8, p. 204: 1. have been studying 2. has been getting 3. had been doing 4. will have been having 5. had been writing 6. will have been raining 7. have been taking 8. had been flying 9. will have been working 10. have been standing

Ex. 9, p. 205: 1. attacked 2. robbed 3. hit 4. choked 5. pinned 6. were working 7. heard 8. shot 9. were trying 10. hit 11. is 12. state 13. is 14. will use 15. pleaded 16. served 17. had previously spent 18. sued 19. was 20. resulted 21. Did McCummings deserve 22. Did the police officers act

Ex. 10, p. 206: 1. bit 2. was 3. had seen 4. had 5. caused 6. begged 7. spent 8. asked 9. are 10. originated 11. suggested 12. attack 13. Does Taro deserve 14. Did Taro do

Ex. 11, p. 207: a. 1. took 2. stayed 3. included 4. did not include 5. spent 6. was 7. took 8. cost 9. was 10. did she spend Answer: $730

b. 11. invited (OR has invited) 12. will have 13. has 14. does (OR will) she need Answer: 2 cartons c. 15. is 16. has 17. buy 18. will have given 19. do they have (OR will they have) Answer: 17 (OR 19 if they buy presents for each other, too) d. 20. lives 21. did he begin Answer: 1990 e. 22. arrived 23. has been waiting 24. will have been waiting (OR will have waited) Answer: 1:10

Ex. 12, p. 209: 1. is 2. became 3. was 4. fought (OR were fighting) 5. were trying 6. held 7. held 8. is 9. built 10. sent 11. defeated 12. outsmarted 13. won 14. faced 15. died 16. outlasted 17. won 18. has 19. speaks

Ex. 13, p. 210: 1. is 2. was 3. was 4. was 5. did not agree 6. appealed 7. said 8. was still not 9. agreed 10. ordered

Ex. 14, p. 210: 1. was not 2. entered 3. was 4. released 5. lived 6. died 7. revised

Ex. 15, p. 211: Answers will vary.

Ex. 16, p. 211: 1. A 2. C 3. B 4. D 5. D 6. D 7. B 8. C 9. C 10. B

Ex. 17, p. 213: Part 1. 1. prefer 2. had 3. had 4. left 5. saw 6. decided 7. had 8. was cleaning 9. belonged 10. refused; Part 2. 1. wrong; has seen 2. correct 3. wrong; have been identified 4. correct 5. correct

Unit 12

Ex. 1, p. 216: 1. How romantic! Amanda said "yes" after Nick had gotten down on one knee and proposed to her. 2. What luck! Khalid was offered a teaching job at Jackson High School after he had accepted a part-time one at King High School. 3. This is par for the course! I had gained 15 pounds over the holidays before I knew it. 4. It was the oddest thing! The orchestra had been playing when suddenly the conductor left the stage. 5. It happened again! By the time Brian had finished his project, it was too late to go to the movies. 6. I've never told anyone this! I had lived in the U.S. for eight months before I started taking English classes. 7. I couldn't believe it! The department store sale had ended when I finally found some time to go to the mall. 8. What a disappointment! By the time we finished biking all the way to the yacht club, the regatta had ended. 9. What luck! Leslie and Scott had just bought their house when construction began on a six-lane highway two blocks away. 10. This is interesting! New elections were held after the government had been in power for three months. 11. How sad! By the time she realized it was a scam, the thieves had taken her life savings. 12. This is almost unheard of today! My dad had worked for the same retail company for 40 years when he retired in 1997.

Ex. 2, p. 218: Sentences will vary. 1. lighten; Painting the walls white will lighten up a dark room. 2. alienate 3. nullify 4. foolish 5. childish 6. dangerous 7. quickly 8. doable 9. professionalism 10. selfishness 11. regularity 12. attendance 13. lively

Ex. 3, p. 219: Answers may vary. Possible answers are: 1. hadn't been sleeping 2. might have heard 3. had heard 4. would have called 5. had caught 6. Had we had 7. would have happened 8. were 9. would put 10. call (OR called) 11. respond (OR would respond) 12. can (OR could catch OR could have caught) 13. leave (OR left OR had left) 14. wear 15. won't leave (OR don't leave) 16. didn't report (OR had not reported) 17. would never have (OR would never have had) 18. catch (OR caught) 19. will feel (OR would feel)

Ex. 4, p. 220: Answers will vary.

Ex. 5, p. 220: 1. I don't know if that's the right answer. (OR I don't know whether that's the right answer [or not].) 2. I wonder if they made it. (OR I wonder whether they made it.) 3. You have to tell me how on earth you did that. 4. I have no idea if she works full time for Microsoft. (OR I have no idea whether she works full time for Microsoft.) 5. She's asking who took the last brownie. 6. Do we know if she'll be moving to Seattle with her family? (OR Do we know whether she'll be moving to Seattle with her family?) 7. She doesn't know if Carlos will be laid off next month. 8. Do you know where in Salt Lake City she works? 9. I'm not sure if my students will enjoy this particular lesson. (OR I'm not sure whether my students will enjoy this particular lesson.) 10. Could you tell me when the final exam for this course is scheduled? 11. I doubt if this team has ever made it to the play-offs. (OR I doubt whether this team has ever made it to the play-offs.) 12. Who asked if we needed more homework this weekend? (OR Who asked whether we needed more homework this weekend?)

Ex. 6, p. 221: 1. The car parked behind yours is mine. 2. Those students qualifying for scholarships must attend Monday's orientation meeting. 3. Although in our price range, the car lacks the options we want. 4. Cannot reduce. 5. I can't believe I fell asleep while watching the news last night. 6. Students taking risks with the language often make the most progress. 7. I can't stand movies containing scenes of extreme violence. 8. Cannot reduce. 9. Cannot reduce.

10. Tallahassee, the capital of Florida, is halfway between St. Augustine and Pensacola, once the capitals of East and West Florida, respectively. 11. Music videos targeted to teenagers don't sell as well in small towns as they do in big cities.

Ex. 7, p. 222: 1. might, could 2. Was she able to see 3. was 4. might 5. used, would 6. had to, would have taken 7. should 8. ought to, would, wouldn't, must 9. was supposed

Ex. 8, p. 223: 1. has 2. is 3. are 4. costs 5. were, was 6. plans 7. interests 8. work 9. are 10. has, says 11. wants, feel 12. lives

Ex. 9, p. 224: 1. to (OR in) 2. to 3. on (OR for) 4. about 5. in 6. at (OR in) 7. to 8. with 9. about 10. in 11. about 12. about 13. to 14. with 15. with 16. by 17. about 18. from 19. to 20. on

Ex. 10, p. 225: 1. comes 2. is 3. had 4. is 5. have been 6. show 7. have raised 8. display 9. taste 10. award 11. win 12. will/might receive (OR receive) 13. should have come 14. had planned 15. showed 16. were 17. were walking (OR walked) 18. eating 19. begged (OR were begging) 20. were throwing (OR threw) 21. knocked 22. would win (OR won) 23. take 24. is 25. will be 26. will have (OR have) 27. experience 28. is

Index

Index to Books 1–4

243

Final Test

Name _____ Date _____

This test has 22 questions. You will receive 1 point for circling the error and 1 point for correcting the error. Perfect score = 44.
Your score: _____ /44 = _____ %
(70% minimum recommended for passing.)

Each sentence contains one error. Circle the error and write the correction on the line. If your answer is long, you may write it above the sentence.

example: _____*have*_____ I (has) a book

Part 1

1. _____   In the 1970s, cloning was the "hot topic" of many science fiction writers who were interesting in exploring the subject as deeply as they could.

2. _____   The Civil Rights Act of 1964 helped to bring equality to African-Americans who had been struggled with the problems of segregation and discrimination for over one hundred years.

3. _____   Tampa, Florida, was unable to host the Olympic games due to the negative impressively from the traffic congestion on the highways.

4. _____   I wish he picked me up on time this morning. As a result of his being late, I was late to work.

5. _____   The passengers look tired because there were such a noisy children on the plane that hardly any of them could sleep.

6. _____   Everyone who teaches a language or who has studied a language would agree that grammar is important in learning a second language is certainly true.

7. _____   Before go to bed last night, I took two aspirin with a large glass of water.

8. _____ I'm sorry I couldn't have gone to your party. I had to work late.

9. _____ Neither the pilots who are working for lower wages at the current time nor the president of the company are ready to agree to the new salary arrangement.

10. _____ While climbing up the tree, the girl got so nervous that she fell out from the tree.

11. _____ In these past few years, medical science, especially the field of human gene therapy, sees an amazing number of new innovations.

Part 2

1. _____ The student's mother told him search the Internet for information about the history of impressionism in art.

2. _____ Christopher Columbus had originally thought that he could sail west to reach Asia; instead, he had found the Americas.

3. _____ Because second-language readers will always be at a disadvantage because of their limited vocabulary knowledge, they must make use of context clues to inference the meaning of the numerous unknown words that they encounter.

4. _____ If John Pemberton did not invent Coca-Cola in 1886, we would not be able to drink it today.

5. _____ Whenever that I have a headache, I take two aspirin with a large glass of water.

6. _____ The insurance agent strongly recommended that Jill does not drive until she gets her driver's license next month.

7. _____ According to the latest weather report, heavy rains will plague us tonight despite that we had such great weather most of the day.

8. _____ I'm so tired I can hardly stay awake today. I guess I couldn't have drunk that espresso at 10:30 last night and stayed up so late.

9. _____ None of the countries in Asia that we discussed in our last class meeting produce much oil for export.

10. _____ Last Saturday I happened to run into Mary in my way home from the supermarket.

11. _____ The party can be a great success if you would make your famous cheese sandwiches.

Diagnostic Test

Name _____ Date _____

Directions: Mark an X on the letter of the correct answer. Mark all answers on this sheet.

			TEACHER ONLY Number wrong (0, 1, 2)
1a. (A) (B) (C) (D)	1b. (A) (B) (C) (D)		_____
2a. (A) (B) (C) (D)	2b. (A) (B) (C) (D)		_____
3a. (A) (B) (C) (D)	3b. (A) (B) (C) (D)		_____
4a. (A) (B) (C) (D)	4b. (A) (B) (C) (D)		_____
5a. (A) (B) (C) (D)	5b. (A) (B) (C) (D)		_____
6a. (A) (B) (C) (D)	6b. (A) (B) (C) (D)		_____
7a. (A) (B) (C) (D)	7b. (A) (B) (C) (D)		_____
8a. (A) (B) (C) (D)	8b. (A) (B) (C) (D)		_____
9a. (A) (B) (C) (D)	9b. (A) (B) (C) (D)		_____
10a. (A) (B) (C) (D)	10b. (A) (B) (C) (D)		_____
11a. (A) (B) (C) (D)	11b. (A) (B) (C) (D)		_____

TEACHER ONLY

SCORING THE TEST

The question numbers represent the unit numbers in the book. For example, 7a and 7b are two questions about the material in unit 7.

Circle the unit numbers below that had two mistakes. These units should be done first.

Underline the units that had one mistake. These units should be done next.

Units: 1 2 3 4 5 6 7 8 9 10 11

Diagnostic Test Questions

1a. *Joe:* How's your reading going? Are you almost done yet?

   Sue: No, no way. Up to now, I _____ only two of the twelve units in the book, but I'll have more time tonight and tomorrow to work on this, too.

   (A) was doing   (C) have to do

   (B) have done   (D) have been doing

2a. *Lim:* Did you enjoy your trip to Mexico City last week?

   José: Yes, it was wonderful, but that wasn't my first trip there. When I was only twenty years old, I _____ there about three times already.

   (A) had been going   (C) had gone

   (B) went   (D) was going

3a. Although the statistics from some years are quite different from those in other years, seventy-three people die _____ from lightning in the United States.

   (A) annual   (C) annually

   (B) extend   (D) extensive

4a. _____ that the restaurant served only seafood, I would never have gone there.

   (A) If I knew   (C) Would I have known

   (B) If did I know   (D) Had I known

5a. Although the invention of the electric lightbulb ushered in a new era in architectural _____ people were at first afraid to have electricity in their homes and offices.

   (A) design, but many   (C) design because many

   (B) design, many   (D) design. Many

6a. What _____ sound intelligent in a second language is a good grasp of

vocabulary and a solid knowledge of English grammar.

(A) does makes a
second-language learner

(B) makes a second-language
learner

(C) does a second-language
learner make

(D) makes a second-language
learner do

7a. Written in central Canada in the early part of the twentieth century,

_____, depicts life in Manitoba.

(A) *The Midnight Sun* was Victor
Frank's last novel

(B) Victor Frank's last novel
The Midnight Sun

(C) which was Victor Frank's
last novel, *The Midnight Sun*

(D) *The Midnight Sun,* which was
Victor Frank's last novel

8a. You're such a wonderful dancer. You _____ lessons from an expert!

(A) would have taken

(B) must have taken

(C) ought to have taken

(D) shouldn't have taken

9a. I have dozens and dozens of folders of documents that we have to look over as soon

as possible, and here _____ .

(A) is your folder with two
hundred documents

(B) are your folder with two
hundred documents

(C) your folder with two hundred
documents is

(D) your folder with two hundred
documents are

10a. Satisfied with the performance of the computer, Steve told the salesperson that he

was interested _____ one.

(A) to buy

(B) for buying

(C) in buying

(D) about buying

11a. Scientists can alter some human chromosomes already and _____ able to

do so for many others in the near future.

(A) will have been

(B) will be

(C) are

(D) will be being

1b. *Brett:* Wow, this soup you made is great.

 Amy: Thanks. Katrina really likes the soup, and _____ .

(A) Jack does too   (C) Jack does so

(B) too Jack does   (D) so Jack does

2b. My neighbor is an intriguing person. I know that it is hard to believe it, but she _____ born in 1906.

(A) had been   (C) was

(B) has been   (D) were

3b. Despite the _____ constant noise coming from the planes taking off and landing at the airport near my house, it does not appear that the city council will do anything to reduce this noise.

(A) seemingly   (C) seem

(B) seeming   (D) seemed

4b. Scientists are not sure of the answer to the question "Where did the sun come from?" If scientists _____ the answer to this question, they would not have to spend so much time looking into this important matter.

(A) know   (C) had known

(B) knew   (D) would have known

5b. Although we tend to think that they are basically the same animal, dolphins, porpoises, and fish are not alike; despite how similar they might seem, these three animals _____ dolphins and porpoises are mammals while fish are not.

(A) different in that   (C) differ in that

(B) different so that   (D) differ so that

6b. Do you believe _____ the single most important aspect of learning a second language?

(A) knowing that the grammar   (C) that the grammar
      of a language is   of a language is knowing

(B) that knowing is the grammar   (D) that knowing the grammar
      of a language   of a language is

7b. Made from a previously unknown plant found only in a remote part of the Amazon

rain forest, _____ .

(A) scientists may be able to develop a new cure for cancer from it

(C) a cure for cancer might come from this new medicine

(B) it is possible that scientists may be able to develop a new cure for cancer from it

(D) the new medicine might be a cure for cancer

8b. This scale has to be wrong. I _____ have gained that much weight in only

two months!

(A) might not

(C) could

(B) can't

(D) would

9b. Of all the books that Jalstony wrote in the eighteenth century, perhaps the best

known of _____ *When Birds Fly Wildly.*

(A) those are

(C) those is

(B) that are

(D) that is

10b. Despite the unexplained noises and the unusual lights, the boys decided to

_____ in the house.

(A) enter

(C) exit

(B) go

(D) leave

11b. Much to the happy surprise of many pet shop owners, the preparation, maintenance,

and enjoyment of freshwater and marine aquariums _____ increasingly

popular in the U.S. so that many families now have an aquarium.

(A) had been becoming

(C) have become

(B) were becoming

(D) become